A DIFFERENT KIND OF BRAVE

A Wife's Journey to Escape Her Husband's Alcohol Addiction

Priscilla Skare

Disclaimer: Some names and identifying details have been changed to protect the privacy of individuals.

Published by Prominence Publishing.

www.prominencepublishing.com

To contact the author about speaking engagements, please email:

Lewismocha1@gmail.com

Author Photography by Brenda B Photography, LLC.

Publisher's Note: This is for educational and entertainment purposes only. This is not meant to represent legal, medical, or any other kind of professional advice. The reader should do his or her own due diligence and seek professional advice when required.

A Different Kind of Brave / Priscilla Skare. -- 1st ed.

ISBN: 978-1-988925-38-7

Dedication

This book is dedicated to all those unsung heroes that were there when I needed them the most; the police, paramedics, treatment technicians, intake administrators, and treatment counselors. You deal with the carnage of addiction every day in your lives, yet you managed to give me a sense of relief and hope.

Table of Contents

Introduction

Writing this book was my therapy. I certainly hadn't planned on writing a book when I wrote in my journals, made notes on calendars, or kept copies of letters. In writing this book I had the hope that others who are in similar situations as mine would find strength and hope, or at least know they aren't alone and that others are going through rough times as well.

Addiction is a killer of life in more ways than one. It literally kills people but also kills the spirit of both the addict and those closest to them. With addiction comes multiple health and mental problems, depression, anxiety, employment issues, financial consequences, and eventually loss of family or their own life.

A tough lesson learned throughout my writing was that for an addict to get better they must hit the full rock bottom. They should have the fear of losing what is most important to them, which often times is everything; their health, the house, the job then the family. A recovering addict and a good friend told me that I was the reason my husband wasn't getting better. Despite all my good intentions, I was still enabling him to continue to spiral down. It was my wake-up call, but it still took me several months, even years, beyond that to make a move.

Those of us that live with addicts are strong people. We have to be or we could eventually end up just like the addict we love. However, we are also damaged. We are as ill as the addict but in a different way. We too are consumed by addiction to alcohol and in a roundabout way have allowed it to control our lives. We do need to remember, however, to take care of ourselves, both physically, emotionally and spiritually. We need to put ourselves first for once. Stay strong. Have hope. Don't give up. Keep the faith.

Chapter 1

How and Why?

Things never turn out in life like you think they will. You aspire to do great things; find the love of your life, live "happily ever after." The sad truth is there are no fairy tales. One may have the perfect little cottage with the little white picket fence. Nobody can guess what goes on behind closed doors, such as the pain, anxiety, and feelings of hopelessness and despair. The feelings of shame that I had let myself end up in the situation that I was in and feeling like I just didn't care. I would just eat, numbing myself with food like an alcoholic does with liquor, not caring about my own health or well-being.

I'm a positive person. I'm a smart person. How did I end up like this in my mid-forties and incredibly unhappy? How did I end up crying on New Year's Eve as my husband laid in the bedroom in a drunken stupor? Cry as I ate rice out of a box to bring in the New Year. Cry as I fell asleep, clinging to my dog.

How did I end up racing up to a Magistrate's office after work a couple of weeks later, hoping I could get court papers and an officer to pick him up before he wakes up? As I sat in the Magistrate's office, waiting in line, I was surrounded by large, scary looking bail bondsmen and a woman with tattoos and ear piercings, who was concerned about her 13-year-old daughter that had threatened to kill herself. I was supposed to be packing for a wedding; packing to go back to my home state for the winter wedding of our god-child. Yet here I was under advisement by his therapist and his family that involuntary committal was my last option. He needed to be "somewhere" getting help for 30 days.

My mind was racing, my heart was pounding, and there was a lump in my throat. Was this for real? He would hate me. The trust was gone. His words meant nothing. Everything he said to me was a lie. I couldn't continue to live like this. I'm a strong person, but even at this point, I had hit my limit. I needed to understand that his issue was not mine. I couldn't control whether he drank or not. He would find a way. He had proven that before.

So, as I sat in this foreign place, with a sick stomach and answered questions about suicidal thoughts, "does he have a weapon" and "has he ever hurt anyone" I wondered... how did I get here?

Chapter 2

High School Sweethearts

Flashback almost 30 years. It was the early eighties. I first saw him at a junior varsity basketball game. We went to rival schools and my school was playing his. He came to my little home town of 400 strong in the Midwest to watch the game, but more so to check out one of my friends that played on the team.

I saw him sitting on the bottom bench of the gym. He had dark hair, along with an equally dark complexion, and wore a letter-jacket. He reminded me of Ralph Macchio from the Karate Kid. He was sitting with a friend, who later ended up being his best man at our wedding. I sauntered by, looking not so sexy in my plaid shirt, jeans, and hiking boots, along with a mouth full of metal. I looked at both, smiled and waved a small wave.

A couple of years later, the summer before my junior year of high school I was elated to get a job waiting tables at a restaurant in a nearby town. I had to work one night during the bar rush, which ran from 10 p.m. – 2:00 a.m. There was a little horseshoe-shaped counter that we put full glasses of water around, to prepare for the drunks that came in after they were done at the bars. Who would have thought at that time I would have more exposure to the world of drinking and drunks than I would have ever imagined?

I was styling a very sophisticated brown, orange and white plaid knit skirt jumper with pantyhose and brown suede shoes, not to mention the overly large logo of a giant chef looking very happy smack in the middle of my chest.

In he walked. It was the guy from the gym that ignored me a year prior. He was with a different guy this time. They arrogantly walked in and sat down at every chair at the counter and took a drink out of every glass of water I had poured. One of the girls that I worked with told me that he was flirting with me and told me his name. Dave. Athlete. Jock. Cute.

A few days later when I was working on a Saturday morning, he came in to apply for an open dishwasher position. Now he was going to be working at the same place I was. He MUST like me, but I couldn't figure out why. He had ignored me before.

I looked forward to those days when we both worked the same shift. One day after I got off work, I went to make the usual drive through town before I went home. There he was shooting hoops at the park all by himself, so I decided to stop.

We talked about nothing, as awkward conversations go, and he asked me out. He said he would come up to my house the next day. I was so excited I could hardly stand it.

I, being the eternal pessimist when it came to self-confidence at the time didn't figure he would show up. However, he actually came!

We spent the entire day together. We first shot hoops, then rode bikes the three miles to a small neighboring town. He then left to go home and clean up. He was going to come back and pick me up a couple of hours later for a real date to include a movie and pizza. I was on cloud nine.

It was a great day. A day I will always remember. Outdoors, pizza, movies and the butterflies in the stomach that comes with the anticipation of that first kiss. After that first date, I felt honored that he wanted to date me and that I was worthy of possibly being his girlfriend. He had that "bad boy" thing going on, but little did I know how that attraction at the time would leave me feeling more than 25 years later.

If only I had listened to my mother. She didn't like him. She had made that quite known from the start. She said he was controlling and I deserved better. And like most teenage girls, the fact that she didn't like him just made me want to be with him more. Sneak out and lie; I did about anything to get to be able to spend time with him. We spent a lot of time together within the first few weeks of dating, which was almost every day until school started that Fall.

I should have known it was trouble when I found out that he would go out and party after he would drop me off or after I arrived home. If I drove home I had strict instructions to call him once I was home. This was, of course, pre-cell phone. After he received my call, he would go out with his drinking friends.

At age 16 I didn't think I was all that cute. My body wasn't great. At a height of 5 ft 3 inches, I wouldn't be called leggy by any stretch of the imagination. I always thought my legs were a little too big for my upper body, which was rather petite. Brown eyes and dishwater blond hair with the mid-80's cut topped off the look. For me, he was on a pedestal at the time. I started ignoring my friends. I had made the cheerleading squad but quit after the first two games as it conflicted with his schedule. After all, the most important person in my life was Dave, right? I didn't want to give him any reason to leave me. I needed to be the perfect girlfriend or else he may break up with me.

As we dated, I was introduced to alcohol. I hadn't drunk much at all prior to meeting Dave. My parents were older

7

and protective since I was adopted and an only child. They thought I should only go out one night a weekend and shouldn't go out at all during the week. I didn't much care for that at the time, which did force me to lie some just to get out of the house. I did what I had to do. I had to see Dave.

Dave was one grade ahead of me, so when he graduated from high school and went out of town to a community college, I felt my life would be over. Certainly, our relationship wouldn't last, but it did.

When I graduated from High School, I followed him to attend the same community college. It was fun living on my own and doing the college thing. However, Dave's version of "fun" and "college thing" was on a completely different level than mine.

We drank together some. I only drank at the bars because he was and the new friends I made were. I hated the taste of the stuff. It was nasty. I didn't like the feeling of not having control of myself, let alone not remembering what happened the night before.

I finished an Executive Assistant program and Dave still wasn't close to being done. Short on credits, low on class load, along with low on motivation equals "never finish Associates degree." He spent more time playing basketball for the school and partying than he did focusing on school.

Chapter 3

Wedding Bells

Logically, the next step was marriage, right? Why not get married at the tender age of 20 back in 1986? It sounded like a great plan! It wasn't and if I had a "do over" I wouldn't do it again. We became engaged in September in a very non-romantic and non-spectacular way, which wasn't a bad thing. We were just so young. We were in his car after going out to dinner and we just started talking about getting married. A few days later we went to a local jewelry store in a mall, where he purchased a $400 bridal set. We planned initially for an April wedding the following year. I was as happy as could be.

Nervous was an understatement when it was time to tell my parents. I swear I think they thought I was pregnant. They took the news better than expected, most likely because I wasn't pregnant and were accepting of their soon to be son-in-law. Unfortunately, we ended up bumping up the wedding to December, as my mother was suffering from cancer. We wanted to be sure she could attend and enjoy the wedding as her health was starting to deteriorate.

Off we went on our honeymoon. We endured a long three-hour drive to our destination. We had some beer and wine coolers while driving on the way. I think we must have drunk some at the hotel as well. Sports fans that we were, we watched a college basketball tournament, ordered room service, "played" in the giant pool style tub, then crashed in the huge circular bed. I don't remember much else from the wedding night though, sadly enough. We had planned to go shopping the next day, but Dave had forgotten pants. All he would have had to wear would have been his tuxedo pants, so we ended up driving back home early.

In our early years of marriage, we both drank some. We drank mostly when we went out with our friends, which was nothing unusual for young couples. We were on our own without much money, but we had each other and we were having fun. We actually spent all the money we had left in savings with the exception of $100 so we could purchase a wicker bar with two matching bar stools!

Chapter 4

A Grown Up World

The newlywed/honeymoon period has to end at some point right? Living in a grown-up world means grown-up fights, which did occur off and on over the course of the next nine years or so. We fought more when he started hanging out with a guy he worked with. They both signed up for a softball league, and then they both started gambling. Bets of choice were on horses and dogs mostly. Dave started drinking more and leaving me behind to hang out with his friends.

He later quit his job after eight years and went into business with another guy. This guy was a heavy drinker and what I would consider the classic loser. During this "business" ownership, much money was wasted, along with much alcohol being consumed by Dave. More fights and more misery. He would be gone for long periods of time. He would come home drunk. It was not a good time in our life. What did I do? I ate. Then I ate some more. I guess food to me was like his booze was to him. I found comfort in my bags of junk food.

I would literally plow through a bag of chips or a package of cookies in one sitting. Needless to say, I started gaining weight. What little self-esteem I had was starting to crumble, at least on the home front. On the work front, things were great. I was getting promoted and getting new opportunities to learn new things.

As my home life became increasingly more pitiful and hopeless, I found myself writing. Writing my thoughts seemed to make me feel better, at least for that one moment in time. Sometimes I would write to Dave and leave him a note, other times I would simply place the note in a hidden box.

August 13, 1996

I look around and want and see

I watch people drive by

Stare at the answering machine

What has become of him?

He says he'll be home

He'll beat me here

I sit and I wait

It is late, he does not appear

What has become of him?

He lies, he promises

That he will stop

He gives me his word

But hope is for not

What has become of him?

I'm still sitting here

Thinking much more how I got to this spot

Always waiting and wondering

What has become of me?

I've lost my looks

I look in the mirror

What looks back at me

Isn't what used to be

What has become of me?

Sometimes I wonder

If I should just leave

Would our lives be much better

A couple no more

What has become of me?

The trust is all gone

There's no romance here

We speak as if friends

We don't kiss goodnight

What has become of us?

I work I come home

He works, he does not

I eat by myself

Where he is, I don't know

What has become of us?

We used to ride bikes, go out or play tennis

We used to hold hands, kiss, and make love

What has become of us?

I don't know if it's the alcohol

Or if it's just me

I want to hope for the future

Should I stay, wait and see?

The days that he circles

Are they really true?

I want to believe him

What has become of us?

I want to erase

The past and the present

Try a fresh start

Like we've tried and failed

What will become of us?

He had started to circle the days on the calendar where he wouldn't drink. I couldn't believe all those circles were true. There was just too much pain in my heart for it to be so.

Chapter 5

Happy Anniversary!

For our 10th wedding anniversary, Dave had a huge surprise for me. I knew we were going on a trip, but I thought we were going to Chicago. I had told him I had always wanted to see Oprah. He kept a good secret. I was completely surprised when we ended up flying off to San Diego, California to stay at the Hotel Del Coronado on Coronado Island. He topped off the trip with a limo ride around the island and La Jolla, then back to an Italian restaurant in Coronado. He could definitely pull off a great surprise when he wanted to.

The Hotel Del was fabulous, full of history and was famous for its random building design with doors and stairways to nowhere. Since it was early December, the hotel was decked out with huge Christmas trees and wreaths everywhere. It was great fun. Looking back at the pictures of us though, we didn't look all that happy.

I remember riding in the limo and seeing the bar fully stocked. My first reaction was to worry about how much he was going to drink and was the night going to end in a good way or in a bad way? Plus, I wasn't feeling really good about myself at the time as I had packed on some extra winter weight, sitting around moping and waiting for Dave to come home all those nights.

We had a very nice dinner and went back to our room, had more late night snacks, and went to bed. The day and night was a success, as was the entire trip. It was nice to break away from the humdrum of the cold of the Midwest and to dream about a different life in California.

Chapter 6

North Carolina
Here We Come!

After our return from our California trip the winter of 1996, we realized there were much better places to live. We bought an Atlas at Wal-Mart and started looking at the map. California had too many people and was too expensive of a place to live. Newport, Rhode Island was nice but expensive and could get cold (we had been there on a previous vacation). Florida was too hot and humid for too long each year. Why not look at moving to North Carolina? This made perfect sense to us. The coast of North Carolina! Nice weather, golf year-round, great college basketball to follow, and the beach. Who could ask for more?

In early March of 1997, we booked a long weekend trip to Wilmington, North Carolina. We stayed oceanfront at Wrightsville Beach. As we ate that first night looking out at the water we knew it was a place we wanted to move to. We drove around and started looking at houses in various newly developed neighborhoods. We found a new one we liked, put a contingent offer on it, and left town three days later. It was a bit impulsive, but we really had nothing to lose.

If it was meant to be, it was meant to be. Who would have thought our house would sell within three days after putting a "for sale by owner" sign in the front yard? Who would have thought we would get a full asking price cash offer? If that wasn't a sign, I didn't know what was. We were in sunny Wilmington by the end of that following April.

Honestly, my thought at the time was that he was drinking so much that if I could get some help getting moved to North Carolina, at least I would be in a better place if the marriage fell apart, or if I left. I learned later that oftentimes moving to a new location was exactly what an alcoholic did.

Moving without jobs lined up probably wasn't the brightest idea. Back in the late nineties, we figured we could get jobs doing about anything. We needed just enough to make our house and car payments. We were young, we would save later.

Everything worked out quickly job-wise. We both had full-time jobs, paying enough for starters within a few weeks after making our move. It appeared that this move was meant to be.

Oprah fan that I was at the time, I tried to follow her advice and keep a "grateful journal." My very first entry read as follows: *December 16, 1997 – I am starting my gratitude journal. I am grateful for the following three items: North Carolina; A 65-degree day in mid-December; Dave's thoughtfulness yesterday.*

I didn't know whether to laugh or cry when I saw my next entry, which was over four months later, which read, *April 19, 1998 – Needless to say, I am not loyal to a grateful journal. I am truly hurting today. My eyes burn from crying too much. Today Dave and I talked about divorce. I have not been happy for the last 6-7 months. He told me he loved me, but he wasn't "in love" with me. He also told me that it is very surprising that a "guy like him" hasn't cheated yet. He is a man. He also told me that he wants to be proud of a good looking woman on his arm. He has broken my heart. He has gambled away and wasted our money, lied to me, and is an alcoholic. I feel very* hopeless. He said he hates it here in NC. He hates the house, the neighbors, everything. We don't talk anymore. The worst thing is that he says he is no longer "in love" with me. I have given him all I have.

Chapter 7

Sad News from Back Home

We soon received horrible news. Dave's father was diagnosed with lung cancer. There we were, over 1,500 miles away and his father was dying. This would be the beginning of the drinking spiraling out of control. It was the true start of the nightmare. I was sure he felt helpless being so far away. He drowned his guilt in booze and started hanging out with the wrong drinking crowd at the golf course, and actually quit his job without having another job for a few months, which turned into one long binge.

It wasn't unusual at that time for Dave to take off on a Friday and not come home until Sunday, leaving me to freak out and worry, not knowing where he was or if he was ok. Oftentimes he would leave a cryptic note. Once in a while, I would get a phone call from him. He would be in a hotel only God knows where and he would always apologize. He would then come home Sunday night and get up for work the next morning as nothing happened.

The drinking wasn't just on weekends though. It was after work as well. His pattern was to drink and drive. He came home one evening with the passenger side window of his truck busted out. He told me he had been driving around and a bullet went through the window. He had all kinds of detail to that story. I found out later that he had been so drunk while driving that he thought he saw a cop, went to throw his beer bottle out the window and didn't realize the window was up. Busted everything. I still can't believe I actually fell for that bullet story.

When he got the call in April 1999 that his dad was passing away and it was time to come home, he took off and drove straight through. Thankfully, he did get home in time to say a final goodbye to his dad, which I think meant the world to him.

When I arrived for the funeral, Dave had been drinking heavily. I found a vodka bottle tucked in the glove box of his car. I tried to be understanding and ignored it as I knew he was going through a very difficult time. I prayed that it would be better once he returned home to North Carolina.

Unfortunately, that was not the case. I remember taking pictures of him passed out on the floor or passed out on the couch. I remember crying my eyes out as I wrote letters to him, begging him to stop, and threatening to leave. I hoped that my tears would make a difference. They didn't. At the time, it hurt me that he didn't even care that I was crying. Now, looking back, I really was naïve. I wasn't fully aware of the power of the drink and how it had gotten control of him, making it more important to him than anything else. I was taking his lack of caring for me personally.

Chapter 8

You Want What?

What does one do when one has a drunk for a husband and feels they have to hold everything together? Sign up for school to obtain a Bachelor's degree, of course! What was I thinking? October of 1999 was the start of my mission for "higher education." Maybe with a four-year degree, I would be able to make more money at work, which meant I could better afford to live on my own.

It was an accelerated program, so my classes were one night a week for four hours each, for a period of 18 months. It was tough starting out and getting back into the school mode again, especially with the home life, as well as working on animal rescue; but I needed to do this for myself.

I was busy with school, dogs, and work. Dave was busy with work, golf, himself, himself, himself, and keeping his consumption of alcohol to the maximum his body could tolerate. The holidays were right around the corner, and with holidays always come holiday plans and fun. Not exactly in our case.

Dave and I took one of our usual morning rides over Thanksgiving. Unfortunately, it wasn't a good one. Following is an excerpt from a journal entry:

On Thanksgiving Day he insisted on playing basketball with his usual group of guys. I had assumed he would be home by around 8:30. He didn't get home until after 9:30. We were supposed to take the dogs to go feed the seagulls. Of course, I was in a bad mood as he was late. I had suspected that he had been drinking. We loaded up the dogs to take the usual holiday ride anyway. During that ride, he got off on a tangent about the reason he drinks is that he has wanted kids for a number of years and I won't do it. He went on to say that he has been empty. What we have isn't a family. He would stop drinking today if I committed to having kids.

Are you KIDDING ME? This came completely out of the left field. I was so shocked and upset I could hardly find words to respond. He gave me an ultimatum. Said if I said "no," he would find someone who would. His words cut like a knife. As I write this, my heart aches and my eyes fill with tears. It was at that point that I realized this marriage was probably on its very last leg. I have devoted myself and sacrificed for him for 15 years and he has the nerve to give me such an ultimatum. Guess who would be stuck raising the kids? Who has to bear the brunt of the ordeal health wise? I am NOT willing to go there for him. I have sacrificed and compromised myself enough.

Turkey dinner was extremely difficult. Later in the afternoon, I left for a couple of hours to spend time with my dad, who we had moved to North Carolina to be close to us. Dave never mentioned that conversation again. I wanted to but I didn't know how it would end.

For some reason, I was naive enough to think that my crying would help, or writing letters spilling out my feelings and emotions would help. Surely he would read these and come to his senses and realize all the wrongs he had done and how much pain he had caused me. Of course, the letters didn't matter, nor did the cards pleading for him to stop drinking. I thought that if I acted a certain way or changed something about me, or stayed glued to his side that he would stop. All of that was just me being a wife that was desperate and becoming a big time enabler.

Chapter 9

Happy New Year!??

When New Year's Eve 1999 was near, all the buzz was how people were going to spend the big night. Everyone had huge plans on what they were going to do during the "once in a lifetime" type of New Year celebration. My 1999 New Year's Eve day was spent home alone as he was a no-show. I finally got tired of waiting and ended up going to a movie by myself. When I got home he was there passed out on the couch. I cried myself to sleep saying to myself I would never spend another New Years Eve like this. Ever. Wrong. Again.

The year 2000 didn't start off any better than the end of 1999. The drinking continued until he finally hit a breaking point on February 10, 2000, and checked himself into a local treatment center for in-patient care. I was so relieved. Finally, he had come to the right conclusion of what needed to be done and that he needed help. I slept well that night.

The next morning, I scurried around to get his bag of clothes ready to take by the treatment center. As I pulled up in the car, he was standing outside waiting for me! He came up to the car, leaned in and stated "You have to get me out of here. I am NOT staying in this place!" Not knowing much about treatment centers at the time I was wondering how they could have let him walk out the front door!? Where was security?! I desperately tried to convince him to stay.

Finally, a counselor came outside and said: "Hey Dave, what are you doing out here?" Dave replied that he was not going to stay. I looked frantically at the counselor and figured it was now or never. I boldly stated "He wants me to take him home and I don't want to let him in the car. Is there something you can do to make him stay?" Dave gave me a look full of daggers but I didn't care. I had to make him stay.

The counselor suggested we take a walk back inside, all together so we could talk about some other options. I was so thankful that there are great people on this earth in this profession. Finally, there was someone on my side!

As we sat in a tiny crowded office, it took a lot of convincing before Dave finally and reluctantly agreed to attend the Day Treatment Program. This meant I would drop him off by 8:30 every morning and would pick him up at 5:00 p.m. This was to continue for ten days.

It wasn't what I was hoping for, but it was better than him coming home and doing nothing. After completion of the ten-day program, for the next three to four months, Dave attended AA meetings 4-5 times a week. He was getting better and so was our day-to-day life together.

Chapter 10

All Aboard!

The end of May 2000 brought us to one of the best times we had ever had! We set off for our first cruise! We had booked a seven-night Western Caribbean cruise that left out of Tampa, Florida. I had lost some weight, I had a little tan, and I was feeling pretty good about life in general. We were getting along great, spending time with the dogs, going to the beach, shopping, dining out. It was normal and it was really, really good.

Dave had been attending AA meetings religiously, and I was no longer obsessing about the smell of alcohol or spending my time trying to find empty bottles. The trust wasn't completely back yet, but we were off to a positive start.

We made the long drive and arrived in Tampa the night before we were to launch. We were exhausted but we wanted to freshen up and go out for dinner. Right before we were to leave the hotel, Dave started acting rather strange. He wanted me to sit on the side of the bed as he had a surprise for me. He told me that he wanted to wait until we got onboard the ship, but couldn't wait any longer. He produced a small box, which appeared to be about the size used for a ring.

I opened the box and there was an absolutely stunning sapphire and diamond ring set in white gold. It was the most beautiful ring I had ever seen and most certainly the most expensive piece of jewelry I had ever received! Not only that, he had put thought into an engraving on the inside of the ring. The initials read "W L F I LUV U DAVE" which meant "wife, lover, friend, I love you, Dave."

I started to cry. He went on to apologize for everything he had done and that he hoped this would help. He had contacted one of my friends from work, who had been in on the conspiracy to help him pick out this ring and get it to him without me knowing anything. It was truly a surprise and I felt so very much loved and honored.

This event started off our cruise on a high note. He was sober and stayed sober on the cruise. We ate our way through eight glorious days at sea and at fabulous ports. We swam with the Stingrays in the Caymans, hit Passion Island off Cancun, and took a swamp tour of the bayous of New Orleans. This was one of the best trips we had ever had.

Upon our immediate return to Wilmington, he continued to attend AA meetings, but less frequently. Unfortunately, by the end of July, he stopped attending meetings and had the attitude that AA wasn't for him. He wasn't like those people. The rest of that year ended up being another round of lies, no-shows at home, passing out, and drinking.

Chapter 11

Fight or Flight

By 2001, Dave had completely stopped going to AA meetings. He barely had any contact with his friends. I could tell he was hiding it. He was continually moody, defensive, and paranoid. Again I had thoughts of being on my own. Could I make it? I thought about how much I would hate to give up the house and the lifestyle I had become accustomed to. I knew I was staying in this marriage for many of the wrong reasons. I sat and thought about how I was in my mid-30's and in an unhappy marriage. No romance. I had no sexual attraction to him at all. He probably didn't have any to me either.

We started talking about investing in a townhouse with the intent of renting it out. I had a terrible thought in the back of my mind. The plus side to buying a townhouse was that if we needed to separate, it would provide a place for one of us to stay.

One day in late July, I received a call from him. He should have been at work but was calling from home. He went on to say once again that he needed help. He had called his boss, who called his Pastor. Dave wanted me to meet him after work at the church.

I met him there to talk with the Pastor. He smelled of alcohol. He had made an unsuccessful attempt to hide it with cologne and gum. He broke down and made a promise that if it didn't work this time, he would commit himself to a treatment center. He promised to start AA meetings again.

To make it through the dry-out, I was to take him to and from work every day for two weeks. We would spend all our time together except when at work.

It was a good two weeks. He felt fatigued, shaky, and would substitute food for booze. I was worn out, as this came at a very busy time for me at work. My stress level was peaked out. However, my hopes were high that he was sincere and this would work this time.

I was wrong yet again. He managed to continually get out of going to meetings. I walked on eggshells, not knowing when it was safe to talk about the issue or not. I was back on the emotional roller coaster.

I knew he had been drinking again. However, we didn't have as many "no shows" as before. He managed to get his boss to pay for a "business" trip to Arkansas. That way he could see his family. He was gone for about a week.

During that week I was much more relaxed. Out of sight, out of mind was a good thing when it came to Dave. I thought to myself there was no way he would drink in a rental car, on a business trip, and with family. Wrong again.

He got back the following Saturday. He seemed very irritable. That night I learned that he drank on the way to his family's house and drank while he stayed there. He voiced a lot of hostility toward his family, stating that they were getting in his business. He was extremely paranoid. He stated things such as "They should stay out of my business. What I do is MY business! I should never have told them about drinking." He was very angry. Of course, I cried. What else was there for me to do? I couldn't make sense of it. I didn't understand. His homecoming night was ruined.

Chapter 12

Cone of Uncertainty

Toss a couple of hurricanes in the mix and the summer just kept getting better. Our first hurricane of the year was Dennis, then shortly after that Floyd. Floyd was predicted to be a big one, and with the high winds we endured in the house for Bonnie the year prior, I wasn't about to take a chance with a Category 3-4 bearing down on us. To make things even worse, it was due to come on my birthday. I had made hotel reservations up in the mountains in Asheville, North Carolina. We figured it would be far enough away from the brunt of the storm if we took a direct hit.

For the two biggest preparation days leading up to Floyd, I tried to get Dave to participate in preparing the house for the storm. That was a futile attempt. I had taken my birthday off for some "me" time, which ended up being spent at Home Depot getting sheets of plywood. Yes, I bought wood for our home windows, putting it in my convertible with the top down, and taking care of what most men would do. What was my man doing? He was drunk. I could barely get him to help me unload them and nail them to the house. I was a nervous wreck.

My birthday that year was a nightmare. He was drunk and passed out by 7:30 that evening. No birthday dinner. No card, not even a "happy birthday." He tried telling me that he only had two drinks. I couldn't leave well enough alone so I pointed out the fact that I thought he was lying and that he had more than two. He told me that I should just load up the dogs and drive to Asheville by myself, swearing at me like I had done something wrong. Needless to say, that birthday evening was spent in tears.

I was watching the Weather Channel constantly to see if Wilmington was in the "cone of uncertainty." Of course, we were. We woke up the next morning early to turn on the TV only to see that Floyd was a Category 4 and was coming right at us!

At least he was sober that morning. We packed up the Yukon, three dogs, and a cat and took off for the mountains of Asheville. Wilmington fared well from Floyd, but we were stranded on the way home in Raleigh due to the flooded roads around Wilmington. We couldn't get back into the city! After we finally arrived back home four days later, I had assumed that after all that, plus having to clean up the yard and unpack, that Dave would be around to help. That was not the case. He said he was going to run into the office to be sure everything was ok. On a Saturday? He took off and I didn't see him until after dark. He had gone out drinking once again. He had left me there with the messy yard, dirty clothes and a sea-salty house to clean up all by myself.

Chapter 13

Mexico

We had planned for a seven-day trip to Cancun early December to celebrate our anniversary, and to stay at an all-inclusive resort south of Cancun near the Mayan Riviera. I was excited about the trip and had booked it several months in advance. I almost canceled that trip, but then figured if it got that bad I would just go by myself. Hindsight is always twenty-twenty, and I wish I had gone by myself. The trip was a disaster.

Upon our arrival at the resort, we were greeted by friendly workers who offered us each a glass of champagne, which we both passed on. The resort was beautiful. Tropical plants and colorful flowers lined the Mexican-tiled pathways to the ocean side of the resort. It was set oceanfront with a very little beach and many jutting rocks.

Our room was oceanfront with a private deck and hammock. The room was completely tiled and included a very large Jacuzzi hot tub right in the room overlooking the water. Fancy towels lined the fully tiled bathroom, complete with a "Happy Anniversary" cake on a table, along with a basket of fresh tropical fruit. Each room also had a mini-fridge, completely stocked with bottled water and of course, Mexican beer.

The food was fabulous, the staff friendly and courteous. We couldn't have asked for a better place to vacation for seven long days. I do mean long. After the first day, Dave indicated that he "needed" to drink that morning. Just the mornings as his body needed it. So, there I sat on the edge of the bed each morning, while he chugged the complimentary beer out of the mini-fridge, knowing full well when we got back to the room later, it would be fully stocked yet again.

Needless to say, it changed the dynamics of the trip. It made me sad and put me in a depressed mood. We laid out some and explored some. We fought some as well. The highlight of the trip was driving into Cancun and swimming with dolphins. Sadly enough, there was nothing romantic or "anniversary" about this trip at all.

Chapter 14

More of the Same

As much as I held out for what I thought would change, it didn't. As much as I said I wouldn't stay and take it, I did. I was raised in the Christian faith and the commitment to honor your spouse during those marriage vows meant something to me. Married people aren't supposed to get divorced. It was a big deal. These things shouldn't be taken lightly.

However, does God expect someone to remain with someone else regardless of what was happening? Did I fall in the abused category? I was not physically abused, but I was so emotionally torn up that certainly, it must be emotional/mental abuse. Would I still be in God's favor if I left Dave behind? Perhaps these questions were why I was still holding out hope. Certainly, God's plan for me couldn't consist of living with someone who puts me in an almost constant state of misery. Or was it? Was it all for the greater good and I would find out later what this plan had been all about?

Following is a letter written to Dave after yet another round of bingeing and lying:

July 2001

Whenever I try to express my feelings, you cut me off or get angry (especially when it concerns issues around alcohol). Last year about this time I had put my ring back on, placed happy photos of us around the house and proceeded to think happy thoughts of security, trust, and marital bliss. A year has passed, the ring came off, photos on the fridge have been removed and the thoughts of marital bliss and happiness have evaporated, leaving thoughts of insecurity, uncertainty, and mistrust.

The ups and downs of living with you are getting to be too much. Last Friday night we had a great time. Saturday, you call me in the morning to tell me about your friend and how breakfast with him went well. I go about my day, looking forward to your return for a fun afternoon. You called me to discuss afternoon plans, call back again to talk movies and more plans. "I'll be home in the half-hour," you say.

No contact. The extreme from the high of the morning to the low of the afternoon and night (and ongoing) can't be described. No word from you. No bag packed. Nothing. It just isn't right. This is the third time over the last few months.

Every time you return you say the same thing. Your next great help is a pill, yet when I ask about it I get my head bit off. It's like living with a ticking time bomb. No rhyme or reason in figuring out when it will explode.

I have regrets. I should not have been so naïve to think that "bliss" is for me. As I sit here on Sunday morning I am thinking about whether or not I can make it financially on my own.

Unfortunately, I am back to thinking of being on my own, proceeding with caution. The lessons I have learned have been tough and painful, but I have still learned from them. These are not happy times. They should be as we have many things to be thankful for.

I'm hurting terribly right now. There may be things here that seem hurtful to you. For that, I apologize. I love you and always will, but I can't be in this situation for much longer, with no effort from you or hope in sight and watch you throw away your life and blessings.   – P

Excerpts from journal entries

- January 14, 2002

I took the Yukon to Walmart. Found more Diet Mountain Dew bottles in his golf bag that included the infamous Dew/Vodka mix. I confronted him when I got home and asked him if he was going to be serious about stopping or not. He got mad at me for looking in his bag. He proceeded to call me a "stupid son of a bitch," among other things. I told him to move to the townhouse. As usual, I slept that night in a different room.

The next morning, we barely spoke. He made the usual comment of "hitting three meetings a week" to which I had no comment. He left to golf at 9:00 a.m. As of 7:30 p.m. he wasn't home. Yet another day wasted in a "wasted" state of mind at the golf course and on the road.

January 26, 2002

Another blown weekend, which usually starts out with golf. He called and said he would be home and we would have a fun afternoon. He never came home. I was told later that he ended up in Charleston, South Carolina and slept in the truck. I packed all his things and took them to the townhouse. He got home the next day, passed out, got up and left to go out drinking again and came home four hours later. He refused to go to the townhouse. He would not leave our house. This horrible weekend led to the following letter to him:

Dave,

I can't take this treatment any longer. It's hard for me to understand how you can continue to look me in the eye and lie. It's not right. Marriage is not supposed to be this way. This isn't loving. Without love and respect for each other, what is there? My heart is torn apart. I cry and worry daily. I see other couples and wish I could be in a relationship filled with love, honor, and respect.

35

I'm tired and worn out. I feel like I'm 50 years old. I think I have matured way beyond my years. I haven't been able to be carefree and light-hearted, for there is too much weighing on my heart and mind.

I have been stupid to get caught up in the thoughts and plans for the future... trips, finances, etc. for it isn't long when the reality of my life slaps me in the face.

The slap might be one of your lies, it may be your breath, or it may be like right now, as I write this, sitting alone at night after hoping you would pull in the driveway (hours ago).

I can't keep up this act any longer. You lie to me, your family, friends, and yourself. I can't watch you destroy yourself any longer. I think it best we live apart for a while as much as I hate it. I hope that during this separation we will both have a chance to evaluate how we want the rest of our lives to be. I hope you choose the road to recovery. If not, you know you will end up killing yourself, either by car or by slowly destroying your body, soul, and mind.

I don't want to see you or talk to you for a few days. I need to get my head on straight. I had hoped it wouldn't come to this, but I can't bear another weekend like this one. I need to stop worrying about things I can't control.

I love you. I always will. I hope you will get the help you need. My efforts and support are obviously not working.

You have a lot to offer when you are sober. That is the man I love. That man hasn't been here since 2000. I wish he would come back. −P

The following Monday he went to work but ended up calling me long after he should have been home. He called to ask me if he could come home and that if he couldn't he was afraid that he would kill himself if he checked into a hotel. He came home.

This incident led to more promises of going to AA meetings. He even said I could go to the "open" ones with him if I wanted. Of course, that all changed the following weekend when he left early to go golfing. He got home at 6:00 p.m. and passed out on the couch. I took his keys and left him there to go to my first Al-Anon meeting. I was an emotional wreck. I was just a mess of tears and could hardly speak. However, despite my emotions, I recalled listening to the ladies at the meeting. They were all telling their stories of their husbands passed out, drunk, etc. These ladies were in their 50's and 60's. I thought to myself, if you have been dealing with this crap for that many years, just LEAVE! I never attended another meeting. Weekend after weekend I would spend by myself while he was out blowing money and drinking himself into a coma.

Chapter 15

In Like a Lion!

Little did I know that the reference to March "Coming in Like a Lion" would mean what it meant for me in March of 2002! It started with a week of the usual drunkenness after work and ended with the typical weekend of golf and being a "no-show." But this weekend was even worse.

I had class all morning on a Saturday. After class, I returned home to yet another handwritten note on the counter stating, "*Will be home by 5:00. I'm sorry. I will call you. This will be the last weekend for this shit, I promise.*" He never came home and he never called.

The following Sunday morning at 5:00 a.m., I received a call from him that he was in jail in Carolina Beach for DWI. They would be moving him to the jail downtown in Wilmington and he needed me to bail him out. There would be a $2,500 bond. He was issued two DWIs in one night! Coming home from some binge in South Carolina he got pulled over on a highway for speeding. He was arrested and taken to jail in Brunswick County. He called a friend in the middle of the night to come to bail him out. In doing so, his friend had to sign a statement that he would not give Dave his keys.

Dave talked his friend into giving him his keys and drove him back to the side of the road to let him drive home! Dave, still being the drunk that he was, decided he would DRIVE PAST OUR DEVELOPMENT and go to the beach, after picking up another six-pack. The DWI papers were sitting on the passenger seat. Dave got picked up at the beach and ended up with two DWIs in one night as well as getting our $30,000 Yukon seized. Gone. Done. Jail. Bondsman. No License. Life Changing Event.

I cried first as I was scared, but then had a sense of relief. This had to be it. This was the wakeup call he needed. This was a costly one, but still. Certainly, he wouldn't drink after all this. It was all over. Life would have some sense of normalcy again once we got past this. The court dates, attorneys, license revocation, were all life changing stuff. However, not life-changing enough for him to stop. Later that day he took off on his bike to ride to a friend's house to drink.

The next few weeks were extremely stressful. We found out the Yukon was gone for good, and that we still had to fulfill the lease payments on it. I had to take him to the North Carolina DMV so he could get a photo ID of himself since he no longer had a license. After that, we drove to the impound yard to pull personal belongings from the truck. Humiliation was an understatement, along with shame and embarrassment. There were Michelob bottle caps strewn all about the floor of the truck along with empty Diet Dew bottles with the still remaining stench of vodka.

A few days later we had an appointment with an attorney, where we learned that 30 days jail time plus three-year license revocation would be likely. We could possibly hope for 7 days of jail time. We both walked out of there with heads down and $2,500 less in the pocket.

Chapter 16

Jailbird

April of that year brought him two court dates, one for each county. Going to court and sitting with other families of "offenders" for God knows what really put things into perspective. As I sat in each of those courtrooms I was still trying to figure out how I ended up there! People from my background didn't end up sitting in court, or so I thought.

Our county left him with no community service, seven days jail (which he could do on weekends), and two years license revocation. The county where he received the first DWI, left him with no community service, no jail, and license revoked for two years. Luckily, the two license revocation periods could run concurrently.

June brought him his first weekend in jail. He had to be there by 6:00 p.m. on Friday and couldn't be picked up until after 5:30 p.m. on Sunday. Those weekends made for some welcomed "me" time, but the days prior to "jail drop off" were always bad. He was still drinking and he would self-medicate himself with Xanax prior to being dropped off. One week leading into jail weekend, he was foul. He said he didn't give a shit about anything and he didn't care any longer. He hoped he "survives" jail.

He was using his weekend jail time as an excuse to continue to drink. He told me all would be better once he got past all the jail time and that he would go to AA meetings again.

Letter to Dave:

July 21, 2002

I have had a lot of time to think over the last few months. I feel like I'm sinking into depression. I don't care about going out. I don't care about myself. I just sit and think about what could have been and what probably won't happen.

I want to be married to someone who adores me and can't wait to see me or do things with me. I want someone who would make me feel special, someone who makes sacrifices for me, someone who will love me unconditionally. Someone who will take care of me and do things with me. I need someone that I can trust, and who won't lie and hide things from me.

Maybe we got married too young, I don't know. I just know there must be a life better than this one. I'm tired of seeing yet another summer go by, with me wishing for more.

You call me on Friday on your cell phone. Claim you can't hear me. You give me a number that won't let me through. You tell me you will call me back from the room phone and you don't. I don't hear from you all weekend.

I think we need to separate. Maybe for a short time...maybe long. I guess we'll just have to wait and see.

It is so over. I am so sad. I cry every day. I can't compete with alcohol any longer. I obviously can't do for you what it does.
- P

My life revolved around him. I had to get him to work and pick him up from work. I had to adjust my own work hours. Luckily, my employer was very understanding. He wanted to go for a ride then I took him for a ride. If I didn't, there would be a fight. I drove him everywhere for over two years. Those were a couple of the longest years of my life.

He had a friend that lived in the development next to ours. This friend had been a recovering alcoholic but had started drinking again. How convenient to have a drinking buddy so close. Dave would ride his bike to his house to drink or to ride to the golf clubhouse and drink there.

There continued to be promises of how it would get better. I didn't have a lot of faith in those promises. One day I went to pick him up after work and he wasn't there. One of his co-workers said he had been gone for almost two hours. I turned to get back in the car to leave, and low and behold he came out from behind the building!

He had walked to a pizza place to drink, then walked back to hang out and wait for me behind his work building?! His boss gave him a letter that morning about going to AA meetings "or else." Guess this was his excuse for the day to go drink. I was so upset I felt like throwing up. I was giving up. There was no hope.

He managed to keep his job. His boss was a very understanding and kind person. Almost too kind as he was getting involved in the personal side a bit too much. We weren't about to complain though as we really needed him to be able to keep his job.

Chapter 17

Time for a Move

Since we were both doing well at work, what better time to move to a larger, more expensive house? At the time we thought it was a logical move. Dave always had a way of sucking me into complacency. He would make me feel safe and secure at the moment and that all was good. He was a masterful manipulator. This other house was closer to our jobs, so it would cut down on all the driving him around I would have to do.

We moved into what was my dream house with a large fenced-in back yard for the pets. It was a classic, very stately looking home about 12 years old that had hardwood floors, tile, built-ins, and a wood-burning fireplace. We were so excited! I was on cloud nine.

Dave's birthday was a couple of weeks after the move. He had taken the day off as we had planned to have some work done around the house. I went to work, oblivious as to what was going on while I was working. I came home to yet another "sorry" note on the counter. He had called a cab and disappeared. He took a wad of cash, not much for clothes, and poof, the day I thought we would be going out to dinner to celebrate his birthday ended up with me crying at home. He did it again. Yet, there I stayed. I waited for his phone call. I pathetically sat on the floor of our bedroom, in front of the open window, staring out at the night, unable to sleep, and waited for him to come home. There were times where

I literally felt that my heart was breaking into a million pieces.

There were good days and bad but at this point more bad than good. I had taken off my wedding ring. I didn't even care anymore and he obviously didn't either. I would sit and try to figure out how much I could afford for rent if I were to leave. I went through this agonizing exercise every year so it seemed.

I recall one weekend after an especially difficult and trying week, I was going to go apartment shopping. I had figured out what my budget was and was determined to find a suitable place for me and the dogs.

I managed to go to two different apartment complexes, both who gave me tours. One was much nicer and I was quite excited. However, they had a pet weight limit and the dogs weighed too much. I wasn't about to leave them home with Dave, so that option was out. I then moved on to a different and not quite as nice complex. A very nice lady took me on a tour of one of their larger units.

It was depressing. The carpet smelled and as I looked out into the complex courtyard, I saw people milling about, some of them smoking, and a few people with pit-bulls. This was so not the place for me, but most likely the only place that I could find in my budget at the time that would take all three dogs.

I followed the manager back to the apartment complex office and sat down for a face to face "interview" along with having to complete the application. Her first question to me was "Why are you looking to move?" Not the question I needed to hear. The reality of where I was and what I was doing hit me. I was an emotional wreck of tears and garbled speech as I tried to respond to the lady. I was gasping some incoherent words like "divorce," "alcohol," and "don't know where to go." I felt bad for the lady as she didn't quite know how to respond, so I ended up just getting up and running out of the office to my car. That concluded that weekend's apartment hunt. I felt trapped and scared. That had to be one of my lowest points.

One day while at work I received a call from a friend of his that I needed to get home as soon as possible. Luckily, I only worked about 10 minutes from the house.

I pulled in the driveway and ran into the house to quite the scene. Dave was sobbing and clutching a 2-liter bottle of what I thought was 7-Up. However, there was very little soda and way more vodka in it. He was sobbing uncontrollably and sweating. There was sticky soda and vodka everywhere in the kitchen and he was babbling about how he wanted to kill himself. His friend was trying to talk calmly to him and trying to get him to hand over the bottle. Dave wouldn't have any of it. He clutched that bottle for dear life. His eyes were big and round and his pupils were dilated.

He got up and stumbled with his bottle to our tiny half bathroom off the kitchen. He slammed the door and locked it. We heard banging and crashing which ended up being him punching a hole in both the door and the drywall of the bathroom.

I called his doctor friend, not knowing what else to do. He told me to call 911. Here enters my first experience with cops coming to my house. The ambulance came, the Sherriff's department came, and even the fire department came. Oh, to be a neighbor on our street that day. So much for the dream house and thoughts of normalcy and friendly outdoor gatherings. I had hoped everyone else in the neighborhood was at work. We weren't able to keep that incident very well hidden.

I called his AA "sponsor" Fred, who came as well. The Sherriff came in and talked Dave out of the bathroom. They loaded him up in the ambulance and hauled him off to the Emergency Room at the local hospital. I can't even recall at this point what his blood/alcohol level was at the time, but it was high. From the ER, they transferred him to The Oaks, which was a psych ward. He was locked in there and unable to have any contact with me. Fred took care of everything from the ER to the Oaks for those couple days until Dave dried out. I don't know what I would have done without Fred at that time.

Chapter 18

Same 'Ole Same 'Ole

He had been drinking again. I could tell by the moods. He came home from golf and went upstairs. He wouldn't stay in the living room with me. Too much Diet Dew was disappearing too quickly around the house. He was drinking right in front of me. I didn't dare ask questions or a fight would erupt.

I came home one afternoon from errands and he was in the living room with "the cup." He was on the phone with a maintenance guy, slurring words, trying to set up a time for them to come. I made the mistake of accusing him of drinking. A fight broke out. He told me he would help me move out. He wanted to remain friends and would help me as needed. He told me he loved me like a sister for the last five years. He told me he wouldn't leave because I couldn't afford the house by myself.

It hurt me so badly. I couldn't breathe. My heart felt like it was ripped in two. The words cut like a jagged knife. Here we went again. I could have made it on my own, but what about the pets? He couldn't be trusted with any of the pets. He lived in a world of ups and downs, drunken stupor to a rational thinker. Back and forth. Back and forth.

I longed for "normal." A spouse that physically hit me would be better than this. I was at a loss for what to do. I told him I was moving out. Dave freaked out, threw his arms around, and hurled the remote control into the cabinet, shattering it into pieces.

I already had the next day off, which was a blessing. I woke up in the middle of the night crying and couldn't get back to sleep. My head was splitting in pain. I started to pack, mentally making lists of things I would take with me. All this preparation, yet I stayed. Again.

He went to work the following day and said he didn't mean any of the things he had said the prior day. I was afraid he would keep drinking. I couldn't control it. I had to just let him destroy himself and try to start living MY life.

He left work early that day to drink. A cab brought him home drunk. He didn't go to work the next day. He was drunk. He wasn't sleeping. I called a mover for Saturday to move to the townhouse. I ended up calling to cancel the mover on the Friday prior. Dave said he needed to "get past this." Yet he never did.

I was so fearful of what would happen. My life had been consumed by him and his affair with alcohol. I was at his beck and call. He had a way of making me believe he was sincere, that things would change. They never did. I wanted my hope to be worthwhile. I wanted "normal" so badly. I didn't think it was attainable.

How sad my life had become, looking for alcohol, sniffing glasses and bottles, and going through drawers. What good did it do? I found it and would dump it. He would get a cab and buy more. What had my life become? Who was controlling my life, me or him?

He had taken yet another trip to Pinehurst, which is a major golfing destination. It wasn't uncommon for him to take a cab the two-plus hours to get there.

Upon his return via cab from this particular trip, he was extremely paranoid. He had golfed with various strangers while he was there but didn't remember who they were or what he may have talked to them about. After going to work a couple of days upon his return, he told me that he thought people were watching him at his office. These "people" were people that he had met in Pinehurst and he must have made them mad. They knew where he worked and they were camped out in various vehicles watching his comings and goings. He said that he thought they may have been mob related.

This is yet another prime example of what long term use of alcohol will do to your brain. It messes you up. It kills brain cells. It can change people forever.

May 2003 – An email Dave sent me from work –

Someday you will be proud of me...I promise.... You are my best friend and soul mate... I hope you understand that all the pain and shit from my drinking would never have occurred without the drink... please understand that my mind is sick just like your dad's is from his Parkinson's. No difference except I have a choice to make and he does not. Sometimes my mind makes me take that choice to drink. I have a lot of regret over my neglect of my family (you, your dad, my dad)... but I have to keep telling myself that I am a sick person....remember... alcoholism is a disease of the mind... I can take the alcohol out but I still will always have the "ism"... that is why I can never quit the meetings. I think I am finally figuring this out. This paranoia is scaring the hell out of me... I hope it is just paranoia.

I RSVP'd for a block party in our neighborhood. He said he would attend. Of course, he stated that in a moment of clarity and sobriety. The party day arrived and he decided to golf. When he came home, I became suspicious. He would back out and a fight would start. He slammed shades, threw things and whined about going. I went by myself, choking back tears as I walked up to 50 strangers by myself. I only stayed for an hour, but when I got back, he was gone. I found yet another receipt for beer/wine.

I shouldn't have but I tossed it at him when he got home and he still denied drinking. He finally said that I made him drink because I wanted him to go with me. He laughed at me because I found a receipt and laughed more at the fact that I would look. I told him that it was what my life had become... looking for receipts and sniffing bottles. I told him I was not the reason for him being an alcoholic and choosing to drink himself to death. I wouldn't stand for it. It wasn't my fault!

He took and took. He was sucking the life out of me. He wouldn't give back to me, yet claimed how good it made him feel to give to others.

October 2003 – I received an email from him at work.... subject line: Commitment

Hello Girl.... After this weekend I have decided that one day will be for golf (mostly Saturday) and the other day will be for us and the family. The only exceptions will be like the Pinehurst weekend or special tournaments, in the case of the tourney's I will always be with you in the morning or the afternoon of the days of the tourney. If I have a tournament on a Sunday, I will not play on Saturday unless you have something planned for just you. If I do play on both days, it will only happen once a month, with no exceptions unless you get tired of me at home. I think this will get us back on the right track and make your weekends more enjoyable. After a while, you may be telling me to go play (lol). Bottom line... I miss hanging out with you on weekends and just taking it easy (yard work allowed). Shopping, etc. -D

Excerpts from a journal entry....

November 2, 2003

Dave says he is going to start going to meetings again on Monday. That is the famous tag line of his. "It's what I need to do" he states. He will golf and be home and we'll have a great afternoon. He promises he won't be drunk but will have "just a couple" at the course. He came home at 4:00 in the afternoon and passed out on his couch.

I took a picture. Passed out. When he did get up four hours later, he came into the kitchen, ran into the center island, and then stumbled up the stairs to bed. I found four Coors Light bottles in his golf bag and found more bottles mixed with vodka in his truck.

I'm so tired. Sometimes tears won't even fall. I drove around looking at neighborhoods that morning, in case I needed to move. I need to think about myself.

All I do is work... at work and at home. He does nothing but goes to work, lie, golf, lie, and sleep. He drinks in front of me and away from me. One of the lowest of the low for me was after another drunken argument, he begged and pleaded...and threatened me if I didn't leave the house and go buy him a six pack of beer. I was afraid of what he might do, so I did. I cried the entire way to the convenience store and back. My shame at myself was intolerable.

Chapter 19

Roller Coaster Ride

Excerpt from a journal entry from 2014 –

January 13 – Chauffeur that I had become, I did my duty to pick him up at the golf course after he enjoyed himself with a round of golf and, no doubt, a few cold ones. When I pulled up, he was clinging to his glass of "Diet Dew." He drank the whole thing. He never drinks all his soda on the way home. VODKA. I had him look me in the eye and answer my questions, "Have you been drinking?" He is the best liar in the world and denies it right to my face.

At home, two hours later he has me follow him around while he supposedly pulls all his "stash" to give to me to get rid of. It was in the attic, sock drawers, shoe boxes, shirt drawers....out comes container after container of vodka. The whole time he keeps saying to me, "Don't get mad. Don't freak out." I choke back tears and refuse to let him see any of my anger or despair.

After that exercise is over, he goes out to relax in his hot tub. Typical, as I'm sure he was just mentally exhausted getting rid of all his stash. Poor fella. Meanwhile, I'm standing at the kitchen sink, dumping out 29 mini-bottles of vodka, 1 water bottle full of vodka, and two Diet Dew bottles full.

New year, same shit! We should have moved out last October. I want to run outside and scream at the top of my lungs. I want to break things. I want to be alone. I can't handle this.

January 16 – He has been drinking by the time I get home from work. I can tell. He knows I know, yet we don't talk about it, which is what our lives have become. We leave to go out to dinner. He says he wants to drive around and talk first. I know it will be bad. He is slurring and not speaking in normal tones. He goes on to rant and rave about his boss putting someone else in charge at work, and that is why he has been drinking. Sure, it is. This is yet another excuse. He wants to tell his boss off. He is bitter about his job situation. Paranoid.... Not rational. Do I believe him? He has used his job as an excuse before then later told me it was a lie. If it is true, I want to say, "What are you, fucking stupid? You made your bed, now go lay in it! I'm sick of your excuses, pity parties, and blame!" Needless to say, I didn't say that.

January 17 – Another wonderful Saturday to look forward to. What will this day bring? Dave left the house at 6:30 a.m. It is dark and 27 degrees outside. He says he is going to golf and he would be home by 1:30.

He never came home. He took another cab to Pinehurst! That cab driver certainly loved Dave as I'm sure all the fares to and from Pinehurst put his children through college! I have GOT to get my money out of the bank. He will drain the account. He is racking up bills on the credit card. He called me at 7:00 p.m. to tell me he was there. He called again at 12:17 a.m. "Do you love me?" he questions. Go figure. He calls again at 7:20 a.m. on Sunday. Raining in Pinehurst and he will come home... he'll be home at 12:30. But no, yet another lie. He got home at 4:00 p.m., went upstairs and passed out. He had a shopping bag with new clothes and he was wearing new clothes. He had taken a cab around Pinehurst to find a store and buy new clothes that he could wear while golfing! I want to take a knife and shred everything. I want to douse his bag in gas and set it on fire. I want to toss everything he has in the front yard.

He leaves the following Wednesday to go out of town. More golf, more drinking, more money gone. I'm so over it. I'm surprised I'm still thinking rationally. Or am I? My despair has no words. My pain and emotion are indescribable. I have lost my best years. My youth is over.

The following Sunday night around 8:00 p.m. he comes down the stairs from the bedroom, fully dressed. He called a cab to have it come and drive him around while he drank. That is the most pathetic thing I have ever heard, next to riding a bike to a store for beer. Been there done that too.

Monday, Jan 19th – He is pacing the floor. He won't stop walking back and forth. He won't eat. A bit before 7:00 p.m. he puts on his shoes and called a friend to pick him up and take him to get booze. He states that he has to get something in his system.

I'm worried about his job. He called me at work the next morning and told me everything was fine with work. He blamed his most recent binge on our dog having seizures. Yet another excuse.

I brought him home food for lunch. He was out of it. He called me later at work that day, crying out gut-wrenching cries that he needs help and can't stop. He is so sorry. He loves me more than anything.

January 23, 2004

After yet another particularly difficult few days, I sent him an email at work in the hopes that he was feeling better, which led to the string of emails:

I am not... very depressed... All I want to do is sleep and forget. Love you too... Dave

Dave, I know this probably won't help, but keep thinking of our blessings that we have each other, family, jobs, and our house. We can have a great year ahead of us. Townhouse going bye-bye...a new start (I know that sounds incredibly difficult for you right now) we can have a great life together...... forever..... P

You must understand that I know this and still have done stupid destructive stuff that can take it all away. Hard to come to terms with... GUILT! GUILT! GUILT! - D

I guess I'll just say, "let go and let God." You can't keep beating yourself up about this. I'll stop now.... Call or email me if you need me.... Love you much.... − P

If there was a God, he would not have allowed me to do the things I cannot forgive myself for. Period. - D

February 2005

After a bad night of screaming and yelling at each other, I received an email at work sent from him.

I am sorry I jumped down your throat this morning. I am just getting to a boiling point over not having any control over anything and no license. Then it seems you always fuel the fire by belittling what I am trying to do with our savings and budgeting and want to take any form of control away. You know, sometimes a man needs to have his ego stroked or at least know that his wife respects and admires him...and it seems you do not have the capacity to do that. We have some serious issues to deal with if our marriage is going to work long term. I think one of two things:

#1 − You have so much resentment built up toward me from my "drinking days" and let it off by your attitude toward me on most issues and by not ever thinking I am capable of handling anything. And not to mention the comments you make about how I have no idea about the timing of bills and cash flow. If I hear that one more time, you will see just how much control I can assert. OR

#2 − You are truly an unhappy and bitter woman...and either take for granted or dismiss what I am doing to make my life better. Believe it or not, #2 is how you make me feel 90% of the time. I truly appreciate all the "wife" duties you do for me

like cooking, cleaning, etc., but it is hard to show appreciation toward you when more than half the time you are bitter or sour toward me or correcting me, or telling me to shut up. I can go on and on. Basically, I am a bother. I think you really need to think about your true feelings and if you really want to be married to me for the rest of your life. You may find that you truly do not need me and our past is just too much for you to overcome. After all, you only have one life to live and it is not too late for either of us to obtain happiness. Sincerely... Dave... Thanks.

To which my blunt reply was:

Gee, that is a nice apology. I was thinking about all this on my way to work. You know, we don't even have anything in common anymore. You think everything I watch on TV is stupid, tell me I continually suck the joy out of your life, go to bed early every night, don't want to watch the news, music taste has completely changed AND ... since you let off a huge puff of steam... you seem to think that since you suddenly got the desire to watch spending that all these years that I have been taking care of finances I haven't been able to save. Let's think about it. how can I save money when you were taking trips all over the place and debiting accounts that I wouldn't know about until a month later when it showed up on the bank statement! You were in a haze and had no interest in what money was being spent on. Now that you are out of your haze, you keep telling me YOU had the ability to put money in savings and I didn't/don't. If I hear THAT one more time you will see a side of me as well. I don't need your hot temper flaring at me and your "F" word continually screamed in my face whenever we have a disagreement.

You can also stop throwing the "I'll just drink again" bit in my face. I have finally come to the conclusion that what you do about that issue is in your control. I used to blame myself for years, and over the last three FINALLY came to the realization that even though you say, "You'll drive me to drink", I know that isn't the case. It isn't in my control and you can't make me think any longer that it was/is my fault.

Yes... perhaps we both have to do some soul searching... that is a point where at least I think we may finally agree. – P

Chapter 20

Graduation

I graduated from college in 2005! To this day I can't believe that I was spending multiple hours a day involved in dog rescue, working full-time AND going to school. I look back at that time and am in actual awe of myself. It was one of the moments I was most proud of... making it through school to obtain my Bachelor's degree. That and all while Dave spent time wasting away with vodka.

I was resentful that it appeared Dave didn't understand what willpower that took. The fact that no matter what was going on with him, I committed to finishing school. I had the option to walk on graduation day and wear an actual cap and gown. When I mentioned it to him he said, "you aren't actually going to walk are you?" I didn't get a card from him. I didn't even get dinner. I went to a local consignment shop and bought myself a graduation gift of two very uniquely carved wooden chests. I received my diploma in the mail.

Chapter 21

Free at Last – Thank God Almighty – Free at Last

After two years with a suspended license, Dave finally got his license back with the restriction of having an interlock device installed. An interlock is a device where one must blow into it before the vehicle will start. If it senses any alcohol, the vehicle won't start, plus it records the fact that someone that has been drinking blew into it.

He had to have the report pulled and read monthly, and the information was then sent to the DMV. He had the interlock for over a year. It was a pain, as it wasn't as easy for me to drive that vehicle, but it was a blessing as there was no way he was going to drink and drive! I truly thought that it helped get him sober along with attending AA meetings.

Soon after the device was removed, he had to start traveling for business. This made me extremely nervous, as I didn't know if he could be trusted to stay away from drinking when he was out on the road and in hotels on his own. I found out later that he did start again eventually, but hid it well. He had convinced himself that he could do so on a business trip, then sober up enough where I wouldn't know once he got home.

Because of all the traveling, he had to do, he finally got over his fear of flying. He also earned many frequent flyer miles. When he was sober, life was great. We had so much fun together in 2010, jetting off to the Turks and Caicos for a week, where we rented a large house on the bay with family, rented jet skis, and dined out at fabulous eateries. A couple of months later, we went to the Caymans for four days and stayed at the Ritz Carlton, took a sunset catamaran tour, and spent hours and hours in the water. That same year we hit London, which was a business trip for him. We toured the city, tried local foods, and walked until we were exhausted, having a blast the entire time. I have numerous photos of us truly happy and having a good time together.

Chapter 22

Cancer Scare

I was not good at taking care of myself and didn't go to the doctor for regular checkups. I had been having some bleeding from my left breast off and on for a few months. I finally scheduled an appointment to have it checked out.

It was a female doctor who basically had zero bedside manners. I found out at that appointment that I most likely had fibroids on my uterus and "gee, couldn't you tell you were bigger down there?" as my doctor so bluntly put it. Not only that, but she freaked me out by telling me I needed to get a mammogram as soon as possible as she had found a lump. She looked at me and said "sorry" and started to walk out the door! I said "Wait a minute! What do you mean sorry?" She softened up a bit, came back and sat down in front of me and told me she was sorry for being so blunt, but that I really needed to get all this checked out as soon as possible.

My mind was a whirlwind. As I put my clothes back on I was fighting back the tears. As I stood in line to check out of the office, all I could think about was cancer. I finally made it out to the car and called Dave at work. I cried through the phone that "she found a lump." I could tell by his reaction on the phone that he was upset as well. He asked me if he needed to come and pick me up, but and I told him I was fine to drive home.

I cried the whole way home. I can't even recall how I got home, past all those stoplights through all that traffic. I must have been driving on auto-pilot. I was in a daze and was scared beyond belief. I didn't know what to expect. I had never had any procedures, mammograms or health issues.

When I got home, Dave was already home waiting for me. He hugged me and assuming I didn't feel like cooking, we went out to dinner. It was weird. We didn't really know what to say to each other and there was a lot of awkward silence like we were both trying to absorb what was going on. We stared at the food and at each other.

He had called a good friend of his that was a doctor, to get the name of a reputable oncologist in town to have a consult with. He went with me to my mammogram, which was scheduled for the very next day. He patiently waited in the waiting room while they did the mammogram along with an ultrasound.

The thing that stuck with me the most though was how very caring, considerate and kind he was to me during this time. He was almost overly protective, but I welcomed the kindness. All I could think about those first few days was how I wouldn't be well for our 25th wedding anniversary and was picturing myself without hair. That was on my mind non-stop. I didn't care about anything else. I couldn't push the thought of me having cancer out of my brain for a moment. Those first few days were the most brutal I had ever had.

Dave's doctor friend managed to pull some strings and got me into one of the top oncology surgeons in Wilmington for a consult. What a relief. It was like a load was lifted off me. He told me he was 97% sure it wasn't anything to worry about. When I walked out of that office, I felt like all the stress of everything had just been removed from my shoulders.

It was determined that I would need to have a surgical biopsy, but they wouldn't be able to do it for four weeks or more! More torture in waiting and the fear of the unknown. It was then that he asked me if I wanted to go to Italy with him on a business trip. He didn't have to go and someone else at work was slated to go, but he would ask if he could go instead.

I know he was hoping to take my mind off everything. We flew into Venice, then drove up to Aviano Air Force Base for two days of work, then back down to Venice for three nights. Other than the fact I got sick as a dog with a bad cold the morning we were to start our fun in Venice, the trip was a blast! We were there during their Carnival time, and the locals were dressed in Victorian costumes complete with full masks and face painting.

We both got our faces painted! Dave got a very cool design painted on the side of his face and walked around Venice all day and night with the paint on! We got great pictures and people were all looking at him and some were taking pictures of him as well. He was looking quite striking with his dark hair, dark complexion and the facial art the face painter applied, complete with glitter! I had the best time. Shopping, eating, and blowing my nose!

A few weeks after our return from the trip, I had my procedure and received the wonderful news that it wasn't cancer!

Chapter 23

Business Trip

The more Dave traveled the more miles it added to his Delta Sky Miles account, as well as adding more alcohol to his system. He would plan an opportunity to take a trip so he could get away and drink.

He left on a business trip to be combined with some personal time to see family in the Midwest. He was gone almost a week, which I thoroughly enjoyed. He was calling me every night to tell me about each day, which were lies. He had gone off on a road trip drinking binge. He did have a meeting in Oklahoma, but canceled another one. He did stop to see family, but didn't stay with them. He stayed in a motel and drank. He told me he was going to leave early to come home as he missed us, which was another lie.

He did leave early, but only drove a few hours then spent the remainder of the day in a hotel room with Vodka. As he was calling me on those last couple days, I had a feeling something was off. What he was telling me wasn't making sense.

A few days later, he told me that he wasn't all bad and there was a good person inside there. He went on to tell me a story about a man he met on the road.

While on his binge trip, Dave had stopped off an interstate to eat at a restaurant. He had spotted a man with just a backpack that appeared to be homeless, hungry and in need of a ride. Dave started to converse with him, which led Dave to invite him to come inside so he could buy him lunch.

They had a nice conversation over lunch, where the man explained that he was on his own, had lost his wife and family and was trying to get back down to Texas to a homeless place he had stayed at in the past.

Dave bought him a bus ticket and took him to the nearest bus stop. Prior to boarding the bus, the man asked for Dave's contact information. He was so grateful and wanted to keep in touch. They exchanged information. The sad part was that Dave lost the guy's name, and had given him a false name and phone number.

Dave regretted not giving the guy his real name and phone number, as he wondered what happened to him and if he made it to the shelter. The way Dave was telling this story I knew it was the truth. He hadn't shared it with anyone else and didn't want any praise or glory for what he had done. He was just trying to help someone else in need.

Who knows, maybe Dave felt deep down inside he could be in need of a hand in the future and someone would pay it forward for him. This tiny little hidden piece of Dave was very special and moments like this made my heart sing for him.

After that tough weekend upon his return home, I received the following email from him at work that next Monday:

Subject: My thought for you today

I wish I was the perfect husband. I pray today to be much better than I am. Sometimes I sit and look at you and am filled with amazement that you have chosen me as your partner, companion and lover. My mind and heart are filled with the memories of the fun trips we have taken over the past 18 months and hope this last month has not soured that for you. I am so grateful for your loyal unyielding support of me during this rough patch I have gone through.

Lord help me to be all the things she needs me to be in support of her work, her life, and her devotion to me. Help me to be honest, dependable and supporting. ☺

Unfortunately, a couple months later things would come to a nasty head, in more ways than one.

Chapter 24

Me Time?

One Sunday evening, after spending the weekend chasing pills with Vodka and soda, Dave arrived home after golfing for the day. He staggered in, practically stumbling over the dogs, went to the couch to sit down and started crying that he needed help.

He called his boss. He told him he needed help and he was checking himself into the local treatment center right away. He was so sorry for everything he had done.

After the call, he looked at me with puffy eyes and asked me if I would call the treatment center to get him in. I called and made the arrangements and packed a bag, hurrying as fast as I could before he changed his mind. The stench of alcohol on him was strong. It was amazing that he made it home from wherever he spent the afternoon!

He was crying and sniffling the entire way to the treatment center. I was driving as fast as I could, as I didn't want him to change his mind. When we arrived, all it took was to sit in the lobby about 10 minutes while waiting for the intake person, before he started to change his mind. The clock crept ahead another 15 minutes, and I was frantically trying to talk him back down off the ledge, telling him that this was the right thing to do, both for him and for me.

He started talking about missing his dog and what would he do if he died while he was there. I still reassured him that all would be fine. He got up and started pacing, stating we needed to leave and he would just do it on his own. At that point, I went to the front desk and said, "Can we get someone out here to take him in the back before he walks out of here please?"

Finally, some in-take person from the back came out to get him. We all walked back to his office. The counselor was very nice, but was way too slow moving for me. They just didn't understand what a flight risk this guy was. After going through the same questions repeatedly, and going off to the bathroom for a urine sample, they finally got him ushered to the residence area.

The feeling of relief that came over me as I walked to the car had me crying almost the entire way home. I needed much deserved "me" time to recoup.

The following morning, I received three phone calls from Dave from the treatment center. The first one was to request certain clothes. The second call was to see how long it would take me to drop off the clothes. The third one was to request $20. Something told me that it wasn't going to be much of a "me" day after all!

As I was sitting in one of my favorite restaurants, I received yet another call from the treatment center. This time it was from a nurse counselor who told me Dave wanted to leave and could I please help convince him to at least stay for three days to detox? She put him on the phone and I tried my best to convince him.

The pleading seemed to work. He agreed to stay for three days. Within two hours I received a call from an unknown number. It was Dave. He had walked out of the treatment center and over a mile to a convenience store. He was calling from a pay phone, telling me that I needed to come pick him up.

One really can't make this stuff up. Fresh off a drunken binge, walked out of a treatment center without ID or his bag, and managed to convince the lady behind the desk of the gas station to let him use her phone. This had started him on yet another path that I didn't want to go down.

Chapter 25

More Pills?

After speaking with his doctor friend, Dave finally decided to enlist the help of a trained psychologist. I was very happy to hear this as I had thought Dave has needed this for a long period of time. Perhaps this doctor could get to the bottom of Dave's issues and he would be able to once again get back on the right path.

After a couple visits, he was prescribed an anti-depressant. I hadn't seen much of a change in Dave after taking the medication. We had booked a week-long trip to Utah to the Grand Canyon for mid-August, but ended up canceling it. He wasn't in a good state of mind and we decided neither of us was really into it. Instead we booked a trip to Gatlinburg, Tennessee to stay in a dog friendly cabin. We would take our two dogs and make a real family vacation of it.

Most of the drive was in silence as Dave was either depressed from the meds or depressed because of coming off his binge drinking. Not sure. In any case, the trip was not a lot of fun, and most of each day was spent in silence.

Dave was so caught up in how wronged he had been by his boss and how nobody respected what he had done for that company, that it literally ate at him. I had hopes that seeing a therapist would help some of the resentment, but it didn't. After gaining trust back, Dave dropped a bombshell on him. He quit and went to work for one of their closest competitors.

It's like he was on a high after he quit. He stated he finally felt free and was excited to help his new employer build the business like he did with the last company. He took a cut in pay. He even bought me a new sterling silver necklace pendant in celebration of him being "free." Being the supportive wife that I was, I tried to be supportive of his decision. I felt if staying with his past employer was causing him so much resentment each day, it would be better to be away from it and to start over somewhere new.

The new job brought with it an opportunity to go to New York City on a business trip. This also meant that I would get to go. The trip was great. He didn't drink. We toured the city, hit a Broadway musical, and enjoyed the excellent cuisine that NYC has to offer.

Hindsight is 20/20 as they say. Not sure whether the pills aided in the euphoria of the thoughts of leaving his job, or whether it was one of the situations where he wasn't really in a clear mind after "stopping" drinking. They say an alcoholic should never make a life changing decision within the first 12 months of sobriety. Not in Dave's case. He was always the exception rather than the rule.

Chapter 26

Happy 25th Anniversary – Not so Much

The days after the return from NYC brought drinking pretty much every weekend. He just wasn't right. He was depressed. He was quiet. He wasn't motivated. He didn't seem to care much about anything, including any preparation or planning whatsoever for our big 25th wedding anniversary.

It didn't help that our sweet 12-year-old dog, Mason, was in very ill health and undergoing kidney failure. I was giving Mason sub-Q fluids every day. Poor Mason got to the point where our vet indicated it was probably time to let him go. He was supposed to be a 65-pound dog but had wasted away to a mere 44 pounds. Every bone in his little body protruded out from his skin. His tail didn't wag much and he didn't have the energy or desire to get up and follow anyone around the house any longer. The vet prescribed some pain medication, which at least made his days more bearable.

Based on our vet's recommendation, I was trying to be the rational one and set something up to end the suffering of our loyal friend. This would be one of the most difficult things we would ever have to do, especially for Dave. Dave and Mason had such a very special bond.

The Saturday we were supposed to take him in was the Saturday prior to our 25th wedding anniversary. Mason was weak but had just a bit more of a sparkle in his eye than he did the few days prior. Dave took Mason out for a long ride, which was supposed to be the "final" ride. When they came back, Dave looked like he was completely out of sorts. He was staggering, slurring his words and speaking incoherently.

He started telling me that he was seeing double. He staggered across the floor and shuffled into the bathroom. I soon heard the water running in bathtub.

Dave had climbed into the bathtub, fully clothed. He had on his shoes, jeans, T-shirt and sweatshirt. He was just sitting in the tub as the water was rising. I screamed "What the heck are you doing?" He replied, "I'm taking a bath." We had a conversation that wouldn't make sense to anyone, me included. He stumbled out of the tub, muttering that he couldn't believe he got in the tub with clothes on. We canceled Mason's euthanasia that day.

Anniversary day basically just came and went like any other day. A year prior, we had talked about taking a big trip to Italy or Greece, or maybe even Australia. Here it was a year later and nothing. I did get a card, which was left for me on the counter. I gave him a card. I took the day off for myself for more "me" time to reflect on what was going on.

That evening we ate at an Italian restaurant. No pictures. No friends. Nothing. It was such an utter disappointment for such a landmark occasion. I made it. I stayed married to this guy through all his shit for 25 years and nothing.

It wasn't like I wanted a huge gift. The connection was missing. Neither of us really cared. We came home after dinner and he went to bed while I stayed up and watched TV. Happy 25th Wedding Anniversary.

Chapter 27

Happy Holidays?

Christmas came and went. Nothing special there either. I didn't even have the energy to fully decorate the house partly due to having two new dogs in the house, but the other part was I just didn't feel very "merry" about much of anything.

We didn't go out. We didn't do our normal Christmas movie marathon. I cooked and we stayed in. By now the neighbors probably thought he didn't exist. He never spent time outside. When he left the house, he would drink. When he came home, he passed out in the living room or went straight to bed. Alcohol was hidden all over the place, with little tiny bottles tucked away safely for their next rendezvous.

We didn't even exchange gifts. Not even a Christmas card or a Christmas kiss. The extra time I took off during the holidays was torture. He would just lie around in a pill and alcohol haze, while I tried to entertain two new dogs, while taking care of our sweet Mason, who was still literally fading away before our eyes.

Chapter 28

Not so Happy New Year - 2012!

The weather forecast for New Year's Eve was a good one, and I was looking forward to having some nice time outdoors.

Dave had stopped eating and wasn't sleeping. He got up one morning for an early appointment with his therapist. He left earlier than normal, which led me to believe he was going to start drinking early.

About 30 minutes into what should have been his appointment time, I received a call from his therapist's office. He was there and he was drunk. The doctor indicated I needed to come to his office as soon as possible and that he had everything all set up for him to be admitted into the treatment center.

Yet another day I had to call in that I wasn't going into work at my job because he couldn't get his act together. Upon my arrival I was escorted back to the doctor's office to find Dave all slobbery and blubbery sitting on the couch.

We stumble out of the office and to my car where we took the 5-minute drive to the treatment center. This was the second time in less than a year. Maybe THIS will be the end of it all.

Chapter 29

Not so Fast

I was in my "thank goodness he is somewhere safe" mode as I drove around town running errands when I received a phone call from one of his co-workers, Mary. She said, "Did you hear from Dave?"

"What?!" I replied. "He is in the treatment center."

Mary stated that he wasn't. He had walked out again, still drunk, and had made his way up to the convenience store a mile away to call her to pick him up. Guess he figured if he called me I wouldn't be giving him a ride. He told her if she wasn't there in 15 minutes he would call a cab.

We were frantic. I made a phone call to his doctor, who had just assisted in getting him admitted to that treatment center a few hours earlier. He panicked and asked where Dave was calling from. It was a matter of who can get across town first, me or Mary. I was racing to get there and as I ran inside the store, he wasn't there. I was deflated. Mary called me back and indicated that his doctor got him and we were to meet them at the hospital's emergency room. It was time to get him back into The Oaks, which was the detoxification center he had been in a few years prior.

As I sat there in the ER with him lying flat on a gurney, I wondered what lied ahead for me…. For us. The past couple months had been a roller coaster of emotions and stress, with more lows than highs, unfortunately. How much can one person like me take? How much abuse in pills and alcohol can his body take before it would is finally shut down? How much embarrassment and failure was he willing to conquer? Was he strong enough to get better? Did he even WANT to get better?

Chapter 30

Locked In

After a very long day in the ER and the "behavioral/psych" process, they finally transferred him later that evening to The Oaks, where you can't just walk out. It was much more secure than the treatment center. They monitored vitals, had very strict rules, and had counseling and activities for the patients.

Another sense of relief overwhelmed me. I finally got some much-needed time to myself to relax and not be on pins and needles, waiting for him to pop out of the bedroom, screaming how he couldn't sleep and needed a pill. It was a great few days. I could even feel it within my own body. I was more relaxed and care free. Even the pets were more relaxed. The poor dogs had been through mass quantities of hysteria, which had been very stressful on them. Animals can totally sense our emotions and the emotional state of the home life was not a good one.

He was allowed to receive two calls a day. There were visiting hours for only a couple hours each day. Patients need to focus on recovery, not on visiting with friends and family. My first visit the following night after he was admitted produced a somber and very defeated looking Dave. He was humbled and embarrassed. During our conversation, he had the nerve to say that he didn't think he needed to stay more than three days. I told him that was for the doctors to determine, not him. He made it clear to me that he could still walk out if he wanted to, it would just be "Against Medical Advisement."

Sure enough, after three full days I received a call from one of the counselors there, indicating that Dave wanted to leave. He was asking for my help to convince him to stay one more day. I tried. They let him out earlier than he really should have been released. He played them. He knew how to play the game and how to manipulate. He knew that it looked good for him to help others there and to be involved in activities. He knew how to tell them what they want to hear. My time to relax and enjoy life was over.

Chapter 31

Committal

So there I was, sitting and waiting for the Magistrate to call me up to the window. Being committed to a hospital was serious business. I was nervous as I slid the completed paperwork through the tiny slot to the Magistrate. The poor man could tell I was a wreck, but then again, I supposed most of those that are filling out paperwork for involuntary committal are!

I sat and waited, not knowing what to expect next. A largely built, rough looking man kept staring at me. He had walked in the room with papers in his hand. He finally caught my eye and said, "Hey, do I know you from somewhere?" "No, I don't think so." I replied. He was another bail bondsman.

I called his therapist to confirm I had the order of committal. I called his family. I called the only friend I figured would be a good choice to be at the house with me just in case, his doctor friend, who would meet me at the house.

Who else will go to the house? Will it be the Police or the Sheriff's Department? What if they beat me there? What will the neighbors think? What will Dave do to me? What did this whole nightmare mean? Was I in a nightmare?

I was told I needed to have the city's Police go since we lived within the city limits. I was to call 911 when I was about 10 minutes from the house and tell the operator that I had an order from the Magistrate for an involuntary committal of my husband.

I sped home, watching the clock closely to be sure I was timing everything just right. I nervously dialed 911 and got dispatch. I told her I was not calling regarding an outright emergency, and gave her the reason for my call. She asked me questions like if I expected him to become violent, did he have any weapons, were there drugs involved, did I feel like I would be in any harm. To all those questions I answered "No." Dispatch told me she would have an officer at my home in a few minutes.

I pulled in the garage and the dogs were all out and about within the house. I had crated the little ones before I left, so this wasn't a good sign. He had woken up. When I had arrived home from work earlier that day he was in bed passed out. When I tried to wake him up, all he could talk about was how he wished he wouldn't ever wake up and how he wanted to kill himself. That was what led me to start the wheels spinning toward committal.

As I came through the door he scared the heck out of me as he was standing in the middle of the kitchen, all dazed and confused looking, demanding to know where I had been. I told him I went out to take care of some things. He was extremely suspicious of me and wouldn't let it go. I told him to just go back to bed and not worry about it. He kept pressing and pressing so I had to confess. He needed to know anyway, as he needed to get dressed for the police visit. He had on underwear, socks and a T-shirt.

I told him that someone was coming to take him to the hospital. I don't think he understood at first what I was saying. Then it hit him. He said "You are committing me? How can you do this to me?" He kept saying it over and over and over and over! He was whining and stumbling around. I went to the front door, anxiously awaiting the arrival of his friend. I really needed him now to help me talk Dave off the ledge. A few minutes later, he arrived.

At this point, Dave was slowly putting on clothes, but continually saying that he didn't need to go anywhere. He was becoming more and more agitated. His friend went in the bedroom and tried to talk sense into him, telling him this was all for his own good and that it was necessary and he needed help.

An hour passed and the Police still weren't there! Dave was becoming more and more upset, pacing the floor and threatening to walk out the front door. I called the Police again, and they told me someone was on their way.

Another thirty minutes passed and still no Police. I called again, frantically explaining that he was about ready to take his keys and leave or walk out the door and disappear. Finally, almost two hours after I got home an officer arrived. I turned off the front porch light as I didn't want neighbors to see what was going on. The officer was thoughtful enough to shut all his vehicle lights off as he cruised slowly down the neighborhood street, looking for our house. I went out to the front sidewalk and flagged him down.

The officer took Dave and led him out of the house to the squad car. He had Dave turn around and face the car, patted him down, and handcuffed him. The look Dave gave me was more than a death look. He was bitter, angry, hurt, and drunk all rolled up in one.

This time he went directly to the ward for psych patients that were awaiting approval to go to The Oaks. How pathetic. This would be the second time to The Oaks in less than 30 days. This ward had a police officer there at all times. There were all different kinds of people there, but none seemed to be like us. Or was I wrong and we really were like the junkies that got arrested in Wilmington on a daily basis?

Many of the patients were highly medicated, which was obvious. Others were demanding more pills. My patient just laid there, either sleeping or passed out or pretending. I think his anger had passed as he didn't seem mad at me. They had already given him something to relax him. After ensuring the staff had all the latest and greatest details from me, I left to go home. I was completely and utterly exhausted and mentally drained.

Chapter 32

Too Easy to Get Out

When I went to see him the following evening he understood why I did what I did. He was more concerned about how long the judge would make him stay. All this was new to both of us. I went to see him each day and he seemed to be getting more of a clear head. He admitted that he played them all the last time, but this time was different. He was going to change. He was never going to go back into any facility again. I would never have to worry about him drinking again. He knew what he needed to do.

Five days later he was out! What good did it do me to go through all the trouble of a committal when all they did was keep him 1½ days longer than the last time he was there? All the doctor had to do was sign a form that was sent back to the judge stating that the patient was approved for release.

He had some prescriptions to take, one of which was Antabuse, also known as Disulfiram, which was a medication that he was to take daily where if he drank he would get violently sick. Drinking while taking this medication could lead to serious reactions, including the possibility of a heart attack. I was thinking this was a great thing as who in their right mind would drink while taking a medication that could possibly kill them when combined with alcohol!?

Dave would. After leaving the house to run a couple errands, I received a panicked call from Dave, where he stated, "You have to come home now! I drank! I don't feel good and I'm scared!" The man drank while on Antabuse. When I walked in the door, he was sitting in a chair in the living room with a pair of shorts and a T-shirt on. The shirt was dripping wet from sweat, his face was fire engine red and looked like it was starting to swell. His heart beat was racing and he kept holding his chest. His breathing was extremely fast. I asked him if he wanted me to take him to the ER or to call 911, and his answer was a resounding no.

Within a few days of being released he was already drinking. Why did they let him out so soon? What about me? Why didn't anyone ask me? I filled out the form. I'm the one that committed him. I felt the system failed me. It failed both of us.

Chapter 33

Gone Again

By early 2012, Dave had gone off his depression medication cold turkey. He spoke of having a clear head and having hope for the first time, finally beginning to feel a little bit more like himself. Other than the side effects from the withdrawal (fatigue, chills, head spins) he felt good. I took Friday off and we had a good three-day weekend. Perhaps things would get back to more of a normal state. Or could this explanation of prescription drug withdrawal be yet another screwing of my mind? I think it was and as usual he was very good at it.

Dave had an appointment with his therapist and told him he had been off the anti-depressants for a week. The doctor was not happy about that. He wrote him a prescription for a smaller dose and pretty much told him to fill it and take it or they may have to "go down different paths." Dave had no intention of filling it and went off another anti-depressant pill that was prescribed to assist with sleep.

Finally, I had a day where my anxiety level had tapered off and it felt like a normal day. Dave was still off work for the week, but had the water heater issue to focus on. The water heater had decided not to heat our water the Sunday prior and he had contacted the plumber. We spoke of what was for supper and how badly we both needed to work out that night. I went to work. We touched base with each other mid-day. Life was finally getting back to normal or at least "our normal."

I returned home after work to the following note scribbled on three small pieces of paper lying on top of the kitchen counter, pushed back and out of the way.

Note:

I have decided to quit my job. I know this will stress you out and make you nervous. But please have faith in me. I have taken off in the Jeep to figure things out. I am not drinking and have no plan to. I will check in with you if you want to talk. Please do not discuss this with anyone at work as they may shut my phone off if you do. I will call you this evening so you know I am ok... love you. I will be back Fri or Sat. Please have faith. I love you. I love you..and I am not drinking... just driving. Trust me. Dave

He left me to "figure things out" and left me without any hot water? I was more upset at the thought he left without resolution on the water heater than I was in the fact that he left again. Sad but true. A few tears were shed in frustration, but then my determination to find a place to move to kicked in. I was going to move out this time. Stand firm. Be strong.

He never called that night, nor did he text. I had no idea where he went but had a very good idea of what he was doing. It was the usual, which meant spending his time with bottles of booze. When he took off, he didn't take clothes or any of his medication. He took nothing but the clothes on his back and the money in his wallet. To this day I still don't know where he went or what he did.

I did get a text from his friend. A simple text: "Hey, how is Dave doing?" I ignored. I wasn't sure how to reply. Was I being an enabler if I didn't call him out and tell his friend he has disappeared?

I received a text from Dave early the next morning "oops... sorry, fell asleep and just got up." I didn't respond. From that point until mid-morning I received four other texts, including one that told me to call him. I ignored everything. I was done. I would not hit another birthday and be miserable.

I received another text from his friend the next morning. "Is Dave doing ok?" My reply was probably what set the ball in motion for what was soon to happen. I stated "I thought so when I left for work yesterday but came home to a note that he was gone. He didn't come home last night. Typical though as he has done this before." Reply from friend: "Ouch."

He rolled on home and stumbled in the door shortly after I returned home from work the next day. This was a complete surprise to me. I hadn't expected him to come home so soon.

Dave came in to find me at the computer with real estate info on the screen. "Why didn't you call me?" he slurred. I ignored. "Hey... why didn't you respond to my texts?" he whined. I ignored. The alcohol stench coming from this man was overpowering. "What are you doing?" he asked, to which I replied quite matter-of-factly, "I'm done with this crap and am looking for a house to rent that was dog friendly." There. I said it. He saw my house printouts on the counter and started following me around the house, whining about how I couldn't leave him, he needed me, I couldn't move out, he couldn't do this without me. He made the comment that he was going to just leave and went back into the bedroom to attempt to put on some clean clothes, nearly falling over in his efforts.

I snatched up his keys, which he had put on the nightstand and went to a different part of the house to hide them, along with my own set of keys. He followed me into the spare bedroom and started looking under things for his keys. I told him to get out of that room and "take a pill and go to bed or else I was going to call the police." I was not about to let this heavily intoxicated, blubbering and whining buffoon get behind the wheel of any vehicle. He finally gave in and went to the bedroom and passed out.

The next morning, I got the typical "I'm sorry… this is the last time… I don't know what happened… you can't move out" crap. After some discussion, where he realized I was serious about moving out, he pulled out a doozy of a manipulation card.

"Fine, you leave then I'll just drink myself to death," he stated. I said "Oh, no you don't. You don't lay those words on me as you stand there and try to mind screw me. You decide to do that it is on your own and has nothing to do with me."

He called me later in the morning and asked me to cancel his therapist appointments for the next two weeks. He didn't want to go. It wasn't doing him any good so why bother? He was done with the meds that made him more depressed instead of helping him. My call to that doctor's office sent off a flurry of events. The therapist called Dave's friend (who was also a friend of his), and then proceeded to call my cell phone five times. He left one message indicating that he heard that Dave had left and he thought I should commit him. In the meantime, Dave was getting calls from his friend, telling him that he needed to be committed. I told the doctor I was done with it and he needed to talk to Dave himself. The doctor called Dave and told him he needed to be committed and go into a 28-day treatment program.

Dave called me. I could tell he had been drinking. He had been driving around all morning after he received the first call, afraid to come home as he thought I would have the police waiting there to take him away again. He started to cry on the phone, stating that he couldn't lose his job, but if he did would I still love him? Did I think he needed a treatment program for 28 days? Sure, I did, but voluntary programs at country club like facilities didn't come cheap, hopefully would take insurance and were most likely completely voluntary. What was the point? He would just walk out less than a week later anyway. Why go through all the trouble?

I convinced him to go home and promised that I wouldn't call the police. When I pulled in the driveway his sponsor was there. They were outside talking in the back, Dave leaning on the Jeep, which was full of empty little vodka bottles. There was much discussion about to go or not to go and beyond "human help" as his sponsor put it. Dave had already changed his mind on going to treatment and instead stated that I could take his money, his keys, and take him to meetings and to work. Like I wanted to be glued to his hip for the next few weeks while he tried to dry out again? However, I agreed that I would be willing to help this one LAST time. This was it.

He then got in his sponsor's car and went to an AA meeting, smelling like a brewery and looking like death warmed over.

Overall, being glued together and keeping keys away from him was easier than I had initially expected this time. Of course, by Saturday he was already telling me that I didn't need to drop him off at a meeting and I certainly didn't need to take him to work. This change in mood was to be expected. I had to continue to remind myself that no matter what I did I could not keep him from drinking. If he wanted it bad enough, he would get to it regardless of how much I wasted my life trying to keep him from it.

He was moody and quiet, but again that was par for the course. Monday morning had my anxiety level high as I fully expected him to take off for his morning ride, blow off work, then text me that he just didn't care anymore and was going to drink. Thankfully, that didn't happen. He went to work and it was a normal day.

There I went again with my silly thoughts of hope and normalcy. Less than a week had passed and he had started drinking again.

Chapter 34

Who Needs Rules?

March and April of 2012 put me at my wits end. The stress within the house was unbearable and our poor dogs felt it too. He had to take his sponsor to work with him so his co-workers and boss could meet him. I had taken the day off, knowing that it may be a difficult meeting for him. He was to meet his sponsor first prior to an AA meeting, attend the AA meeting, then go to work for the other meeting.

Roughly two hours later I received a call from an unknown number to tell me he was leaving soon.

An hour passed, then another 30 minutes. No Dave. No call. I called back the unknown number that he had last phoned me from. One of his co-workers answered. It was his work phone and I didn't know it. However, they said that he had left over an hour ago.

After about another 45 minutes he pulled in the driveway. My guard was up. Had he been drinking? Did the meeting go well? I asked him where he had been and he indicated that he went to his sponsor's after the meeting, then took a drive which in my reality meant "grabbed something to drink and drove around." I told him that his co-worker indicated that he had left the office over two hours ago. He lost it and freaked out completely. He said I had blown it and how dare I call the office as now they would think I was checking up on him and they would think he was drinking. His eyes got wide with the veins in his neck starting to pop. He stormed around the house, angry and screaming at me as to how stupid I was and all he wanted was to come home and take me out to dinner and tell me how the meeting went. His face became more and more red. He went into the bathroom and screamed into the mirror at himself. He then picked up his large hair brush and hurled it into the tub, breaking off the handle into little pieces. He picked up what was left of the main part of his hair brush and with the backside of it proceeded to bash in his forehead with five blows.

I was speechless. I had cried my eyes out. My eyes hurt from all the tears. He got ready to grab his keys and told me that he was so furious he couldn't breathe and that I needed to get out of his way so he could leave. I knew exactly what that meant. That meant that he would take off and drink. I grabbed his keys, shoved them in my purse and held my purse close to my chest, telling him I was not letting him leave the house like that and that I knew what he would do. He got up in my face and I told him I would call the police. He screamed angrily "For WHAT?!!" I told him I would report to the police that an intoxicated person was leaving the house and give the license plate, make and model of the vehicle.

He then stomped off to the bedroom and slammed the door. What a great afternoon off I had. I had wasted yet another day. I woke up that morning with hope and in a great mood, left to deal with his shit once again. He did later come out and apologize, for whatever that was worth. He told me, quite angrily, that his boss had laid stipulations on his return to work. He had to provide a note if requested, from his sponsor to verify that he had been attending meetings. He was to work from 9:00 a.m. – 5:00 p.m. with two hours off for lunch and a meeting. He could not have his phone back nor could he take his computer home. I thought he should be grateful he had a job to go to, yet he was pissed that he had rules to follow.

Chapter 35

Saved at Last!

Upon his return to work, I felt relieved. There would be no more of him hanging out on his own during the day while I went to work. He would get back into the swing of things and it would get better. Really. It would be back to normal before I knew it.

That was my "glass half full" optimism speaking. It was either that or a big-time enabler in full denial of what was going on. The next two months were spent with me thinking I smelled alcohol, him telling me it was cough syrup as his throat hurt, me wanting him to take a Breathalyzer (yes, I purchased one, sadly enough), me finding Halls cough drops scattered about the bedroom and Jeep, and of course always taking his set of keys to bed with me. Weekends were spent with him in bed mostly as he "needs to sleep." When not in bed, he was fowl, sour, depressed and on multiple occasions stated that he hated himself and his life. HE hated his life? Mine was certainly no walk in the park. I was eating myself out of house and home. Eating to fill a void or eating just to eat. I didn't care that I had gained weight. The comfort and happiness I got from shoving that giant cupcake in my mouth was like heaven.

Health problems galore, it didn't seem to matter to him. The most recent excuse for sleeping and being a lump on a log (and I do mean LUMP... the guy had gained so much weight it was unreal!) was his digestive system. Food just sat there midway and he was miserable. After he would eat (if he ate at all while at home) he would go to bed and try to sleep.

He had become so manic about sleeping that he would freak himself out. He would take Benadryl as I made the mistake of saying that it made some people drowsy. He would take Unisom more than as directed and drink half bottles of Vicks cough syrup. He went to see his primary doctor, lied to him about drinking and came home with a prescription of Seroquel.

He woke up on the morning after taking two 100 mg Seroquel within four hours of each other along with adding Benadryl to it, and wondered why his heart was racing. He looked at me all sad and scared and held his hand to his chest, as he attempted to sit up in bed. "My heart is racing" he said softly and slightly out of breath. I replied "Hmm.... No surprise there." He had the nerve to ask me if I was mad, to which I replied that I had to get to work.

Later that day, all came to a head once again out of the blue. I was at work and received a text from his co-worker around 11:00 a.m. "We haven't heard from Dave today and we have a hard and fast deadline that we need to ask him about. Can you get this message to him?" My heart stopped. Here we went again. He was blowing off work.

I called him right away and he answered. He sounded normal. I asked him where he was, and he indicated he was on his way to work. I asked him why he didn't go in at 9:00 a.m. like he was supposed to and he stated that he had "things he was working on." I asked what and he said we would just talk later that evening.

Low and behold I received a call at 3:00 p.m. from Dave stating he was going to check himself into another treatment center, which was three hours away. He had planned for the 3-hour ride so I didn't have to worry about it. All he needed was for me to call the insurance company and confirm coverage. When he dropped that info on me, I simply replied "ok". He wondered why I didn't say much and asked if I was mad about it. Selfishly, all I could think about was how nice it would be to have some time away from him as I needed a break. I needed some space for my own recovery.

All was going to be covered by insurance so I called him back to let him know. He started to break down on the phone, asking me if he was doing the right thing. My response was this exactly, "Well, prior to this you had two options. One, you are dead. Two, I am gone. So, given that I would say this third option is a pretty good one." I received silence. He started crying more and indicated that he was really worried about Mason and what would Mason do without him there. Mason was failing in health and we were grateful for each day we had with him. I coldly responded "You haven't BEEN there for Mason for the last six months. We'll do fine without you at home." That was it. End of phone call.

After I hung up the phone I felt like this larger than life burden had been lifted off my shoulders. I could look forward to going home from work this day. I was almost giddy with excitement that he wouldn't be there. All the things I could do. I was already planning on taking a day off to have a real "me" day. The past few times I had tried that had ended up with me staying close to home, thinking that doing so would somehow prevent him from drinking.

When I got home I was almost scared to go inside as I had this horrible thought that he may have changed his mind and would be sitting there in the usual spot on the couch, or worse yet, all covered up in a drunken ball in the bed. I looked around for any signs of life other than the dogs and saw nothing. It was going to be a good night. It was going to be a GREAT night.

I was like an energizer bunny, picking up all his dirty clothes and throwing them in the wash. I cleaned his sink and put all his stuff in the cupboard, stripped down the bed in the master bedroom, cleaned off the counters and put away all his doctor notes and miscellaneous notes to himself. I was up watching my favorite programs on TV and hopping up during every commercial break to do something else. It was like I was erasing him from the house.

Thursday, the day after he entered the facility, I received a phone call after work from an "unknown" number. It was Dave. He spoke in almost a whisper, telling me he wasn't supposed to call but that he wanted to be sure I knew where the bills were. He also wanted to let me know that this was a good place and he would stay as long as they told him to. I asked him why he was calling me when he wasn't supposed to have contact for seven days and his response was, "You know me and rules."

I had the best weekend that I had had in months. The freedom I felt was incredible. My attitude was good and I wasn't even emotionally eating. I took the following Friday off from work and enjoyed walks in the park with the dogs, errand running, and chilling out in the back yard with the dogs.

By the following Wednesday, a week since he admitted himself, I was wondering why nobody from the facility had contacted me with questions, or sent me anything to fill out. Certainly, he couldn't be trusted to tell them everything that has been going on and what all his issues were.

This was also the day that he could officially make a phone call to me. My cell phone rang at work mid-afternoon. The first thing out of his mouth after the basic "Hello" was "How would you feel if I didn't stay here the full 28 days?" This was the first thing he wanted to say. My heart sunk. I told him I didn't think that was a good idea and what happened to "I'm going to stay here as long as they say I need to?" He answered by telling me that he missed us terribly, the place was dumb, and that he was worried about Mason. No more time for this discussion though as he had to go to class.

Later that evening the "Unknown" number called again and he proceeds to take off from where he left off on the LAST conversation a couple hours earlier. I begged him to please stay at least three weeks, where he agreed to "not speak of this again for another week." He promised me another week in treatment. I half expected him to show up at the front door that following weekend, having taken a cab home.

After my calling them, the facility finally sent me a five-page questionnaire that included all types of questions related to how his problem had impacted our finances, marriage, work, home life, kids, etc. I spewed it all out, including the brutal truth. The answer to the question "What will happen if he doesn't get better and sober?" My very straight and to the point answer was: Divorce. Period.

I sent the questionnaire off to his counselor, who thanked me for convincing him to stay another week. She also indicated that what my questionnaire indicated was close to what he had disclosed to her.

Another Friday rolled around and "Unknown" called once again. He told me that the counselor had shared the entire questionnaire with him. He told me it broke his heart to hear everything on the questionnaire and why didn't I tell him this before? I replied that I did tell him and that he either wasn't listening or wasn't in a frame of mind to care.

After his first two weeks in treatment, our sweet Mason started declining further in health. His kind old eyes were losing their sparkle and the tail was constantly draped straight down his hind area. He had no excitement over anything and was becoming increasingly weaker, falling in the house, down the stairs, and even falling as he tried to urinate outside. I was helping him to get up constantly, carrying him up and down the stairs, and to top it off I had Dave calling me every day asking how he was doing. I lied. He told me that if anything happened to Mason while he was gone, he would just as well drink himself to death.

We were just a few days short of Dave officially completing the 28-day program. I wanted to know if he could leave a few days earlier, primarily because of the state of Mason. He wasn't doing well. I prayed each night before bed that I would wake up and he would still be alive.

Mason and I made our way up to the treatment center to pick up Dave. It was a long drive for a sick dog, but he did well. I was nervous at seeing Dave again. It had been about 24 days since we had last seen each other and he hadn't gone 24 days without drinking in probably over a year. This was a very big deal.

It was kind of awkward at first. I didn't want to ask too many questions as it may seem like I was prying for information.

The following Saturday we took the dogs for a ride, a walk, then came back and went for a bike ride. He helped me trim bushes in the back yard. It was like what normal couples do. I was thinking this was good. Life was good again. As long as he went to meetings and finished his readings, he would stay on the good path. He would, right?

Chapter 36

Back to the Grind

Mason's health started declining again and Dave was the one to mention that it may be time to say goodbye. How would he ever be able to stay sober with this weighing on his mind? He didn't stay sober. He drank. He tried to hide it, but he drank. Within about a week of Dave's return home from treatment, we tearfully said farewell to our best friend on Sunday, May 20, 2012.

The following day I was a bundle of nerves as I left for work. He told me he was going to go to work normal time. An hour and a half later my phone rang. He wasn't going to work. He couldn't deal with the death of Mason. Couldn't handle emotions and no way could he focus on work.

When I got home from work, he was in bed. He was slurring his speech and attempting to tell me that he hadn't had anything to drink. It was revealed later that even though I took his Seroquel with me to work so he wouldn't take too many, he went to the pharmacy and filled the last prescription of it! He took multiple pills prior to my arrival at home. When I asked him where the pills were he told me it wasn't any of my business.

A confrontation began when I started questioning him about drinking after he asked me for another pill. He had hidden the pills from me but couldn't remember where they were. He was frantically pawing through his drawers trying to find the bottle. Things escalated and he threatened to leave. I couldn't find his keys and wasn't going to let him leave when he was under the influence of something. At that time, I wasn't exactly sure what it was other than pills. There was pushing and shoving. He slammed the bedroom door. The "F" word was flying. I told him I was going to call the police. He spit back at me, "Why...because I'm not acting NORMAL in my own home?" I took his phone as I wanted to call one of his sponsors. He started chasing me around the kitchen for his phone, screaming at me.

I gave him his phone back and he hurled it down onto the hardwood floors at full force, shattering the entire phone in multiple pieces. He stormed off into the bedroom and slammed the door. By this time my breathing was heavy and my heart was pounding. I picked up the pieces of the phone and put them on the counter in a pile. He came out of the bedroom a couple minutes later; all chilled like nothing happened, and picked up the cracked and broken phone and asked, "Does it work?"

I looked in awe at him, amazed at the strange transformation that occurred in such a short period of time. I didn't reply and he held the shattered and so obviously busted phone up and asked me again if it worked. I told him to take his phone and try to call a friend.

My saving grace later that day was a phone call I made to Fred, the guy who drove Dave to treatment. Thankfully he was near my end of town and said he would be right over. He arrived and I left him and Dave to talk in the bedroom. The plan was for Fred to come back over in the morning and take Dave to work. He would pick him up for a meeting and I would pick Dave up from work and bring him home. The goal was to get him through one more day so he can work the day before going out for surgery for acid reflux.

Not surprising, Dave had once again mixed booze with pills. Between 7:30 a.m. and 12:00 p.m. when I got home, he consumed a six pack of beer and a 10 pack of airplane size bottles of vodka. As I was digging through the drawers while Fred was there, I found the bottle of pills, as well as one empty vodka bottle and a lid and straw in another drawer.

When I woke up the next morning, as awful as it sounds, I had half hoped he was unconscious. I didn't want to face another day of unknowns with him. It was time for me to go. I needed to follow through with my promise that one more mess up and it was over. As I found over the past years, this was much easier said than done. It was more of the same.

Chapter 37

A Looonnnggg Summer

The days all blended together. Summer was supposed to be a time to be outdoors and enjoy the air. Would it have been too much to go for a walk with the dogs after work? Was it too much to ask to do anything other than sit in the house and watch re-runs on cable?

I was so very tired of coming home to the same thing, day after day after day. For the last few days, my radar had been up as when Dave got home he appeared to be a bit out of sorts. I had learned to rely more on my gut instinct at this point and something wasn't right. I couldn't even stand to look at him lying on the couch.

As I drove around with the pups, I was planning what my next step would be. It was definitely time for me to leave. No sense in me staying in this marriage and going through another round of misery. I debated on whether I should approach the idea with a letter to him, or whether I should talk to him the next day. As the Kelly Clarkson song "Stronger" came on the radio, I cranked the volume and started belting in unison with her "What doesn't kill you makes you stronger, Stand a little taller, Doesn't mean I'm lonely when I'm alone, What doesn't kill you makes you a fighter, Footsteps a little lighter, Doesn't mean I'm over 'cuz your gone! Stonger, Stronger, Just Me, Myself and I!"

I didn't sleep very well that night and had one of the strangest nightmares. It started with a large buzzing bug with wings and a stinger the size of a large sewing needle coming after me. I was swatting frantically with my arms and hands to protect myself, when suddenly I was on all fours spinning on top of the bed. I was levitating above it, but spinning out of control. No matter how hard I tried to stop spinning I went faster and faster.

I thought I was moaning, but I had been screaming so loud that it woke up Dave, who came over to my room to see if I was ok. From that point, I drifted in and out of sleep for a couple hours, then woke up bright and early. Could a nightmare like that possibly mean that my life was spinning out of control?

Dave didn't sleep well the following night. He wanted to talk and I agreed that we needed to. He got concerned and asked what we had to talk about. I told him I didn't want any more of what had happened the night prior. He said that he thought the night was fine, just that he came home and needed to lie down.

I told him how he acted and how his eyes were red and he was incoherent. I described to him that I couldn't live like this and I was not happy. He asked me what he could do to make me happy, to which I replied "Get some help. I have given myself until my birthday as I'm not going to go past another birthday like this."

Dave said, "What do you mean by your birthday? What happens then?"

I responded, "I decide whether I'm going to stay here or leave." There. I said it. I had been afraid to go there for weeks, but I finally said it. I got it all out there. He said nothing, got out of bed and put on a pair of shorts. As he looked for his T-shirt I asked him what he was doing.

"I'm not going to stay here and listen to you talking about leaving," he stated.

I replied, "So that shows how much you care about how I feel. You show me that by just getting up and leaving. I'm trying to have a conversation with you so we can talk through this and you just want to leave. I have major trust issues. I don't believe a word you say. I'm a nervous wreck, afraid I'm going to get a text or a call that you have wigged out again and haven't shown up for work." I was crying at this point. "I hate my life and I want the old Dave back."

He stated, "So what do you want me to do to make you happy?" I told him it wasn't about making ME happy. It was about HIM getting better. About getting the help that he needed. Professional help. It had been obvious that he couldn't do it alone. He talked about hating his job and being depressed. He talked about how it wasn't like him to not want to do anything or care about anything, but that was just the way it was. He thought he was getting a little bit better. However, there was something that he had been doing that he hadn't told me about. I was thinking to myself that it must be prescription related and was right. He had filled another prescription of Seroquel without my knowing it and had been taking a full pill in the afternoon to "take the edge off." That explained my radar being up and my gut telling me there was something going on. Sneaky bastard was self-medicating with prescription pills and alcohol instead of just alcohol. It was all the same for me. Same end result for me, selfish as that may have seemed. The conversation ended on that note. It was awkward but I didn't want to beat a dead horse about it so I asked him about plans for the day. He wanted us to go to the beach with the dogs.

A few hours later we loaded up the three dogs and headed for the beach. I could tell he was trying to be in good spirits, showing me that he was normal. It was a good that he made an effort and appeared to hear what I had to say. We had a great day that day, enjoying time with the pets, eating junk food, and even laughing a little.

Meanwhile, I still day dreamed of being on my own. Oftentimes on my way to work, I just wanted to put the top down and keep driving south, past the office, far away from the places and memories that were too quickly becoming more negative than anything else. What if I were to re-invent myself? Move away, change my name, my hair, get a tattoo and just become someone else? Maybe it wouldn't really be to "become someone else," but rather to really "be myself."

I felt that I had lost myself. I didn't really know who I was as a person. I had always been with either my parents or with Dave. I had never had the opportunity to live on my own and explore my own dreams, crazy as some of them may be. Shouldn't everyone at least have a chance for that?

Chapter 38

Therapy

Given all my thoughts of moving away and escaping my current life as I knew it, prompted me that it may just be time for me to seek a bit of professional help myself. I had a spring in my step and a plan. I needed to find a therapist that I could talk to. Maybe I needed someone to TELL me what to do. Give me the kick in the pants that I had needed for years. GET OUT!

After researching and reading bios, I found a therapist that had grown up the child of an alcoholic. She was also a published writer. This was meant to be. The stars were all in alignment and this would be my sign.

I finally got the nerve to call and make an appointment and found out she was no longer practicing. My quest was over. I had lost my nerve again and figured I could work through this on my own.

After yet another day of coming home from work and having Dave return to lay on the couch, watch continuous re-runs of Seinfeld, then take a pill, I had to get out of the house. I loaded up the dogs and went for another long drive. I had found that these evening drives by myself with the dogs really gave me some good time to think.

Sometimes thinking wasn't such a good thing as I realized once again how very unhappy I was. I felt stuck. I wanted to leave so badly. I wanted to have a little place by myself with my dogs. As I drove through the beach, watching the happy vacationers, with their sunburns and inappropriate swimwear, I longed to be one of them. What would it be like to be in a relationship where everything was normal? What WAS the definition of normal? I would think just having a nice time, good conversation, taking a walk, staying up late, sitting on the porch, walking the dogs, and laughing would be normal. Was normal too much for me to ask?

I had given myself until my birthday to decide on which direction I would go with my life. That was only a month away. I really wanted out of this. I wanted to re-invent myself. I wanted to be happy. My marriage was toxic.

Chapter 39

Soul Mates?

Dave and I seemed to have a fairly good time on weekends. I wasn't sure if it was because we were together the entire time and he couldn't slip a drink or take a pill, but in any case, it was better. One weekend while having a conversation over our favorite slice of pizza, the subject of "soul mates" came up.

Dave was talking about some friends that had told him they were having problems with their marriage, one cheated on his wife indicating that he had now, after over 30 years, found his soul mate. Dave said "Like with me and you. I have found my soul mate. Don't you agree?"

I replied, "I don't know if I believe in soul mates." The look on his face said it all. I had to recover and keep talking so as not to make him feel bad. I was very unhappy, but I certainly didn't want to hurt his feelings. I rambled on "Well for me, soul mate is like that once-in-a-life-time connection with someone where all the stars align. The puzzle pieces fit together perfectly and everything just jives. It's like they can't stand to be apart from each other. Maybe I'm reading too many Nicholas Sparks books, but I'm not sure if my definition of soul mate even exists."

That seemed to make him feel better, as he stated "Well, no I wouldn't think any such thing exists either."

Chapter 40

Fired!

It is said that one of the stages of severe alcoholism is job loss. I guess that meant that Dave was still in the severe stage, as that now applied to him. As if my stress level could handle much more. We had never been in a position where he had been fired from a job.

The letter that arrived via UPS at the house indicated that he was fired since he was told to work 40 hours a week and he didn't. He had been told on numerous occasions to do so, and wouldn't. His company phone was de-activated and he was given the rest of the week to schedule a time to come by the office and pick up his personal items, as well as turn in the company equipment.

This was humiliating. I was sure it wasn't easy for him at all, but I was also humiliated for him and for me. Was that selfish? I was also very angry. I had always done the responsible thing in just sucking it up and doing a good job at work, no matter how much I hated it. No matter how unfairly I felt I was treated, I continued to keep my chin up and go to work every day with a plastered smile on my face. Somebody had to be responsible. Somebody had to be sure the bills were paid and things were taken care of.

Dave said he was glad it was over. He just couldn't work there any longer and wanted to get a job somewhere that didn't know his history. Granted, it would be very difficult to work somewhere when you had to constantly try to gain everyone's trust back, and anytime you had a bad day they thought you were drinking; but then again didn't he put himself in this situation in the first place? Why did I have to suffer?

The first full day he had off he wanted me to make him a list of things to do. "You will be so surprised at all the things I'll do while you are working," he stated with a smile. "Make me a list and you'll see."

So, I made him a list small enough to handle for day one. Get a phone. Clean out your personal emails. Exercise for 30 minutes. Lay the pine straw. I got home and he was gone "to an AA meeting." Yeah, like I believed that. He didn't do anything on the list but did go so far as to lie about it. He had crossed off the list "exercise for 30 minutes" as well as "clean out personal emails."

He came home and told me he took the dogs for a walk and they had great fun. He took them on a neighborhood stroll. I went back to where the leashes were hanging and they hadn't been touched. He told me he exercised for 30 minutes, no, actually 45, detailing out how he did three 15-minute increments. He lied about that too. I ran my finger on the peddle of the elliptical machine and made one nice finger mark down a 1-inch layer of dust. No foot print. He hadn't been on that machine at all.

The list wasn't the issue or the problem. It was the lying. If he lied to me about such little things and made up detail to his story, how could I even come close to trusting him on the big stuff? To make matters worse, he had picked up a new prescription of Seroquel on his way home and had supposedly taken a pill about two hours prior to arriving home.

He appeared to be under the influence of something, slurring his words. He could hardly keep his eyes open long enough to eat supper. I told him I hated the pills and hated coming home to him being in a stupor. He stated, "It is what keeps me from drinking." It appeared my choices for marriage were either deal with him drunk, deal with him self-medicating with prescription drugs so he doesn't drink, or drinking and taking pills. Those were my options for continued peace and happiness.

And there we were. About three weeks into Dave's joblessness and there was no improvement. I had a feeling that he continued to drink occasionally and I thought that was most likely evident in the reason as to why he was fired. On top of everything else, he now had the stigma of being fired from a job.

I had hoped that after our trip to the mountains with the dogs, things would change. I had hoped that during that week away from home that we would have some deep and serious discussions about what his plans were, as well as our marriage. Needless to say, that didn't happen. He didn't say a word to me for the over six hour drive home, which was very frustrating. I had hauled my laptop along as we were going to work on his resume and file for unemployment. Didn't do that either. He had no interest in it at all.

He kept saying he was getting better. He wasn't. He didn't take care of himself and he continued to lie to his friends as well as me, and ignore his family. I was feeling trapped. I wanted out so badly. This was sucking the life out of me, still. I was less than a week away from my 46th birthday. It was this birthday deadline that I set for myself to decide as to whether to stay in this rut of what was supposed to be a marriage, or leave and take my chances as to what happened to him.

I had to remember that what he did to himself was not my fault. But what happens if he drank and drove, killing someone? How did that impact me and assets? I needed to protect myself. Was I selfish for feeling that way?

I had a good job with a good salary and could more than support myself on my own. I would not let him suck me dry while he continued to sit, lie and drink. I was desperate at this point. I was so unhappy and disappointed yet again.

Chapter 41

Happy Birthday to Me!

I took the Monday after our return from vacation off as a wind down day. It was a beautiful day without rain. I had hoped it would be the start of a week where Dave would change. After all, he said he would, right? We took the dogs for two long walks at the park, went to the dog park, and out to lunch.   However, he started shutting down in the afternoon and got quiet. We had planned to go out in the evening for dinner.   He indicated he was going to go to a meeting, and that he wasn't really all that hungry so would I mind if we just ate at home?

While he was gone to the meeting I decided I was going to enjoy the final hour of my vacation in the hot tub. As the smell of chlorine churned around me, I was deep in thought about my self-set birthday deadline. I was thinking that I would continue to give him a chance.

Bad idea. It happened again. He came home and walked passed me, going straight into the bedroom to change clothes. I followed him in and told him I was going to go ahead and call in some take-out. He looked at me with a blank stare and said, "But I don't want noodles." I replied, "I know, I'm just telling you that I do and I'm going to call in an order and go pick it up." He was still staring at me. I asked, "Are you ok?" I was starting to sense something was off once again. As he looked at me with slowly blinking eyes, it hit me. He didn't go to a meeting at all. He had been drinking. All these "meetings" he had been attending had been nothing but a lie. He would simply go drive around and drink.

I stepped away and he came out into the living room smelling of mouthwash. I figured I was opening a can of worms but went for it anyway. I blurted out, "Why did you brush your teeth?"

He replied, "I didn't." I shot back, "Then why did you use mouthwash?" He said that he always used mouthwash when he came home. We argued back and forth and he started giving me a very poorly orchestrated lie that he ate. He ate noodles. Where? "On the way from here to there" was the answer. I asked him where he got the noodles and he couldn't really answer. As he sat on the couch, he pointed at the news on TV and told me to "Watch, I ate there." The dude was out of his mind. I was out of my mind, arguing with a drunk person about noodles.

Needless to say, the last day of my vacation did not end well. I ended up crying with the dogs in the backyard while he fell asleep on the couch. All he could manage to say to me during my grand inquisition was, "What is wrong with you?" and "You are blowing this out of proportion." Months after the committal and the inpatient treatment and this shit was still going on. I hardly thought I was blowing anything out of proportion.

I wanted to be single. I wanted to just enjoy my life, take care of myself, have some fun with friends and find myself again. I was lost. I was depressed and I wanted to eat.

Waking up the next morning jarred me back to the reality of yet another day of misery in this marriage. I couldn't help it. The tears started flowing. As I laid there balling my eyes out in my pillow, Dave peeked in and asked me if I was ok and said that I sounded sad.

Who wouldn't be? We went around and round about the previous night. Noodle night as I liked to call it. He continued to deny drinking and after a few minutes confessed that he had taken two pills before he went to the meeting. Pills? How could that be? I was the keeper of the pills. They were on lock down and I would divvy one out each night for bedtime, like a parent would do. He stated that he had some stashed and he took the last two. He told me weeks ago that stash was gone.

My birthday week was supposed to be all about me and fun. Instead I was crying every morning, not even wanting to get out of bed. How depressing was it that I was in my mid-forties and feeling completely trapped in a marriage that I wanted out of. I knew there were people that had it worse than me, but emotionally I could only take so much and after over 25 years with this guy I thought I had finally met my limit. I loved him as a person and I cared deeply for him. I just wasn't IN love with him any longer. There was too much history and unhappiness. Sound familiar?

My birthday arrived and I'm awoken by Dave calling the dogs to go outside. I was anticipating my birthday dinner that evening with our neighborhood friends. I knew he was very anxious about going out with them as it had been a year since we had all gotten together.

On my way home from work that day I kept saying to myself, "Please let him be ok. Please let him be normal," over and over again. I had a feeling that something would screw up my birthday plans. I got a text from him that he was at a meeting. Right. Earlier in the day he had texted me and stated he still had nausea.

Long story short, he bailed on dinner out. He used the excuse that he had extreme nausea and was running to the bathroom every 30 minutes and he just didn't feel good. I put on my game face and told him it wasn't a problem and that I understood. Fake it 'til ya make it, right?

Chapter 42

Job Yet?

We were approaching the fourth week of Dave being unemployed. I didn't want to be a nag, but please. At least DO something when you're home right? He just stayed in bed or laid on the couch and watched re-runs of sitcoms. It took him almost four weeks to finally update his resume and apply for a job. He had zero motivation and initiative.

When I was busting my ass at work to support both of us, the least he could do was try, like clean the garage, help around the house, or maybe even look for a job!

One morning I woke up after having a dream the night before. I had dreamt that we were both at someone's house for some sort of social gathering. There were people there that I hadn't seen in a long time and some guy came up to me and gave me a hug. He had on a double-breasted suit, shirt and tie. By the feel of the hug, he was healthy and physically fit. In the middle of the hug, he nudged me away a bit to look into my face and stated "It's me. I'm back." It was Dave. It was Dave in a suit, being happy and confident and social. Being normal.

I can honestly say that I had a feeling of happiness and contentment while in that short dream, so much so that I was brought to tears after waking up. If only some dreams could come true.

Chapter 43

No Sweat, Afternoon Golf and a Day Off!

Just when I thought things might be making a turnaround, I once again got smacked in the face by the cold hard truth of a major reality check. We had a few heartfelt discussions where he spoke of not having self-confidence. I responded with my usual uplifting words of encouragement, etc.

He said he was going to go golfing with his sponsor and a couple other guys. I was glad as I thought it would be good for him to get out and enjoy a nice day with friends. I went about my afternoon, taking in all the fresh air of the first official weekend of fall.

Later that afternoon, Dave came home. He walked in the door, past me without making any eye contact and went straight to the bathroom. Oddly enough, this seemed to be a regular routine for him by then, but only when he had been out by himself. This never happened when we had been together.

I followed him into the bedroom to chat about the day. I asked him if he had fun and he said he did. I had a feeling that something was up and he was lying. I assumed he thought I would fall for it. He sat in the bathroom for what seemed to be eternity, complaining about what a bad stomach ache he had. He finally came out of the bathroom, keeping on his golf socks and golf shirt. However, he changed out of his shorts and put on a pair of gym shorts.

You see you must understand the pattern of consistency with him. He was a creature of habit and I could always count on him doing the same thing every time he came home from golf. He was usually soaking wet, very tired, and either hopped right into the hot tub, or took a bath.

Not this time. I moved into sleuth mode. The shorts he golfed in that he left on the floor weren't even dirty. They weren't sweaty and they hadn't spent the day walking 18 holes of golf. I asked him why he was leaving on his golf socks and his golf shirt. All he could keep saying to me was, "My stomach hurts." As I continued to question him, pointing out that there wasn't a speck of dirt or a blade of grass on his socks or ankles, all he could say through slowly blinking eyes was, "What is WRONG with you?"

There you have it. He either drank or pilled up. Not sure which, but my guess was that it was pills this time. He didn't appear to smell of alcohol. He was mumbling incoherently and it got worse the more I tried to talk to him. I called him on it. I told him he didn't golf and he insisted that he did. I asked him why he lied to me still and did he think I was born yesterday. He replied, "Yes." I couldn't leave well enough alone so I went out to the Jeep to inspect his golf clubs. I realize that sounds incredibly ridiculous. They were clean as a whistle as well as the towel he always took golfing. Not a speck of dirt, moisture, or grass on anything.

He left at 11:00 a.m. and came home at 4:30 p.m. and expected me to believe he was golfing. Where he was I didn't know. I probably will never know. It was clear this pattern was coming back again. A couple hours later I checked on him in the living room and he had passed out with his leg crossed above his knee and his head falling to one side, practically drooling. I tried to wake him up and he would babble things like, "Yes, the interstate" or point to the TV

120

and state, "Yes, the table is there." I finally got him to remove himself from the couch and go to bed.

I left and went for a drive. The day after was supposed to be a fun day as I had taken the day off. Instead, I once again did a lot of soul searching. It was about one year ago exactly that I had shopped for apartments to move into, swearing it was the last time. I was so disgusted and disappointed with myself in more ways than one. I was not liking myself. I didn't like how I felt or looked. I couldn't even stand the sight of myself in any window reflections. I felt the bottom half of me was disgusting and repulsive. I blamed him for my demise. Was that wrong? I was the one shoving food in my mouth, not him. I let myself go. I didn't care. Why?

I was sinking into the depressed mode again. I had just turned 46, which was only four years away from the big 50. As I was thinking about how old I was and how so much of my life had been spent in a state of turmoil, wouldn't you know that a bus full of assisted living people pulled up next to me. As I watched the mini-bus pull away with all the happy gray-haired elderly heading out for their trip to Walmart, I thought I was only about 30 years from being in one of those buses myself! I started to cry.

Chapter 44

Club of One

My sadness was gone and I was just flat out pissed. I was back into my fighting mode. I was now officially the Founder and sole member of the Self-Preservation Society of One. This was a very exclusive club where only the most pathetic enablers of all time could join. It was now time for survival of the fittest. I would not let him suck any more life or health out of me. Not going to happen this time. I would win!

He whined about how he was "coming back" and how I just needed to be patient with him. I had been patient. We were now past one month of unemployed, pill-popping, laziness that I was not going to sit around and watch any longer. I had been patient all year, waiting for the almighty turnaround that would take place where "fun" Dave was back.

I didn't think it was going to happen anytime soon. It was getting worse. If I had to come home and see his butt on the couch watching cable one more time, I was going to break something of value. It was time to contemplate seeking out a therapist for myself, again.

Chapter 45

Knock Yourself Out

My life continued to be more highs and lows. This day off started out with a fun walk in the park with the dogs, followed by a bike ride for lunch. This same day ended with him taking off to a "meeting" and coming home with one eye looking bigger than the other one along with some slightly slurred speech. The following Saturday brought the admission that he had been lying all along and had been keeping the pills stashed, not taking them at night when I gave it to him. He waited later to take them during the day when he felt anxious. He had taken two.

I gave him the bottle and told him I was done trying to help him with medication. He could take the bottle and knock himself out. He took more pills and spent the entire day in bed. My thought was if he overdosed at least it would lead to the hospital where he could get some help. I was tired of his lies and his excuses. I wished he would just cheat on me. It would make it easier for me to leave, as odd as that sounded.

Was this really part of God's plan for me? Continuing to ride the roller coaster of highs and lows with this man? Was my life supposed to be sucked and drained on a daily basis? It didn't seem fair, but then again life isn't always fair. I spent most of my day in and out of tears, but when needing to run errands or running into someone I knew, flipped the brain switch and thought of something different so I didn't become emotional. It was all part of the lie.

I didn't want to spend any time in my front yard, as I didn't want any neighbors to ask how I was or how was Dave. At this point, I was about ready to spill all my emotional guts if some poor soul asked me.

I wanted to leave. I was still feeling trapped. He lied about everything. About finding a job, pills, even small things like taking the dogs for a walk. Our entire relationship was now nothing but a lie. I was so miserable and stressed out. I felt like my life continued to slip away before my eyes. How much more of this could I take?

Did I just resign myself to the fact that this was what this marriage had become, checking out mentally, and staying in it and just do my own thing? Did I stay committed and continue to use all my energy to build him up, check on him, worry, and continue to ride his roller coaster of lies? Did I take a chance and tell him I was leaving, all to have him tell me he would just drink himself to death or kill himself if I did? Should I have continued to live the life of more emotional extortion? Did I take his threat as an exaggeration and leave anyway, to find my own peace again?

So, yet another Saturday night was spent with the bedroom door shut, him lying in the bed behind it, pilled out and drugging away his life. I lit my candles, popped in a movie, and tried to find a sense of normalcy.

Chapter 46

Depression

It was so very difficult to watch someone you cared about lose all sense of what was important in life. To watch what used to be a person with confidence, goals and initiative turn into someone who really wanted to do nothing but sleep.

My concern for Dave was enormous. I felt sad for him each day that I went to work, knowing he was just there by himself without any desire to DO anything. He constantly made doctor appointments then canceled them. He often said, "I don't feel like being around people." He turned his phone on vibrate and ignored calls from his friends and family. I was afraid at some point he wasn't going to have any friends left to care.

He had lost all desire to care about himself. He didn't bathe regularly and stayed in the same clothes for days at a time. He wouldn't exercise, could go all day without eating, and went to bed early every night. He rarely laughed and even more rarely smiled. I didn't think he was drinking any longer, although I couldn't be sure. This was a different battle, equally as bad as drinking.

I was at a loss as to what to do to help. I couldn't make him go to a doctor. I couldn't make him care about himself. The Dave I once knew was gone. I honestly felt that he would never come back.

Chapter 47

Depression Times Two

Complacency was not a good thing. One's day could start out on a great note and as usual soon end in disaster. Stumbling through the door after attending a "meeting" was not how I expected his return home on a beautiful Saturday morning. Between no eye contact and slurred to non-existent speech it soon became quite apparent Dave had once again been drinking.

He was not the same person that had left the house an hour and a half earlier. I soon found out why when I went searching in his Jeep and found a large empty bottle of Jack Daniels.

I was destroyed. He had sat there and lied to me continuously. I was disappointed in myself for once again getting into the comfort zone. Shame on me.

A year ago, one of the worst times of our marriage had started. Here I was a year later dealing with the same shit I promised myself I would not put myself through again. I was so upset at myself as the realization came to light that I was still in this life-wasting situation that I just couldn't seem to get out of.

I wanted him to leave. I had decided I could manage to pay the house payment on my own by adding some of the money I saved over the past year. He needed to go. Would he?

He never thought I was serious and for some reason he seemed to think that continuing with this emotional extortion was acceptable. I had allowed it all these years, why would this time be any different?

When I stated my marriage vows "through sickness and health, through richer or poorer" I meant it. But I just couldn't take it any longer. I was disgusted and hated myself for continuing to allow this.

Another weekend shot. I was still living with, married to and evidently enabling my alcoholic of a husband who now had no job, no motivation and had apparently changed to a new drink of choice.

As expected, the following morning started with, "I'm sorry" and "I just had a slip." I went through my usual speech, this time trying to be sure he understood where I was coming from and to take me seriously as I was speaking from my heart.

How should someone react when they are told by someone they care about, that they think of ways to kill themselves every day? I was at a loss as to how to respond when he told me that. He said that he sits and goes through different scenarios as to how he could kill himself without it looking like it was a suicide. As long as he did it without it being an obvious suicide, I would receive the payouts from his life insurance and would be set for life. He went on to say how he hated the very sight of himself in the mirror. He hated himself for what he had done to screw everything up. He prayed every night before going to bed that he would just die in his sleep, of a heart attack or something. Die of anything other than alcohol as he "doesn't want to die an alcoholic."

This conversation made me so very sad. I knew he was in a dark place but to hear him speak so openly to me about wishing he didn't exist made it very hard for me to comprehend.   That level of darkness was something I couldn't pull him from.

We spoke further of professional help and going to church. He agreed that we needed to start going back to church and we would start the following weekend. He said that he would turn it around. He would call the therapist, set up an appointment, and get his head on straight. As always, time would tell.

I couldn't leave now. How could I possibly leave when he told me he went to bed every night praying he wouldn't wake up? How could I in good conscience leave him? Or, was this yet another case of emotional extortion?

Chapter 48

Mission to Leave

I had made it my mission to find a new job and do what it took to leave the company where I worked at the time. Over the course of a few months I had applied for jobs across the country, in Orlando, Tampa, Houston, Dallas, and of all places, Provo, Utah. I wasn't happy at work or at home so it was time to make things happen. My thought process was if I were to get a job offer out of state, I would have to move. Now if he would make the move with me was a different story.

I got my first boost of confidence when a recruiting firm in Houston called me regarding a job in Houston. We had an initial phone interview, then another screening Skype interview. Nothing came of that one as they opted to hire locally. However, the fact that someone was interested in my work experience gave me the confidence boost to keep trying.

After a few particularly bad evenings at home, while falling asleep I prayed to God for a break. I wanted one good break. I wanted something good to happen; something positive. I needed it desperately. The next day, I received a call from Provo, Utah. The phone screen went well and they wanted to fly me out to Utah for an interview as soon as possible! I was stoked. I wanted the job so badly I could taste it. I wanted a fresh start. I wanted to start over somewhere new and leave all the memories and grief of this city behind me. Maybe this was the one good break that I had prayed for.

Chapter 49

Be Careful What You Wish For

After months of talking to Dave about making an appointment with a therapist, he finally did. It may have been the fact that I pushed and pushed, made the calls, and told him I would basically leave if he didn't try getting this type of help that finally pushed him to go. Whatever it was, he went.

He wanted me to take him. To be sure he went, I agreed to do so. On the way there he asked me if I would fill out his paperwork, as he "hates that kind of stuff." To avoid a fight, I agreed to complete the paperwork, which included all kinds of questions related to how he thought his marriage was, what kind of thoughts he had, medical history, etc. I finished up the paperwork and got ready to leave and he then asked me to stay and wait. He didn't want me to leave and come back to get him. Again, to avoid a fight or him walking out altogether, I agreed to sit there and wait.

About 40 minutes after he went in the back to see the doctor he came back out with a handful of prescriptions and a free 28-day sample of anti-depressants. They set up two other appointments, one with an addiction specialist for the following week, then another one in two weeks to see the doctor. Dave seemed a bit wary of all the prescriptions, but after we got home indicated that he had a plan now and would follow it.

He was given prescriptions for Ambien for sleep, Luvox for depression, Gabapentin for anxiety, Naltrexone, which is a deterrent for drinking and a bottle of Phenergan for nausea. He was also supposed to take Ativan in extremely high doses for the first three days, and then taper down. The cocktail of drugs made him zombie-like. He had slurred speech and acted like he was drunk. He had no memory and said things that didn't make sense. After being on the full doses of medication for two days, after supper one evening he shuffled into the kitchen where I was standing at the sink. He had food spilled all over the front of his sweatshirt and stood there staring at me. I looked up and asked him what he wanted. He said, "I want the spoth." I replied, "What?" He said, "The full thing. I want it." I looked at him like he was nuts and said, "What the heck are you talking about?" As he tilted his empty milk glass in a drinking motion, he said with much conviction that he "Wanted the full spoth."

He put down the glass and shuffled off to the bedroom. The next couple days were more of the same. I had already planned on taking the day off on that Friday after his appointment, and was quite glad that I did, as Dave was not in a state of mind to be able to drive.

I later noticed that when he had driven the day prior, when pulling into the driveway he had misjudged and mowed down the sprinkler head in our front yard. He later plowed over a shrub when pulling into the driveway. That Friday late afternoon, after appearing to be somewhat coherent and awake, he stated that he wanted to go to a meeting. I was a bit wary about letting him drive, but to avoid a fight like I typically tried to do, I gave him his keys.

He was gone for an hour. It was dark when I noticed the headlights pull back into the drive. He seemed to be taking a very long time in the driveway. I was going about my business in the laundry room when I heard a loud metal thump. I ran to look out the back door and saw that Dave had pulled up right against the garage door, hitting it. Not hard, but enough to where the garage door wouldn't open until he backed up. When he came in the house, he was staggering and said he felt dizzy on the drive home. I told him he hit the garage door and he denied it.

He sat up long enough to eat, then staggered off to another drug induced sleep in the bedroom. I went out to get his phone, as he had left it in the Jeep. He was supposed to be applying for jobs every week to maintain his unemployment status and receive unemployment. I knew he had received some email confirmations, so I thought I would print them out for his records, just in case he needed them.

I didn't mean to snoop on the phone, but the first email I saw was one from EHarmony.com. I scrolled down further, and there was another one from eHarmony. In reading them, it appeared he had signed up with eHarmony and had agreed to receive emails.

I was devastated. Seriously? The man was out on the web looking for dates? Well, he certainly was a catch, now wasn't he? Wouldn't they just be climbing out of the woodwork to have an opportunity at this guy? All those little ladies out on eHarmony could just knock themselves out getting to him. Heck, I would have paid someone to take my place so I could get out of Dodge. It was very hurtful to me, and brought a few tears to my eyes, but in the grand scope of things, nothing surprised me that much.

As I sat at breakfast the following morning, I reflected on my overall situation. Our situation. His situation. Would he ever get better? Did the rest of his life mean pills and unemployment? Did I want to live like this? As I reflected, I was put a bit at ease in the thought that if I were to leave, certainly one of his family members would take him in and care for him. He could go live with one of them.

I dreamed of my interview in Provo. I really wanted it. I needed to make it happen. I envisioned myself in Utah, renting a cute little place with a fenced in back yard, meeting new friends, and trying new things. I pictured myself in winter-wear and boots, learning how to ski. I pictured myself snowmobiling and walking my dogs on trails. I wanted this chance at a new start. A "do over." I had never been by myself in my entire life and I was more than ready to make it happen.

Chapter 50

The Man Without a Brain

A few days later, the panic calls to his cell phone that went unanswered should have been a clue that something wasn't right. I had a gut feeling that he was drinking. However, I still wanted to give him the benefit of the doubt that he wouldn't be that stupid while on all those new medications.

I was wrong. I received a call from one of those non-descript 1(674) numbers that made my heart race. It was him calling me to ask me to come get him out of jail. He had been pulled over on yet another DUI offense.

I spoke with the arresting officer who explained what would happen with him next. He would blow a test in 30 minutes then see the Magistrate. The officer didn't think a bond would be posted but didn't know.

So off I went on a rainy and cold Sunday night before Thanksgiving to get him out. As I pulled into the parking lot of the jail, I shut off the car and cried. There wasn't much more I could do other than cry. Bail bondsmen cars were parked in the lot and I started to have that foreboding sense that I had been there before. Like someone stuck in a bad Lifetime movie, I was parked in this same parking lot less than a year ago to commit Dave to treatment.

Why me? I prayed for something good to happen to me for once and I got this? I just wanted something to be over-the-top excited about. I would not call this the answer to my prayers. I thought I was a good person that always tried to do the right thing. Why was this happening to me? Was this

God's way of telling me to leave and just let Dave deal on his own with his family to take care of him?

I was at a loss. I was feeling so hopeless at that time I didn't know where to turn. Was this really part of God's plan for me? They say God only gives you what you can handle. What about Dave? He clearly wasn't handling this at all. I hated my life on so many levels.

As I sat in the lobby of the Sheriff's department, I was numb. Staring at the cold tile and watching the officers behind the desk made me feel sick to my stomach. The TV was on but with no sound. As the words scrolled across the bottom of the screen I had thoughts of just getting up and walking out the door. Let him be someone else's problem. Not sure why he had to be MY problem any longer. However, I didn't. I stayed and waited.

Happy holidays didn't seem to be in the cards for me yet again. I wanted him committed. Jail would be good at this point. It wasn't like he had a job to worry about. No income since August other than the measly unemployment checks he started collecting on a weekly basis.

Maybe the Magistrate would order him to treatment. Maybe I could persuade him to commit him to treatment again but this time for more than five days! The system failed me once before, would it possibly fail me again?

Sitting and waiting as people walked in and out, some looked at me and politely smiled. Others looked as miserable as I must have looked. I wondered why they were there. Were their husbands' drunks as well? Was this their first time? I didn't feel like I belonged there. This wasn't the type of place someone like me should have been.

My holidays would be filled with court dates and attorney fees. All the excitement of my trip to Utah had vanished. He had even taken that away from me. Did they seize the Jeep? Did they take his license away again? Bond? Some old distinguished-looking guy in a black cowboy hat and long black trench coat strolled in giving greetings to those at the front desk. Guess he was a regular. Was he a bail bondsman? Was he there because of Dave?

The clock kept ticking as the air in the lobby got more chilled. I was cold. I needed a hot bath so I could just sink into the water and lose myself. Finally, the front desk officer told me I could "go back." As I made my way back through the industrial looking hallway, noting that I was on camera as I walked, I wondered what bad news awaited me.

I walked into the small room called the "visitation room." There were three glass windows where I could see through to a holding room of those being held on various offenses. It was just like you see in the movies. Hard plastic chairs to sit in looking through little paned windows. There he sat on the other side of the glass, peering through the window at me. He looked ashamed and drunk.

I picked up the phone on my side of the window and he picked up the phone on his side. He asked me if I had $1,000 cash on me for his bond. Like I drive around with wads of cash stuck in my purse anticipating the need for bail bond? I was told by the officer that they couldn't take a check, and I could certainly call one of the bail bondsman numbers so conveniently plastered on the outside wall.

I went to the wall and reviewed the names. I picked a female bondswoman. She told me she wouldn't take a check either as she couldn't verify on a Sunday night that my check was good! Guess this meant I had to go back out into what had become a tropical depression and head for the nearest bank to get cash.

I was learning more and more through each of these experiences. Who would have thought that the most I would be able to get from my bank's ATM was $800! That was a waste of my time so I drove the extra few miles to go home.

Pulling $1,000 cash out of my "get out of here" stash was not what I had planned for the evening, but I was glad I had money available to me. A lesson learned for the day was to always have a decent amount of cash stashed at home for emergencies.

Back at the Sheriff's office I was instructed to take paperwork to the Magistrate's office where I could pay the bond. More sitting and waiting. There was one other person in the room with me. A 29-year old black woman who just witnessed her best friend's boyfriend beat her in front of her kids after returning from a trip to the Bahamas. She was there to make a statement as a witness. We had a nice talk about life in general, her nerdy kid, drunks and people that beat other people. She was originally from inner city Newark, New Jersey and moved to Wilmington 10 years prior. She said she had seen a lot of bad things growing up and wasn't a very good kid. She had grown up and found God. I told her I was from the Midwest originally, was an only child, was a goody two-shoe growing up, but fell for a bad boy that turned out to be a drunk. We laughed and it felt good.

After the judge signed the paperwork, took my cash and gave me a receipt, I was informed that I would have to take a sobriety test to prove I was a sober driver for my drunk husband. More waiting. I passed the test and was told to go back out to the lobby and wait until they finished processing him. I watched a pizza delivery driver come and go.

Finally, he was processed and shuffled through security, holding two baggies with his personal belongings. We walked in silence through the blowing rain to my car. As I pulled out of the parking lot he told me he was sorry and this was the last time and that he would get help this time. He was met with silence. He kept talking and even told me to, "Just get mad now and then get over it." I was so wiped out emotionally that I didn't even have the energy to respond.

It was a long drive home. He had been pulled over within a few miles from our home for swerving into other lanes and not making a complete stop. He had stopped at a bar and had "two shots" which meant he probably had four or five. Adding alcohol to the already fully sedated and drugged state he was in from prescription medication certainly didn't help, but may have helped his case in court. His license was initially suspended for 30 days and the Jeep had been towed to some holding yard where it needed to be picked up.

The first words out of his mouth once we got home were, "Where is my pill? I'm feeling anxious." Nice. I cried myself to sleep, then woke up the next morning, remembered what had happened the night before, and cried some more.

Chapter 51

Happy Thanksgiving!

The days leading up to Thanksgiving did not lend hope for a very happy one. He was spending most of his time in the bedroom, barely coming out long enough to eat anything. He hadn't had a bath in at least three days. He was demanding, uncooperative, and basically just existing on a daily basis.

My saving grace was that I finally called a therapist for myself. She was taking new patients and indicated she could see me the week after Thanksgiving. I had a lot to work through. My life had been even more turned upside down than it was a year ago.

I guess one of my biggest faults is that I am too quick to give someone the benefit of the doubt, especially when it came to Dave. Every time he hits a new bottom I thought this was it, when he told me he was sorry and would turn it around, I believed that he would.

He told me that we would have a good Thanksgiving; just us and the dogs, and we did. He still slept in late due to all the medication, but got up and ready in time to eat at our annual Thanksgiving buffet. We walked the dogs and watched a movie. This day seemed normal. However, he was sucking me in and I didn't even know it.

I wasn't much in the Christmas spirit, despite the numerous commercials and radio stations playing non-stop annoying Christmas tunes. It took everything I had to put out a couple wreaths in the front of the house. I had to keep up appearances for the neighbors. I certainly didn't feel like decorating the house at all, except for a tiny eight-inch tree with lights that was already decorated. I put my little tree on an end table and set my Christmas figurine of a Black Lab with a Christmas robe on next to it. That was the extent of that year's Christmas décor.

The day after Thanksgiving started out being a bit more difficult. Dave didn't want to get out of bed, and after he finally did, went back to bed within a couple hours. He said he felt like he had been hit by a MAC truck and I "have no idea what he is going through." Like what I was going through was better. He asked me if I was excited about my interview and trip to Utah. I told him I was and he said, "I hope you get the job." I asked why to which he responded, "I'm ready to move and have a fresh start." I looked him directly in the eye and told him that I didn't want to be a caregiver in Utah. He assured me that he was making the change. This was it. He was going to turn his life around, get healthy, and get a job.

A few minutes later, he was putting on his warm clothes to ride his bike to the AA meeting about a mile away. He would call or text me once he got there so I knew he made it.

I received a text about 15 minutes later that he made it safely. I had a gut feeling that something wasn't right. He usually texted me in the middle of some of the meetings, especially if he had just gone back after being absent from them.

I waited until about the time I figured he should be home, then made a call to his phone. He answered the phone after a few rings and indicated he was home. I asked him where and he said he was outside by the gate. "Why didn't you text me?" I asked. He replied that he did.

He certainly didn't. I knew the minute I saw him outside by the gate that something was wrong. He didn't go to a meeting. He rode his bike to go drink somewhere. There was a convenience store and a small lounge on the way to the meeting, and he visited one of those. He staggered into the house, almost ran into the wall when he tried to make a turn into the kitchen, then almost fell when he turned to walk into the bedroom.

I should have known better, but I continued to follow him into the bedroom and asked him if he had been drinking. He told me he hadn't. His movements were staggered and his speech was slightly slurred. I knew the minute he said, "You are blowing this out of proportion," that he had been drinking. I told him, "Fine, then you won't mind taking a breathalyzer."

I pulled out the gadget and while waiting for it to show the "ready" light, we battled over him lying down or sitting up. The machine was taking forever! I just needed to see. I needed confirmation that I WAS NOT blowing anything out of proportion. I needed confirmation that he was lying to me again. After everything that had happened this year, after spending four hours at the Sheriff's Department the previous Sunday to bail him out of jail and after making numerous calls to the Police Department and the Sheriff's Department to try and find his Jeep, I needed proof. After calling a cab and taking a ride with a toothless driver to Earl's Towing to drop another wad of cash to get the Jeep out of impound, I needed proof. Was it wrong for me to really want proof before I just threw in the towel? For real this time?

He blew into the machine and blew a .24. Right or wrong I brought my right arm back and swung it forward as fast and hard as I dared to slap him across the face. It didn't even faze him. I screamed at him through tears, "How could you do this to me? How could you after everything this week? How can I trust you with anything? How can I trust you to even take care of the dogs when I go to Utah? You need to get out of this house. You need to get on your bike and phone a friend to go stay with as I don't want you here!" By the time I was finished ranting, he had passed out.

It was time for his family to come out here and deal with him. There was nothing else I could do. I was hoping his family would come before I left for my trip. I took off my wedding ring and put it away. I located the checkbooks. I needed to find out what the balance was and take some before he depleted the entire account.

I lit my Christmas candle, plugged in my tiny tree, dried my eyes, and tried to muster up some holiday spirit as he laid on the other side of the bedroom door, once again in a drunken and prescription drug induced state.

Chapter 52

Up Up and Away!

Thanksgiving Sunday was a day I had been looking forward to for weeks. I was to fly out to Utah for my long-awaited interview! Dave and I had a nice lunch together, dining outdoors at one of our favorite restaurants, talking about normal and everyday types of things. We even laughed a little. On the way back home from lunch he wanted to stop by the bank to get some cash. I was wondering in the back of my mind why he would need cash. I was only going to be gone one full day, he didn't have a license, the fridge was stocked with food and he didn't have anywhere to go. He took out $100 cash.

My flight left late Sunday afternoon and Dave and I kept in touch via text. Since I was the pill police, I had stashed his pills in various locations throughout the house, planning on texting him at pill time to guide him to where he needed to go to get his pills. He seemed normal as we texted and conversed via phone.

My interview went well, albeit very rushed. It was a very long day, as I didn't arrive back home until the following Monday, close to midnight. I was excited to come home and tell Dave all about my interview. We had been texting off and on throughout that day and I was hopeful of some good conversation when I arrived home.

That was not the case. When I got home he was already in bed with all the lights out. I tried to tell him about my interview, and received some disinterested mumblings back.

He claimed he was tired. I was exhausted, so didn't think much more about it.

After unpacking and crawling into bed, I dozed off into a deep sleep. Within an hour after going to bed, I'm awakened by the dogs growling. A few seconds later I heard a bang and shattering glass.

I followed the sounds through the master bedroom to find Dave on his hands and knees, in the dark, attempting to pick up pieces of glass off the tile. I turned on the light to see that he had fallen against a large picture in the bathroom, which had crashed down on the tile, shattering all the glass out of the frame and all over the floor. One of Dave's knees was bleeding profusely as he had chunk of glass in it.

He was completely out of it. He had no idea what was going on. He couldn't speak other than jumbled words and sentences. I was trying to get him to hold a towel to his knee to stop the bleeding, but he just wasn't getting it. He kept rubbing it up and down and making it bleed worse. I was sobbing as I was on my hands and knees, picking up pieces of glass while my drunk husband sat on the side of the bathtub, completely out of his mind.

Why did this happen? What did I do to deserve coming home from what I thought was one of the most exciting interview opportunities I had in my life to a drunk ass husband, a broken picture, and me on my hands and knees at 1:00 a.m. cleaning up a bloody mess? Ruined. The experience, the excitement, the everything. Ruined.

After the floor was free of glass, Dave stumbled to the bed and passed out flat on his back. I went back to bed and cried myself to sleep.

Luckily the next morning I had already planned on going in late due to my flight getting in so late. I did what I had promised myself I wouldn't do again. I did a dumpster dive to find out what, if anything, he had drunk. I found two large empty bottles of wine hidden beneath a layer of garbage. I checked his wallet. He only had $40 of the $100 left. He must have taken a cab, hit the liquor store, and spent the day drinking at home. I was devastated. Why I seemed surprised at this, I didn't know. Why it always hit me like a brick, I can't explain. I was stupid and forever hopeful that I would see the Dave I used to know come back.

I was fortunate in that my very first appointment with a therapist happened to be scheduled for noon the day after my interview. This therapy thing was all new to me and I didn't know what to expect. She was a nice lady and very welcoming. She even had a couch. As I sat on the couch, I looked around her office, which was filled with books and paper, complete with a couple Kleenex boxes. As she reviewed my paperwork, I wondered how many people had sat on that couch and bawled their eyes out. I wondered if her other patients were like me, or worse and what kind of conversations had taken place in the small office.

All she did was ask me why I was there and what I wanted to get out of the visit, and I lost it. I completely broke down into a sniffling and snotting mess, looking frantically for one of those Kleenex boxes. I told her that I had basically come home from a quick trip out of town and had spent my time in the middle of the night cleaning up broken glass after my drunk husband fell and broke one of my favorite pictures. I told her I wanted to leave, but didn't know what he would do if I did. I needed her help in dealing with the guilt if something were to happen to him after I left.

After getting all that off my chest and just spilling my heart out to a total stranger, I felt better. My time was up 45 minutes later and we scheduled an appointment for the following week.

Chapter 53

Drink No More?

The day after the shattered glass night, was the start of another attempt for Dave at sobriety. He admitted to me that he didn't remember a thing about the night prior. I told him I would be happy to help him remember by showing him the video of the whole thing off my phone.

The next few days he was miserable, going through detoxification at home once again. He was going through the chills, sweats, shakes and the depression that comes with coming off another binge. Despite him not feeling well, he seemed to be trying to show some consideration and respect for me. He was making me feel like he was really trying this time, which he hadn't for years.

A week later, he had an appointment to see the therapist that he had stopped seeing earlier in the year. I took time off work to drive him to his appointment, since he still didn't have a license. When he came out of the office, he had a list on a piece of paper from the doctor. He was supposed to cut back on some of the medication the crazy doctor had prescribed, go to AA, seek out a substance abuse counselor, and attend the next appointment with me. That seemed to depress him even more; as once we got home he wanted more pills and wanted to go to bed.

The next few weeks were spent with him continuing to be sober, trying to be social with me by staying up and watching TV, taking an interest in my day, etc. I continued to feel hopeful.

Meanwhile, my therapist was telling me I needed to learn how to set boundaries and reminded me that I was an enabler. He needed to "put on his big boy pants" and I needed to stop doing everything for him. If I stated that his drinking again was a deal breaker, then I better be ready to step up and move out.

Chapter 54

Happy Anniversary: Again

Having an OB/GYN appointment and topping off the evening with an appointment with a DUI attorney wasn't exactly my idea of a way to spend my part of our 26th wedding anniversary, but it was better than the prior one. He was sober!

On the way to the appointment with the attorney, Dave acknowledged that he figured I probably didn't much care to spend our anniversary in an attorney's office discussing his DUI, but that he, too, felt it was better than the prior year. I agreed and told him that I would rather be doing this with a sober Dave, then going out to dinner and faking it with a drinking Dave.

My body was tense as I sat and listened to the attorney explain that a judge most likely wouldn't care about prescription medicine while drinking. He blew a .08, which was over the legal limit, so the best thing this lawyer could do for Dave was to shop judges and hope for the best. He eased Dave's anxiety by telling him it was highly unlikely that he would have any jail time.

We topped off our evening by grabbing some pizza at one of our favorite pizzerias, having some good conversation, and toasting with cokes to a "happy anniversary."

Chapter 55

Merry Christmas and Happy New Year?

We were having the first sober Christmas in two years. Granted, there weren't any parties to go to and we weren't exchanging gifts. We never even talked about exchanging gifts, but none of that mattered. He wasn't drinking. That was the best Christmas present I could ever ask for. I had fun Dave back.

The day after Christmas, Dave had his first appointment with his clinical addiction specialist. I was nervous, yet hopeful. I really wanted him to go and for it to go well. I figured if he kept an open mind, it might do him some good.

He went and texted me that it was a good meeting. I was dying to ask questions, but didn't want to pry. I figured if he wanted to share anything with me he would do so on his own. However, when I got home from work he seemed a bit withdrawn and distant. He claimed he was really tired and ended up going to bed at 6:30.

The following day I came home to something similar. He seemed withdrawn, had a growly look on his face, and my gut was telling me that something was up. It looked like he had been drinking again.

I kept prying as to why he was tired, but he ignored me and continued to stare at the TV. I did something my therapist probably would not approve of. I picked a fight. I asked him if we could talk. The "talk" didn't accomplish anything, as he wasn't in a coherent state of mind.

We received a call late afternoon on New Year's Eve that Dave's mom had suffered a stroke . She had been admitted the day prior due to pneumonia, and had a stroke in the hospital the following day. It impacted her speech, and at 80 years of age, a full recovery from a stroke did not look very hopeful. Dave tried speaking to her on the phone, but she wasn't very responsive.

After he hung up he told me he would have to think of going back. We agreed that decisions would be made after getting further prognosis information from his family.

Chapter 56

Grief and Mourning

A couple weeks later I received an unexpected call from his family. They had just arrived at the hospital where their mother was. They had planned to go down for the weekend to move her things from the assisted living section of the center to the more skilled care wing. Upon their arrival they were told that she had suddenly developed a very severe infection and they didn't expect her to make it through the weekend.

They called me, as they wanted me to be with Dave when he found out that his mother was declining in health very quickly. He seemed abnormally "normal" given the news I gave him so he had to have been under the influence of something.

He couldn't get a flight out that Friday evening, so he booked a 5:20 a.m. flight the following Saturday morning. Neither of us slept very well, as I was obsessed about getting up and getting him to the airport, and he was worried about getting a call in the middle of the night that his mother had passed away.

I was worried. Worried for all the wrong reasons perhaps, but definitely worried about him traveling by himself. It was too soon. However, I shouldn't have been worrying about things that were beyond my control. He had choices. If he chose to drink, there was nothing I could do about it.

I got him to the airport about an hour early, and he was delayed by an hour two different times due to fog. This gave him more time in an airport to sit at the bar. It was all I could think about. The fog delays meant that he wouldn't get to his Mom by noon, but rather late in the afternoon.

He called me when his flight landed. He had his rental car and it was starting to snow. It seemed to take him a VERY long time to get his car from the time his flight was to have landed. It should not have taken an hour and a half. I was immediately suspicious.

The next few hours were spent on the phone with his family, giving me updates as to how quickly their mother was declining. Dave was telling me he was pulling off the interstate to a hotel, due to white out and blizzard conditions.

Within a half hour of Dave getting a hotel, I received a call from his family that their mother had passed away. We all felt we should not tell Dave until he made it there the following morning.

Meanwhile, despite my efforts to redirect my thoughts and NOT worry about what Dave was doing in a hotel room by himself in the middle of a blizzard, I was a nervous wreck. I knew she was gone. He didn't know. How could I carry on a normal phone conversation with him knowing this? It was eating me up inside. We chatted about the football game, his ordering pizza, and the grossness of the roach motel he ended up staying at.

The next morning, he hit the road after what he indicated was a great night of sleep. All this time his family was telling him their Mom was still hanging on. They told him to go to his family's house before going to the hospital once he arrived. As usual, Dave never did what he was supposed to do. He went directly to the hospital.

The moment I heard his voice on the other end of the phone after answering, I knew that he knew. I asked him where he was and he sobbed that he was at the hospital. He had gone directly to the hospital to surprise her, only to find out by hospital staff that there was no longer anyone there by that name. After everything, that was how he found out his mother had died, alone in a hospital, without family, by some staff. We cried together over the phone. My heart ached for him. I felt so bad. He beat himself up for not continuing to drive through the storm.

I told him that even if he had continued to drive 35 mph on the interstate through the storm, he still would not have made it. There was a reason he wasn't supposed to be there to see her take her last breath and to see her in the condition she was in. Flight unavailability on Friday, fog delays on Saturday, blizzard; this was God's plan. It was hard to understand at the time, but it was all part of a master plan.

We agreed that I would fly out the following Tuesday. Dave would drive to his family's home outside of St. Louis, spend the night on Monday, and then pick me up at the St. Louis airport on Tuesday.

My flights were on time and everything was going as planned. I was picturing Dave meeting me at the baggage claim in St. Louis, with me hugging him and telling him how sorry I was to hear about his Mom.

As usual, things never go as planned. As I landed in St. Louis, I texted Dave and asked him where he was. His text back to me indicated he was at the bar in the airport. I texted back, "You are joking, right?" His response was, "No, meet me at the Pasta Bar after you get the bags."

The sick feeling in the pit of my stomach was indescribable. My heart was nearly pounding out of my chest as I made my way to baggage claim. As I arrived, there was no sign of Dave.

I got the heaviest baggage that I checked, and then sat on a bench and called him. "Where are you?" I asked once he picked up the phone. He responded with, "I don't know." "What do you mean you don't know? I was waiting for you in baggage claim." I replied. He replied, "Bring your bags and meet me here."

I hung up. I was in tears. I was sitting in an airport I had never been in, had no idea where my husband was, and I was supposed to have a 7-hour drive with him. I dragged my bags to the nearest car rental booth and asked them if they knew where a bar called the Pasta Bar was. They pointed up the hall, directly around the corner from the baggage claim area.

As I made my way to the Pasta Bar, I saw him sitting at the bar, drinking. It was him and one other "happy drunk" sitting there shooting the shit like they were old friends. I stumbled in, eye make-up no more, as a sniffling and snotty mess to him turning around to look at me while he took a big long drink. I told him to put the drink down as we had to go. He kept drinking. I told him to please put it down. By now the bartender was looking at me. Two other people started to look at me. I didn't care. I was oblivious to the public humiliation that was in progress. Happy Drunk started to tell me it was ok, and blah blah, to which I responded through tears, "No, it is not ok. He is drunk and he is supposed to be sober." Happy Drunk apologized to me and stated, "Hey, I'm just trying to make conversation." At this point, I was crying. The bartender came over to me and gave me a hug, telling me she was sorry. I clung to her and told her thanks and shared with her that he was an alcoholic. I'm not sure why. Perhaps it was to make her feel bad for being in such a profession that continued to serve poison to very sick people.

Dave was blitzed. He was out of it completely. I got the key to the rental car and asked him where he parked. He didn't know. He couldn't remember. More humiliation as we roamed around in circles, not even sure how to get out of the airport and where the parking lots were. I flagged down some poor unsuspecting airport worker (Airport Lady 1) and told her my husband was drunk, I just got in, and could she tell us where the exit was to the parking deck. I was losing it emotionally, crying yet coming up for air long enough to hold a conversation with this kind woman.

She took me over to the transportation desk, where I explained to Airport Lady 2 that my husband was drunk and we needed help finding the rental car. Her eyes filled with pity for me. I was humiliated once again. I didn't want people to feel sorry for me. Should I have just left him there to fly back home, leaving him for his family to deal with? That wouldn't be fair to his family, after the death of their Mother. I sucked it up. Airport Lady 2 made some calls to transportation people outside regarding the situation.

Airport Lady 1 stayed pretty close, and kept her eye on Dave to ensure he wasn't taking off to wander around the airport. She came back to me to take us out to the parking deck. Dave was dragging behind and didn't seem to grasp the concept of what was going on at all. The three of us were standing out in the parking deck with various levels colored green, yellow and red, as well as columns with a lettering system of A-Z.

Airport Lady 1 asked Dave if he could remember going in through a certain drive, or if he remembered a specific color. He stared blankly at her. As we continued to wander around trying to get him to recall where he parked, I flat out tripped on the sidewalk and did a complete face-plant onto the concrete. My purse flew, but luckily, I caught myself with my elbows. This was just more humiliation to add insult to injury. The entire time I was sprawled flat on the concrete with Airport Lady 1 coming to my aid, my drunk husband was about 10 feet behind, stopping long enough to cough up some nasty phlegm crap that sounded like a cat choking on a hair ball.

Onto the scene arrived Airport Lady 3 in an airport transportation vehicle. Airport Lady 2 explained some of the situation to her co-worker, and motioned for me to get in the truck. I looked at her and said, "I'm afraid to leave Dave. What if we find the truck and upon my return he isn't here?" She assured me he would be safe with her.

To that point, I crawled in the cab of this truck to ride around with Airport Lady 3 as we drove from level to level, with me holding the key out the window into sub-zero temperatures, pushing the panic button, desperately hoping that I would hear an alarm go off. Airport Lady 3 looked at me with a bit of disdain, and said sarcastically, "So what is going on? What is the story, you can't find your car?" I replied with, "My husband's mother passed away a couple days ago, he was supposed to meet me here as I flew in from North Carolina, he is supposed to be a recovering alcoholic, but I found him drunk out of his mind at the bar in the airport." Her face softened immediately, and she told me she was so sorry and that "We need prayers." She went on to say that she had been married to one for 27 years but left him. I asked her, "Are you happy now?" She replied, "Yes, most definitely." Was this yet another sign that I should leave this man? After a few more circles around the various levels of the parking deck, constantly hitting the key remote, we were successful in locating the rental car.

Thank God for navigation or I would not have been able to make my way out of the St. Louis area. Dave wasn't passed out. He was just sitting in the passenger side of the car, sunglasses on, gazing out the window. As I made my way through traffic toward the suburbs of St. Louis, I began once again to cry. I had just been through one of the most humiliating experiences in my entire life. I had been left completely and totally emotionally vulnerable to multiple strangers in a public place. This was a new low.

Hour after hour crept along as we drove in silence. There was no conversation. Instead I was drifting in and out of sob fits. He remained oblivious to my emotions and pretty much everything around him. Suddenly, he started messing with the auto window. He looked at me and said he had to pee. At this time, we were out in the middle of nowhere so I told him to wait until we got above the hill to see if there was an exit. If there wasn't I would pull over on the side of the road. He looked back at me and started screaming that he had to pee NOW and if I didn't pull over he would jump out! I pulled over and made my way up a little gravel road and before I had even stopped he had opened the door and stumbled out. He didn't even go behind the vehicle. He stood right there, front and center for what seemed to be five long minutes peeing in the freezing cold, for the entire world to see. One must try and see the humor in how some things play out. About one half mile after the pee stop, we crossed over a small bridge with a sign that said "Peeno Creek."

A few more hours passed. As I drove on, looking at the flat land spotted with a farm house and silo here and there, and even a field with wild turkeys roaming, I wondered what my life would have been like had I stayed in my home town. Would things have turned out the same? Would I have left Dave and married a farmer? Would I be living in a tiny Midwestern farm town?

I had hours to cry and mourn. I was ashamed to say I wasn't mourning the death of his Mother, but rather the death of our marriage, along with the death of the Dave I used to know. He was gone and it made me sad. It was a loss for me as well as his family. He was the fun guy of the family, playing with the nieces and nephews, acting silly with them. He was

157

the successful guy that would help anyone that needed a hand. He was the athletic one, that as he aged, refused to give up on playing basketball and tennis. However, too much had happened. I didn't think that version of Dave would ever be back.

Many thoughts were going through my mind as I continued to drive my drunken husband to his Mother's funeral. I had hours to contemplate what my next move would be. We were about two hours from our final destination, when I decided it was time to pull over for gas and a break. As we pulled back onto the interstate he told me that he just "woke up," and did he just fill the tank with gas? He said the entire five-hour drive at that point had been a black out for him. He didn't remember anything that happened at the airport or anything that he did or said until we hit that stop for gas.

I asked him if he wanted the abridged version or the one with all the details. He indicated he wanted all the details. Details I gave, every last one, with every word spoken. I ended the story saying, "I will never be humiliated like that by you in public again. Ever. It will not happen. Do you hear me and understand what I am saying?" He indicated that he understood. He said he took a sleeping pill at some point prior to arriving at the airport. He said he went to the baggage claim to meet me, but since my flight wasn't there yet, decided to hit the bar. That was all he remembered. To top it off, after he heard the details of those past few hours, he stated, "Man, I have to get off that medicine." I replied, "Seriously? You don't need to get off the medicine. It isn't the medicine that makes you do this. Stop drinking!"

The next morning in the hotel, after waking up from a deep sleep due to utter exhaustion, it started to hit me as to what had happened the day prior. I cried. Then I cried some more, attempting to muffle the sobs in the cushy hotel pillow.

After the funeral the following day, as we were walking to the car, his brother gave me a hug and said, "You are a Saint. There is a special place in heaven for you." Quite honestly, I didn't want a special place in heaven. Heaven would be wonderful, but all I wanted at that point in time was to be happy. I just wanted normal. Hopefully that day would come and when my time for heaven rolled around, I would be greeted at the gate with open arms.

Chapter 57

Knowledge is Power

Arriving home brought me hope that his promises would stick. You would think I would have learned my lesson by then. I guess I was a slow learner. More of the same happened, with him going to "meetings" and coming home acting much more differently than he did when he left. It was time. It was time for me to get my ducks in a row and look out for myself. Knowledge is power and it was time for me to meet with an attorney to see where I stood in the middle of all this mess of a so-called life I had.

I should have met with an attorney months ago. I felt empowered as I left her office. But I also felt depressed. In the eyes of the law I was screwed either way as it appeared I had condoned his behavior all these years. Should a divorce go to court, the judge would most likely ask what had changed versus 10 years ago when he was arrested the first time? Why did I stay with him all those years? My answer to the attorney was simple. "I refuse to continue to live with someone who drinks and drives. I will not be financially liable and have everything taken away from me due to his drinking and driving, which could lead to vehicular homicide of some poor soul out there. I won't stand for it and want to protect myself." My attorney seemed to like that answer and her opinion was that a judge would as well.

A separation agreement would protect me financially from any future debts he incurred, including lawsuits, etc. Even if I didn't have a signed agreement and we had just started the dialogue around a separation, if he were to go out and kill or seriously injure someone as a drunk driver, I would have 48 hours to contact her where she could put into place an emergency injunction which would protect me. That was a load off my mind. It gave me time to think through everything more clearly and prepare for what I had to do.

A couple weeks later, Dave agreed to attend a counseling session with me. It was absolutely brutal, with me crying and him making excuses along with stating he didn't have a plan to change anything to get sober. Even me telling him I saw an attorney didn't seem to trigger much if any emotion from him during the session. He just sat there, looking down and avoiding eye contact with me. He spoke softly and honestly. The honesty of him stating he didn't know what he could do to get sober hit me like a ton of bricks. He stated he hated God. He hated Him for taking his Father, his Mother and his beloved dog, Mason.

This brutal honesty from him made me see how far he still had to go, which made it very hard for me to continue to have any hope of our marriage working. It appeared a separation was in the near future for us, and that made me feel defeated and hopeless. Walking out of that counseling session together to the car in silence was very awkward. He didn't have anything else to say to me, nor did I to him.

The day of our counseling session he had to leave for an appointment with his doctor related to a routine physical. During that appointment, the doctor thought Dave may have a spot on his lung and ordered him for a breathing test and x-rays the next day. What else could possibly happen? Right when I felt like I had a plan of action to leave, there was news of a possible spot on his lung.

I couldn't leave someone who was sick. How could I even think of such a thing? If he were to be diagnosed with cancer, he certainly wouldn't stop drinking. He would most likely drink more. How selfish was I to even think of these things?

Chapter 58

Huh?

Valentine's Day came a few days later and he asked me out to dinner. This was a surprise as he never wanted to go anywhere at night. He met me at the restaurant and was in a good mood. On his way to the restaurant he had received a call from his doctor's office and heard the news that he didn't have any spot on his lungs. He was cleared and in good health lung and heart-wise to exercise and get better. It was all on him now.

That following Friday I took the day off. He had an appointment with his therapist and indicated it was intense. On the way to lunch, he put his hand on my leg, patted it and said "I love you. You are special." We reminisced about high school and people we knew back in the day when we first started dating. It was a special moment. A normal moment.

Later that day he left for a 5:00 p.m. AA meeting, which was just five minutes away from the house. Over an hour later I texted him that supper was ready, which triggered the following exchange of texts:

Dave: Sorry, I am waiting for approval. They know nothing.

Me: Approval for what? What are you talking about?

Dave: Sorry. I am talking bout them.

Me: I just tried to call you. What are you talking about? Thought you went to a meeting.

Me: Where are you?

Dave: I'm talking bout them. I did. Just finished.

Me: Where are you?

Me: There are cops on our road.

Dave: On way home. No worries.

Me: Do I need to come get you?

Me: Why do you not answer your phone?

Thankfully, he rolled in the driveway 35 minutes after the end of an AA meeting that was supposed to be five minutes away. I could tell he had been drinking. I asked who he was getting approval from and he responded by handing me his phone, mumbling away things that made no sense. He crawled into bed and that was it. I spent my evening writing down assets, debt and what he could take when I kicked him out, or perhaps more properly stated, when we "separated."

The following morning, he woke up and asked me what happened the night prior. He had read the texts on his phone which made no sense to him. He stated he didn't drink but he had taken a Seroquel an hour prior to going to the meeting. He didn't remember any of the texts or what was said after he got home. He had evidently once again mixed Seroquel with booze.

A couple weeks later, after a rough weekend, most of which was spent in bed and with Sunday ending in him stating he was messed up and something had to change, he stopped. He stopped drinking.

Over the course of the next few weeks he came out of his shell of a life. He started contacting friends, making appointments, seeking employment, and taking an interest in life again. He said he finally had a feeling of hope and that he thought the medication was finally working. He had lunch with friends; returned phone calls, and took an interest in his appearance. He got on Facebook and started contacting friends and family from the past. He even for a period of time took an interest in looking for and applying for jobs!

When would the next shoe drop? When would the next sucker punch come? What would trigger the next episode?

Chapter 59

Always an Excuse

It was just as I figured. It didn't take long for that next shoe to drop or for that next sucker punch to come. For this addict, and maybe for most, there was always an excuse to drink, but never a reason strong enough to stop! Not sure what it would take.

The excuse this time was due to an out-patient surgery procedure at UNC Hospital in Chapel Hill. Dave's voice had been hoarse and at times non-existent for over two years. He was supposed to have seen a specialist over a year ago, but blew it off due to drinking. He had seen the specialist, received optimistic news about some ways to treat it successfully, and now was scheduled for the second part of a two-part surgical plan.

We enjoyed a nice weekend together prior to the procedure, which was scheduled for a Wednesday. When I got home from work on Monday I found him in bed. He indicated he wasn't hungry and had a stomach ache. I knew something was wrong as he always blamed his feeling bad on his stomach. He evidently thought I kept buying that story, but I didn't. It was a huge red flag for me.

Upon my arrival home on Tuesday, he wasn't in bed but he also wasn't himself. He was blinking his eyes slowly and repeating himself.

On Wednesday while on our way to Chapel Hill, I asked about it. He admitted that he had been drinking and it was because he was nervous about the surgery. He was scared about being put completely out then having a tube stuck down his throat. I thought this shouldn't be any big deal after all the medical procedures and tests this guy has had. It was an excuse.

However, I didn't want to rock the boat or create a stir on the way to surgery, so I kept my opinions to myself. The surgery went well and we were on our way home a few hours later with a prescription for 15 Hydrocodone pills that he was supposed to take as needed for pain. They didn't seem to be helping much so the next day I called the surgeon's office. They said he could take two at a time every six hours, which meant he would run out more quickly.

I called on Friday and after much discussion, they agreed to call in more pain pills that he could take every four hours. Later that evening I picked up a prescription for 30 of them. It was more Hydrocodone, with a different mix of Acetaminophen. For the next few days he was on those things every four hours like clock-work.

I learned yet another lesson. Doctors should never prescribe any type of opiate drug to someone with an addiction problem. They must not have looked at his chart. I should have known better, but for some reason I was thinking Hydrocodone wasn't a very potent drug. I was wrong. In Dave's case it was, or was it?

When I got home from work the Monday after his surgery, he was not himself again. He indicated he was hungry, but by the time supper was ready he was in bed. He came out of the bedroom around 7:00 p.m. and told me he was going to go to a "meeting." I could tell by his eyes that he had either pilled up or had been drinking before I got home from work. In any case, I was not about to let him get in the Jeep and drive.

It was rather pathetic as I side-stepped back and forth in the kitchen, blocking his path to the garage. I pushed on his chest, I started crying, and I grabbed his keys. He pushed past me and grabbed the keys back. I pulled on his arm to come back out of the garage and into the house and to please not leave in the Jeep, as there were cops out everywhere due to a local festival. He finally gave up and went back into the bedroom.

I was mentally and physically exhausted, but I was not about to let him drive in the state he was in. Not sure what exactly that state was, but he wasn't right. Needless to say, I went to bed with his keys that night.

A few days later, he was supposed to have had an unemployment review meeting with the Employment Security Commission. It was a routine meeting that occurs for people that have been on extended unemployment. He was also to have sessions with both his therapist and his counselor. He woke up that morning with the excuse that he felt bad from not having Hydrocodone, was a no show to both appointments and called to postpone his review meeting. He told me later he was nervous about the review meeting.

So, this guy couldn't handle anything anymore? Every meeting or appointment freaked him out to where he had to drink or take pills just to get past it? How could he ever get a job again? How could he ever hold a job again?

Coming off a week of Hydrocodone for him was worse than going through detox from alcohol. He may have been feeding me a line and he may have drank while on the medication, which wouldn't be that much of a surprise, but by the following Friday night, he was restless, freaking out, shaking, nauseous, had diarrhea, and was almost begging me to take him to the emergency room.

I was cold about it, but that came from having gone through so much of this crap with him. I gave him a mix of pills that I thought would calm him down, told him to calm down and take some deep breaths, and try to sleep. Luckily, we made it through that night with the help of some Gabapentin and Seroquel.

The following Tuesday gave us another opportunity for a drive to Chapel Hill for his post-operative check-up. The plan was for me to work in the morning, get home by noon, get on the road, grab a bite on the way, and head for Chapel Hill.

When I got home he wasn't ready and wasn't hungry, which was odd since we planned on grabbing a bite to eat together. He seemed to be quite attached to a large Styrofoam glass from a local fast food joint. First, he told me he wasn't hungry because he had a late breakfast, then five minutes later told me he didn't tell me that, but instead just got a soda from that place. The red flag devil was waving his little flag at me again.

Within 30 minutes of inter-state driving he was out like a light. He slept in the passenger side, head bobbing from side to side as I switched lanes. It was quite clear he had been drinking something that morning. This was made even more evident when we stopped to get gas. He stayed in the car with the ignition turned off while I pumped gas. When I opened the car door to get back in the car, the odor of alcohol was strong as he had sat in there and sweated for about 10 minutes. I once again chose to keep my mouth shut and my opinions to myself.

Shortly after arriving home and settling in, we sat down to relax and watch some TV. He became restless and said that he would rather not watch TV as his "mind was full." I pushed a bit further and questioned what he meant by that. He made some motions with his finger around his head and says, "I just have a lot of stuff swirling around in there right now."

What the heck? We got home and he started to wig out again? Within five minutes he was stating he was going to go to a 7:00 p.m. meeting right around the corner. "It's just 5 minutes away" he said. It was 7:15 p.m. so he was already late. I said, "Really? There is a meeting right around the corner?" as I walked to a drawer where I had stored the print outs of local AA meetings by day of the week. "According to this, there isn't a 7:00 meeting around the corner," I stated as I walked back into the living room. "What? I don't mean around the corner, I mean the 7:00 meeting in Ogden," he replied. I flipped the page and examined the schedule. "Wrong again. There isn't any meeting in Ogden at 7:00 either, nice try." I replied.

He asked me what I was looking at. I told him it was the schedule of all the AA meetings in Wilmington and surrounding communities. He seemed very surprised that I would print off a schedule! I said, "Hey, I don't do drive byes, but after last week's stunt of saying you were going to a meeting as I begged you not to, I figured I should see for myself when and where the meetings are."

He didn't like that one bit. He went on to say that everything I was looking at was wrong, then took his keys and left for the fake meeting. This meant that he left long enough to find a drink and get it into his system, all to return within the hour to make it LOOK like he had been to a meeting.

While he was gone, I did it again. I decided I would search for bottles. My gut was right. I found one of the infamous Styrofoam glasses hidden on a shelf, with the lid and straw and just enough liquid in the bottom to give the stench of booze, in his closet. I also found another empty soda bottle under his bathroom sink. It was as I had figured. He was drinking continually again and lying about it.

When he got home, he staggered into the bathroom for his also fake stomach problem, then as he held his chest, stumbled across the living room into the bedroom to pass out.

A couple weeks prior I had received a follow up email from the attorney I had met with earlier in the year. She was checking in to see how I was doing. My response to her at that time was:

Thank you for the follow up. Things are going well and he has been sober for over a month now. I definitely have your contact info in my phone. He knows we met and that may have been the message he needed to hear from me. I so appreciate your time with me. I left there with knowledge and knowledge is power, which is exactly what I needed.

Unfortunately, it was time to refer to her number programmed in my phone.

Chapter 60

The Ride that Never Ends

He stopped, he started, he stopped again, he started back up again. The weekends were fun and normal but somehow Monday's were always bad. That particular Monday ended with him going to one of his fake meetings and coming home a little over an hour later with a large jar of peanuts.

Normally, someone coming home with a large jar of peanuts wouldn't be any big deal. In this case the carrier of the nuts shuffled in, holding the jar of nuts in one hand and holding a half drank bottle of Diet Pepsi in the other. Sometimes being a creature of habit can burn you in the end, as it did with Dave's lie this time. He would never drink a soda out of a bottle, let alone one that wasn't cold. He always had a glass with ice in it.

He wouldn't for the life of himself put down his bottle of Diet Pepsi.

"What are you doing with the soda?" I asked.

"Drinking it!" he replied as he tried to guzzle what was remaining in the bottle.

"You never drink room temperature soda out of a bottle, what is in there?" I asked as I grabbed for the bottle to take a sip of a Diet Pepsi and Vodka mix.

"What is WRONG with you?" he screamed. This was yet another red flag as the only time he screamed that at me was when he had been drinking. He stormed off into the bedroom, skipping the supper I had made, slammed the door and locked me out of the bedroom. The dogs had all taken refuge in the bedroom so they were also locked in there with him.

I was not about to have him lock me out and keep me from my dogs, so I went a bit psycho, standing at the door, pounding on the door screaming "let me in," more pounding, "let me in," more pounding, "let me in." It felt like a bad imitation of Sheldon knocking at Penny's door in Big Bang Theory! He finally unlocked and opened the door.

I continued my tirade to the garage in search of more proof that he had lied and had been drinking. Why I kept putting myself through this exercise was beyond me. I continued to do the same thing and expected a different result.

My quest for proof was validated once again. He had changed it up this time. Under the driver seat of the Jeep there were two Diet Pepsi bottles full of a liquid. I knew right away this wasn't Diet Pepsi as both bottle caps had been opened, then screwed back on again. I brought them into the kitchen for a closer look, opened one of the bottles and took a swig. He had poured out some of the soda and replaced it with alcohol. I dumped the bottles out and put the empty bottles in the sink. I wanted to be sure he could see them and know that I knew what he did. This seemed to give me some sense of personal satisfaction that I couldn't really explain.

The following morning Dave was apologetic. He told me I should take his keys and his money. He was going to detox himself again. "This is the last time," he stated. I was non-responsive as I took his keys and his wallet and walked out the door.

I was on a constant roller coaster of emotional highs and lows. He was sober a week, then drunk. He was sober a weekend, then drunk. Bottom line was he was still drinking.

Quite honestly it appeared he was still drinking and driving as well, which was supposed to be my hard-stop. Drinking and driving was supposed to the final straw that would lead me to kicking him out and filing a separation agreement. I failed again. I wanted it to be over and I wanted him out of the house, but I was afraid of what the immediate reaction by him would be.

A year ago he had been locked away in an in-patient treatment facility. A year ago, I had a little hope that when he got out things would be different. He would make an effort, go to meetings, stop lying and most importantly, stop drinking. There I sat, a year later, wondering why I continued to ride the ride. When he was normal, life was really good. When he drank, it was so very bad. The bad was still outweighing the good. After all the sessions with the doctors, the meds, the therapist, and the counselor, it was bad.

It was time to have the conversation. It was time to see if he loved me enough to just leave peacefully and stay away for a few months. I needed it terribly. I wanted it desperately. I wanted a life. I wanted MY life BACK!

Chapter 61

Not a Good Liar

Today I would write a letter. Today I would make my choice. I would choose to no longer have the life sucked out of me by an addict. I would write a letter to Dave as whenever I tried to broach the subject of our marriage or him moving out, he walked away or shut me down.

I felt good about my decision. I left the letter on his nightstand around supper time. He had spent his day in bed. A beautiful Friday that I took off so we could have a fun three-day weekend and he chose the bottle and lies over his family once again.

This wasn't the first time but it would be the last. The day started out with him not getting up on his own. It was going to be another hot day, so I wanted to get the dogs out for a long walk before it got too hot. He just wouldn't get up. I left and took the dogs for an hour-long ride.

As I got ready to walk out the door he decided to sit up in bed. I told him I was leaving to run errands and to grab lunch. He got up, walked to the bathroom and told me he would meet me there.

I ran my errands and went to one of our favorite places to eat, sitting outside to dine. After waiting 20 minutes I texted him `"I take it you aren't coming."` `"Just getting ready to call you. My tooth is killing me,"` he replied. Seriously, his tooth?

I figured he wouldn't show up. I finished my lunch then ran a couple errands. He texted me about 45 minutes later, `"You coming home soon?"`

`"Why?"` I replied as I was very suspicious.

He sent me a picture of my dog, Lewis and texted that Lewis missed me. I ignored him.

I arrived home about 30 minutes later and noticed the Jeep had been out. He had left and returned. He managed to leave in the short amount of time I was gone. I decided to confront him.

He was faking sleep when I entered the bedroom. I asked him where he went. He said "Nowhere."

"Really?" I replied. "That is so weird because I KNOW you went somewhere."

He acted like he suddenly remembered that he did go somewhere. "Oh yea, I went out to get a Diet Pepsi."

"Really, as I don't see an empty bottle anywhere. Nothing in the Jeep. Nothing in the kitchen. Nothing in the bedroom. You went to the liquor store!" I claimed.

"I did not" he replied. "You are unreal. I am not drinking."

I knew he was lying. I left again to treat myself to a Mother's Day shopping spree, justifying that I deserved to spend some money on myself. I returned home and he was still lying in bed. Before I left to shop, I had put an empty toilet paper roll under one of the rear tires of the Jeep to see if he had left again. He had not.

As I sat in the back yard on this most gorgeous spring day, I decided I had had enough. It was time to write a letter to him.

Dave,

I'm writing this in the hopes that you will read this with an open heart and an open mind. I have a choice to make. It is one on whether to continue to be an enabler for your addiction or whether to set myself free to have a life of my own. At this point, I need to set myself free.

The lies continue. It's a roller coaster ride with you that I can't handle any longer. You know what I am talking about. I don't need to give specifics. I never know when I get up in the morning or when I get home from work which "Dave" I will get. There isn't any initiative to get a job. You don't even really try nor do you seem to care. I'm exhausting myself at work while you do nothing. This nothing has been going on since last August. I'm done.

No matter what I do, I can't make you stop or make you change. Only you can do that. I will not continue to have the life at age 46 sucked out of me. A year ago, at this time you were in treatment and I had prayed that it was finally the one thing that would help you get on the track to sober living.

You still need help. I can't make you get it. You must want this enough for yourself. I have poured my soul into 57,000 words. As I read those words, I realize that this same cycle continues to happen over and over again. Yet here I stay.

I'm sorry to write this, but we can't ever seem to connect for a conversation without you walking away from me. Please be open-minded about this. If you truly love me like you say you do, then you will understand why this has to happen. If you truly love me, you will take this time to do some inner soul searching and get the professional help that you need.

I placed the letter on his nightstand and went into my closet to get a basket of laundry. I put the laundry basket in the hall and when I bent over to pick it up I noticed a partially empty

178

bottle of Diet Pepsi under the bed! He had gone to get booze, mixed it with soda and was drinking in bed. When he had heard me come home earlier he had tossed the bottle under the bed. I opened the bottle and sure enough. This reaffirmed my decision. I felt at peace with it and quietly set the bottle on the corner of the letter that I had placed on the nightstand.

Chapter 62

Been There, Done That

I'm not sure if it was my letter or if it was the fact that he was already too far gone, but by 1:00 p.m. the following Saturday we were on our way to the Emergency Room at the local hospital. His Saturday morning had been spent drinking a fifth of vodka out of multiple mini airplane-size bottles he had purchased from the liquor store that morning when I was running errands. By the time I got home shortly after lunch he stumbled from the bedroom to the kitchen to eat some soup. Shortly after he finished he started gagging like he was trying to throw up, stumbled back into the bedroom and within 60 seconds had fallen hard, flat on his back.

I walked in to see him on the floor, half in the bedroom and half in the hallway to the bathroom. He reminded me of a giant beached whale. He was only wearing a pair of gym shorts, was bloated, puffy in the face and everywhere else, and completely incoherent. He also smelled like a dirty old sponge soaked with vodka. I asked him what happened, to which he replied, "I fell."

"Why?" I asked, very curious as to what his response would be.

He didn't answer but attempted to get up on his own as I stood and watched. I didn't feel like giving him a hand, as I was tired of it. After he finally got up off the floor he tried climbing up into the bed, almost fell backwards, then tried again. Upon getting on the bed, he sat with his legs dangling, looked at me and burst into tears.

"I can't stop. I'm sick and I can't stop drinking," he cried. He went on to speak through his tears that he had no hope. If he had a gun right then he would shoot himself in the head. He didn't want to exist any longer. He wanted it to be over. He kept making the gun shape with his fingers and pointing at his temple.

I looked at him and simply said "Get dressed, we are going to the ER to get you admitted for detox." There was no crying by me. Everything was very matter-of-fact with me. I had been through this drill before and had heard the same thing from him repeatedly.

It was a beautiful and warm spring Saturday. This was the kind of day I would spend outside enjoying some gardening, enjoying the warm breeze of the air flowing through my hair as I drove with the convertible top down, the kind of day spent playing with the dogs. Instead, on this great day I was about to spend seven hours in the ER. Not exactly what I had planned, but then again, my life with Dave hadn't exactly turned out like I had planned.

As we checked in and walked to the little room right inside the ER doors, I found it oddly humorous that we were told to go inside and wait in the same exact room he was in over a year ago. I could even picture what he was wearing that day and the condition he was in. It was the same thing in a different year, which was pathetically ironic.

After waiting for over an hour, the attending ER doctor finally stopped by for a visit. The mention of suicidal thoughts did come up and Dave started to cry. He admitted he wanted to hurt himself but did not have any thoughts of hurting anyone else. Another 45 minutes passed before the behavioral health nurse came into the room.

She looked at me then looked at Dave, then back at me. This nurse looked very familiar. She was the same nurse that saw him on two different admissions over a year ago. Sadly enough, she remembered us. As we spoke of why we were there yet again, the expression on her face was priceless as I nonchalantly rattled off all the medications he had been on since the last time he had been admitted. Since he had confirmed with the admitting doctor and the nurse that he had thoughts of hurting himself, the doctor wrote him in for an involuntary detox committal. He was not allowed to leave until he was medically released from detox.

He needed detox and an extended treatment program of 30 days. Even Dave initially stated that. The hospital decided they were going to send him outside of Wilmington to a different facility for detox this time. My guess was due to his history locally. He either walked out or managed to convince the doctors that he was fine and ended up getting released too early.

The following Sunday it was determined he would be sent to a facility in South Carolina. When asked how he would get there, the nurse replied with "A ride with the Sheriff's Department."

"In cuffs?" he asked with his eyes getting bigger by the minute.

"Sure," she replied, "Certainly you have been cuffed before if you got a DUI or committed."

That was the end of that. I was trying hard not to feel sorry for him at that point. All the crap he had put me through and I was feeling bad that he would take a two-hour ride in the back of a squad car!

While Dave spent his Sunday waiting at the hospital in a gown and socks for his handcuffs and transport vehicle, I spent my day eating lunch outside, playing with the dogs, and topping off the day with live music at a marina and a boat ride with friends up the Intracoastal Waterway. We even saw a pod of dolphins! It put it all in perspective for me. This was what every day of my life could be like, minus the boat ride and dolphins of course. I could be enjoying my day, doing my thing, and having a life.

My friends as well as Dave's friends and family continued to tell me they couldn't believe how strong I was. They couldn't believe I was still with him, how amazing I was, and how devoted I was. I didn't see that at all. What I saw was someone that didn't have the guts to follow through with what they had wanted and needed to do for many years. I saw someone who was gullible enough to always believe and give the benefit of the doubt to a master manipulator and liar. I saw someone who was a very good faker that life was good. I wasn't amazing. I wasn't a saint. I was just an extremely slow learner!

Chapter 63

One Flew Over the Cuckoo's Nest

By 11:30 the next Monday morning I received a phone call from a "Blocked" number. I assumed it was Dave calling from his new temporary home in South Carolina. I answered the call and he asked me if I was at home. "No," I replied, "I'm at work."

"At 3:30?" he asked.

"It isn't 3:30, it's 11:30 in the morning," I replied.

"On Tuesday, right?" he asked.

"No, it is 11:30 in the morning on Monday" I replied.

He proceeded to tell me how deplorable the conditions were there. "There are men and women sleeping in the same rooms and sharing bathrooms," he whispered under his breath. "They won't give me my medicine and I'm miserable. My legs are jumping out of their skin. This place is crazy. I'm going to talk to a nurse to get me sent back to Wilmington."

Great. Here we go. Less than two days after entering ER, he wanted to bail. I tried to calm him down and told him that since he had just gotten there the night before, that they had to have time to process him as a patient, and that he needed to be patient and give it a few more hours.

The following Tuesday morning I was in a meeting, having left my cell phone at my desk. I was only gone for 30 minutes

184

to return to four missed calls and two messages on my cell phone along with one message on my work phone. The messages on my cell phone were:

Message 1 - "You got to be kidding me. Not picking up the phone after last night. I'm worried stiff and don't know what is going on. Pick up the phone."

Message 2 eight minutes later – "Why are you not trying to pick up the Goddam phone, Hun? They had me so drugged out last night. I don't know what happened. Someone told me Ripley got shot and I'm fucking sitting here dying."

Message 3 one minute later – "I can't believe you won't pick up the phone after everything last night."

I waited at my desk and within 10 minutes he called again. I picked up the phone to him saying, "Why don't you pick up your phone?!"

"I have a job. I was in a meeting and can't always take my phone or take calls in the middle of a meeting," was my cold response.

He started to rant, "After everything that happened last night. Cops and everything were here. You should have seen it. Ripley got shot and nobody would let me see him!"

I calmly replied, "Ripley didn't get shot as Ripley was home with me last night."

"What? What time did you get home? Didn't you come and see me last night and bring Ripley?" he questioned.

"No Dave. Nobody came to see you last night. Ripley is fine. Everyone is fine and nobody got shot. I think you either hallucinated or had a dream that you thought was real due to the medication you are on. Everyone is ok." I explained.

"What time did you get home last night?" he asked.

"I got home after work and stayed with the pets. We ate and watched TV. Nobody went anywhere and everyone is fine," was my reply.

"I don't have any shoes. I only have one sweatshirt. My shoes are gone. My jacket is gone," he stated.

"Shoes? Where are your shoes? What happened to them? What are you wearing on your feet?" I asked.

"Stolen. You should see this place. I'm wearing socks and my flip flops. I don't even have any money for a soda. They are stealing things from me," he whined.

I must say that was one of the strangest conversations I had ever had with him and I had had some crazy ones. I wasn't sure what to believe. He lied so well. Also, the effects of high doses of Ativan will do that to a person. I resorted to thinking that it was the medication and perhaps they took his shoes since they had shoe laces, and one could hurt themselves with long enough shoe laces.

Later that evening I received a call from one of the counselors at the facility. They were calling me to get a baseline on Dave. In other words, he was acting like a crazy person and they needed to know if he had any history of schizophrenia, paranoia or any other mental illness. He had been saying things to everyone that didn't make sense. He had been "intrusive" with others. I told her that it must be the medication he was on and that typically as a patient he was kind, compassionate, considerate and an all-around good patient other than wanting to get out. While on the phone I took the opportunity to ask her about men and women in the same room, people lying in the halls, etc. and she assured me with a bit of laughter that was not the case.

Wednesday mid-morning hits me with yet another phone call from Dave. "Good Morning!" he said cheerfully in response to my answering the phone. "How are you?"

He sounded much more like himself. He told me he had "great news." He had met with a doctor that morning who indicated he had completed the detox portion of the program and they were discharging him the following day. They were recommending and referring him to outpatient treatment. He told me that it would be different this time. This would be the fresh start. He would do what he was supposed to do with treatment and would attend AA meetings and everything would be good. My heart sank. I thought for sure he would at least be there a full week. I had been enjoying my time to myself. I had been enjoying the fact that I didn't have to think about him drunk, driving, or over-medicating himself.

He stated, "This place isn't a place for a 28-day program. You have to trust me." I asked him if he would be open to going back up to the Greensboro center that he had been to the prior year, for a 28-day program. He wouldn't have any part of it.

That evening he called again during his allotted time to make a call. He wanted to confirm what time I would be there to pick him up. I broached the subject of treatment again and basically told him that he must agree to allow me to be part of the initial care. I needed to have access to the facility where he would be having outpatient treatment and I wanted him to work with his counselor to determine the most appropriate place in Wilmington for his outpatient treatment. I asked him if he remembered receiving the letter I wrote that was left on his nightstand. He indicated that he did and he understood if he didn't follow through that he would be out. He said he understood completely and would have to prove himself with "actions." To me it sounded like

he had picked up on the appropriate buzz words during some
treatment/therapy sessions.

Chapter 64

Home Sweet Home?

I was deep in thought as I drove the 83 miles to pick Dave up once again from yet another facility. As I followed my GPS through the turns I wondered what would happen this time. Would this finally be the time where he had hit bottom? I would think spending four and a half days in a facility with some hard-core addicts, mentally challenged old people, and literally a few crazies of the Carolinas would do him in and he would think enough was enough.

The directions on the facility's website were wrong and I ended up in the middle of a university parking lot. As I circled around and parked to get my bearings, I spotted two parked police cars. Both officers were outside their cars, chatting. I pulled over near them and asked for directions to the facility. One officer was kind enough to give me a personal escort to where I needed to go. I had to chuckle at the irony of it all. Dave had made his way to this facility in the back of a patrol car and here I was getting a police escort to pick him up!

He looked clear-eyed and once again eager to embark on a journey to sober living. He couldn't wait to tell me about what had happened the night he thought Ripley had been shot. He had evidently been on a psycho tangent thinking that I had come to visit with his entire family and had brought Ripley. During our visit, Ripley got out through an open window. I went out to look for him and Dave had heard gun shots. He thought I was stuck outside unable to get into the facility and Ripley was somehow stuck up in the ventilation of the facility and had been shot. Nobody at the facility would allow him to see Ripley or to get out and find me. He and his family were stuck inside while I was stuck outside and Ripley was bleeding to death overhead. This went on for a couple hours until finally the staff decided to go along with his story to calm him down. They told him they had found me and Ripley and that we were both fine, which calmed him down enough for two orderlies to each give him an injection of valium in each arm. He was then out like a light.

He went on to tell me that one of the employees didn't complete the check-in and logging of his bag and belongings and had stolen his new shoes, bag, and a jacket. After Dave kept hounding everyone and getting up in the face of a very large man, the shoes and bag suddenly reappeared, minus the jacket. I hated that jacket anyway as he always wore that thing when he was drunk. If it hadn't been stolen, it soon would have found its way to the garbage container.

As we drove home we talked about his plan of action. He assured me he would attend meetings every day and would consider an out-patient day program after he spoke with his counselor. He said that he knew he had said it before and that this time the proof would be in his actions, not his words.

I was hopeful, but doubtful.

Chapter 65

Ain't No Proof in this Pudding!

Needless to say, the meetings didn't last long. He attended a meeting along with a friend the day after he returned home, had me drop him off and pick him up from one on the following Saturday, but didn't go on Sunday. I had to trust that he would go to meetings during the work day when I was at work. In the back of my mind I was thinking that he would give me a reason to kick him out this time. He wasn't serious enough. He still hadn't hit bottom.

We decided it may be a good idea for both of us to take a little trip to Florida to see his 10-year sober friend. I got the time off work, planned for a dog sitter, and we booked our hotel and started making plans. This would be a nice diversion and spending time with his friend would be good.

However, that first full week back from detox was not good. He continued to be lazy, not making any effort to find a job, most likely not attending any meetings, and basically just existing and spending time with the dogs. This was the week leading into Memorial Day weekend. We had planned to take the dogs to the beach on Friday afternoon before all the tourists made their way into Wilmington.

He was just off, but I couldn't put my finger on it, plus he wanted me to drive, which was strange. I pushed it out of my mind, not wanting to ruin the long weekend. The holiday weekend was full of fun, spending time walking the dogs, biking, working in the yard, going out to eat and dining outdoors. We had a great time, until the following Wednesday, when the little red warning flag was once again raised. Little did I know what would be in store the next day.

Chapter 66

The Straw that FINALLY Broke the Camel's Back

Thursday morning was when my car was going into the shop for an oil change. The plan was to leave it there for the day and that Dave would take me to work, and then pick me up. I had an uneasy feeling that he was going to hit the liquor store once it opened.

I texted him around 4:00 pm to remind him to pick me up. He didn't respond. I texted him again, and he didn't respond. I called him and he didn't answer. Finally, shortly after I hung up he answered my text with, "Of course I am."

It seemed like it took him forever to arrive. He was 20 minutes late. He pulled up in the Jeep with all three dogs barking and shrieking out the windows. As I climbed in I caught a scent of something strong. Could it be that sweaty booze smell that happens when the alcohol seeps out through the pores of the skin or was it just my imagination again?

It didn't take long for me to find out. About three minutes after getting on the freeway, he was driving extremely slow in the left lane of traffic, causing a back-up of traffic behind us. He started to swerve to the left, crossing over the painted line and way too close for comfort to the concrete barriers that lined that section of the freeway. I screamed, "Dave, what are you doing?" He jerked the Jeep back in the lane. I told him he needed to speed up or move over and let the traffic go around. He was going 45 mph in a 55-mph zone during rush hour. He started to shift into the right lane without looking and almost side swiped a car that was approaching our right side. I screamed, "Look out! There is a car there! You can't shift lanes now!" He hadn't even looked. His response to me was, "You told me to!" As the road curved and started a slight decline, his speed went from 45 mph to slightly over 70 mph.

I was hanging onto the roll bar for life at that point, white knuckled the entire way. After a few more comments from me on what was going on he pulled off to the side of the road and onto the shoulder, slammed on the brakes, ripped off his seatbelt and screamed, "Do you want to drive?" I was scared to death to have him get out on the driver's side as traffic was flying by and he hadn't left much room to get out without getting hit. I didn't know what I was thinking, but I let him continue to drive me to get my car, which was about a mile and a half away.

He dropped me off then left with the dogs. Would he go straight home the back way where there would be less of a chance of seeing a cop? Would he be dumb enough to drive around? As I waited for my car, I held back my tears.

When I got home about 15 minutes later, I heard the dogs as I pulled into the driveway. However, they weren't outside. They were all still in the Jeep with him in the garage. I found this odd. After I pulled in and shut the gate, he got out, steadied himself on the railing to walk up the stairs to the laundry room, and then steadied himself again on the dryer before walking into the kitchen, straight through the master bedroom and onto the toilet, sunglasses still on.

The hiding out in the bathroom thing had become a pattern and the sunglasses still being on his face didn't help. I got the Breathalyzer. I thought he just needed to give me the reason to kick his ass out. I knew he had been drinking prior to picking me up based on the ride home, but that wasn't good enough for me. As I held the gadget in front of his mouth telling him to blow, he tried to push my hand away and missed.

He got up, stumbled to the bed and flopped flat on his back saying nothing. I went back out to the garage to check the Jeep. Certainly, there must be evidence there. I was not disappointed. In the center console compartment there was a half full bottle of Diet Pepsi, missing the lid. I took a drink. It was soda and vodka. Mission accomplished. I was done.

I stormed back into the house, ranting my words of anger and hurt all bundled together and screamed, "You are drunk! You picked me up drunk! You drove with the dogs and you picked me up and drove me drunk! How could you? I hate you! How could you! This is it. No trip, no us, it is over. I'm done." He laid there and looked at me and defiantly said, "Yeah right." That was about all I could take. I took the bottle in one hand and used my other hand to attempt to open his mouth, trying to pour what was left in the bottle down his mouth. He sputtered and tried to sit up while I continued to pour it on his face.

Probably not the best way to handle my hurt and anger but it felt good. After a call to his family and our friend in Florida, I called my attorney, who luckily could squeeze me in the following morning. This would be the beginning of a new start. Finally, and a long time coming!

Chapter 67

Stay Strong

Waking up the following morning with a splitting headache forced me to immediately recall what had happened the night before. I didn't sleep well which wasn't a surprise.

Sitting at the table waiting for the attorney four months after my initial consult had me reflecting on why I waited four months. I guess it was stupidity or insanity or just plain cluelessness. Be strong, I told myself as I sat there. Don't cry and be a weak mess of tears. I could do this. Be strong.

Janet, my attorney came in and after initial pleasantries she opened my file. "You know what notes I wrote in your file last time?" she asked. I replied, "She'll be back?" "No," she stated, "I noted that it would take something major happening before you would come back." She was right. I needed to value my life more than I had been and him picking me up drunk had to be the final straw.

She told me that she wanted to be sure to let me know that leaving him was brave, but not only that leaving him was brave, but also staying with him this long had been brave. Many people don't say that but she wanted me to know that she felt I was brave. That was all it took. Where was the Kleenex box? I was nervous, but reserved. I was scared, but strong. I was anxious, but resolute. I was strong. I needed to do this for myself and no matter what he said or how hard he tried to suck me back into his web of lies, I would be strong. I would not fail. I was too important to fail.

I received instructions on what I needed to do with bank accounts and credit cards, signed a client agreement, slapped $1,200 cash on the table for payment, and took notes as to an email I was supposed to send him after I told him he needed to move out.

Chapter 68

Stress Ball

Stressed was an understatement for how I felt that Friday on my way home from work. Would he be home or would he be gone? Would he be drunk or would he have feelings of guilt and try to make it up to me as he had in the past, mind-screwing me every step of the way?

He was home in the bedroom. The dogs were completely hyper, so my guess was he had spent the day in the bedroom with his supply of booze. How could I have the conversation with him if he was passed out? I couldn't send the email until I talked to him. I was a nervous wreck. Finally, around 8:30 p.m. I walked in the bedroom and tried to wake him up. He finally looked at me with bloodshot eyes. The sheets smelled, he smelled, the entire room smelled. I told him we needed to have a conversation and that he needed to understand that I had hired an attorney to work on drafting separation papers. I told him that picking me up at work drunk was the final straw. He still denied being drunk.

Before I left the bedroom and as I was finishing my speech, I opened the nightstand drawer next to the bed. I was not surprised to see an empty soda bottle and another one that was half full. I put both bottles on the nightstand and calmly stated, "Well here are a couple bottles. I'm not even going to dump them out. You just stay in here and enjoy your beverage. This just confirms that I made the right decision in hiring an attorney." I went to the kitchen to send my email.

Dave,

I told you on May 11th on the way to the Emergency Room that if you drank again you were out. When we spoke on the phone while you were in detox, I told you if you drank again you were out. I told you that as a condition of returning home, you would need to stay in a treatment program, which you did not. You indicated that you would attend AA meetings every day once released from detox and that your actions would prove themselves. You have not attended AA meetings daily and you drank again.

When you picked me up from work with the dogs yesterday (May 30th), you had been drinking. On the way home you drove oddly slow in the left lane of an interstate, and then swerved left over the line toward the concrete barrier. When I called you on it you swerved back into the appropriate driving lane. When I told you to move into the right lane of traffic to let commuting traffic pass, you proceeded to swerve into the right lane without looking, almost side swiping a car that was approaching on our right. When I asked you if you were drunk, you yelled at me and indicated you were not, as you proceeded to speed up at a speed of 70 mph as we were rounding a declining curve.

When we arrived home, you refused to take a breathalyzer and passed out in bed. I checked the Jeep and found a half drunk bottle of Diet Pepsi that had been mixed with alcohol.

You put my life as well as the lives of our dogs in danger. I have to protect myself physically, legally and financially.

I have hired an attorney to work on our legal and financial issues.

Priscilla

That night I locked my bedroom door and hid his keys. He didn't come out all night, nor did he the next morning as far as I could tell. My attorney told me to make plans to be gone a lot and away from him over the weekend. That wasn't difficult at all when he was passed out. He was making it very easy for me. I would have felt guilty had I come home on Friday to him cooking or wanting to go out to dinner.

As I was sitting in the backyard with the dogs, I happened to look down at my hands and noticed my wedding ring. The tears started flowing. When I stood at that altar 26 years ago and said the words "for better for worse and till death do us part," I meant them. I think God will understand why I had made the decision I had. In a way death was involved. It was the death of my spirit. I hope He understands that I have done everything I possibly could to try and make it work. There was nothing left for me to do. It was in God's hands completely as to what happened to Dave.

As I headed back to the house, I tried to be quiet as I didn't want to wake him up. I was not in the mood for a confrontation and I figured once he woke up he would be looking for his keys. About an hour later, the bedroom door opened and he shuffled out, looked around the corner, rubbed his bare belly and shuffled back into the bedroom. About 30 minutes after that he came out in his flip flops, shorts and a T-shirt, and staggered to the kitchen, using the kitchen counter to steady himself. He opened the fridge and stared inside. He looked horrible. I watched him out of the corner of my eye. He hadn't shaved, he smelled, and he looked like a blowfish, both in the stomach and in the face. He took some left-over chicken out of the fridge and leaned over the counter, fridge left open, and started eating the chicken with his hands. He was chewing slowly. He hadn't eaten in three days.

I wasn't completely cold hearted and asked him if he would like me to make him something. He looks at me all puffy-faced and whispered, without eye contact, "Yes, if you wouldn't mind." I made him some peanut butter and jelly toast with milk. I watched him eat. He was the true picture of what you would see in a movie of a drunk. He was slouched, could barely keep his eyes open, and then suddenly looked up and around like he was seeing something flying. He finished, and went back to the bedroom.

I stepped outside for a bit and when I came back in he had come back out into the living room with his hat on. I asked him, "What are you doing with your hat on?" He replied, "I put it on."

"I know that," I said, "but why are you wearing it? Do you think you are going somewhere? Do you think you are leaving?"

"Yes," he mumbled.

"I don't think you are leaving to go anywhere. I'm not giving you your keys and you aren't driving anywhere as you are drunk. I can't stop you from drinking but I can stop you from driving. Do you need me to take you somewhere? You can always call a cab or ride your bike but you are not going to drive. Period," I stated.

With eyes barely open, he whispered, "Yes, take me." He then held out his hands to show me that they were shaking. He NEEDED it.

I drove my alcoholic drunk of a husband to the nearest ABC store so he could get a stash. As I sat in the parking lot waiting for him to buy his booze, I tried to hold back my tears. This was disgusting. I watched bloated, red-faced men walking in and out of the store with their brown paper bags of booze. I was disgusted at myself for taking him there. I was ashamed that I had offered to take him. Maybe it was the easy way out for me, knowing deep inside that if he boozed up at home, I didn't have to mess with him. I could just shut the bedroom door and shut him out.

Chapter 69

The Family's Turn

Through all the commotion on Friday and into Saturday, many texts and conversations occurred between me and his family. I made it clear that I was finished with this part of my life and I started the process to move on. They made it clear that there wasn't one person within Dave's family that blamed me and I shouldn't feel guilty about it.

Guilt. That was the problem. Being fed up with the life being sucked out of me for the last two years did not negate the fact that I still cared for and deeply loved Dave. However, I had been married to two different people over several years of our marriage.

When Dave was not drinking, we had the best time. We had a lot in common, rarely fought about anything of any substance at all, and everything was very comfortable and easy.

However, when Dave was drinking, he was a completely different person. He wasn't a mean drunk, but he wasn't considerate either. He was selfish, self-absorbed, lazy, and most of all, a liar. The lying was the worst. I couldn't believe a single thing he said about anything. He would even lie about something as small as if he ate or what he ate.

Guilt was something I would feel if something should happen to Dave if we split. My therapist tried helping me with that feeling a few months prior, but bottom line was I would feel guilty about it. It was for that very reason that I hinted to his family about them coming out to help in this "transition" situation. It would either be to be here with him while he heard the official news of separation, as well as assist him in getting out and getting a place of his own; OR it would be to try and convince him to go back to the Midwest and stay with family.

It made me feel better about my decision, knowing that Dave at least has family there for him and he wouldn't be all alone. Selfish as it was, he could be their problem now as I was tired of dealing with it and was not going to deal with it any longer.

So, the planning started on timing. How soon would they get here and what was our plan?

Chapter 70

The Last Drunk Day?

The following Sunday started much the same way that Saturday did, with Dave shut in the bedroom with his booze. I went about my day and had lunch with a friend, only to receive a text around 2:00 p.m. from Dave stating, "I need something to eat," which I ignored. By the time I got home about 30 minutes later, he was passed out. I left once again, taking the dogs with me for an afternoon ride.

At 3:50 p.m. I received another text from Dave stating, "I liv u. I am going to kill myself," which was followed by another text at 4:01 p.m. stating, "Where u going," followed immediately by "??? Where are you?" By 4:23 p.m. I had yet another text stating, "Where are you? ???," almost immediately followed by, "I am going on my bike." I also had two missed calls and a text from his friend. I had turned the sound off my phone to enjoy this afternoon ride with my dogs and everything was coming to a head. Dave had also texted his friend that he was going to kill himself, which resulted in multiple calls/texts from him.

I called his friend while heading back home, who frantically stated "Dave just sent me a text that he was going to kill himself!"

"I know," I responded, "I don't mean to sound cold, but he has done this before. I'm on my way home plus he just texted me again that he was leaving on his bike, so he clearly hasn't killed himself." The fact was I had been hardened by Dave's actions, threats and behaviors over the past two years.

When I got back home he was still there. He was lying flat on his stomach in the middle of the bedroom floor. I poked at his leg with my foot and he didn't move. I poked a bit harder and he did move that time, raising his head slightly and moaning. I asked him, "What are you doing on the floor?" Dave replied, "I'm laying here." After I saw that he responded and moved, I left the bedroom and shut the door.

A few minutes later he shuffled out to the living room and headed toward the kitchen toward a box of crackers. He looked horrible and was more bloated and red than the day before. He took his box and shuffled back into the bedroom, leaving the bedroom door open.

Shortly thereafter he came back out into the living room and told me that he wanted me to take him to get more alcohol, to which I firmly replied, "No." We continued to argue back and forth, him whining and begging for me to take him to get booze, and me standing my ground and refusing to do so. I told him I would be more than happy to get his bike out of the garage if he wanted to ride his bike somewhere. He stood and looked at me with an incredulous look on his face as I went outside to get his bike.

After returning to the house, I said, "There you go. Your bike is ready so off you go." He refused to leave the house on his bike. He continued to whine so I offered him my stashed bottle of wine.

"Do you want a bottle of wine?" I asked.

"You don't have any," he replied.

"Oh, yes I do," I replied. "I got a bottle as a gift and hid it for a special occasion so I could try it. Do you want it?" I asked again. I felt like I was bargaining with a child.

"No, you don't. I drank that a long time ago," he slurred.

"I bet you didn't," I replied and off I went to produce the bottle. I came back into the living room and triumphantly handed him the bottle. "Knock yourself out trying to open it as it has a cork. Enjoy."

I sat in the living room, watching this most pathetic looking individual mutter to himself as he spent ten minutes trying to find a cork screw. He looked everywhere and even attempted to open it with his teeth. He took a sharp knife out of the drawer and tried digging the cork out of the bottle. This scene made me very sad but not sad enough to cry. I was officially out of tears.

Suddenly I heard Dave state triumphantly, "Found it!" He had found the cork screw in the back of a junk drawer. He opened the bottle, got a glass, and went to the living room to sit in a chair, bottle between his feet on the floor, literally guzzling the wine he had just poured in the glass.

After chugging two glasses of wine, he sat there looking around, burping, running his hands through his hair, and shaking his head. He was shaking his head, repeatedly, like there was something wrong with him or like when a dog has an ear problem and keeps shaking their head. The ceiling fan in the bedroom was on and the circulation from the fan caused the bedroom door to slowly swing shut.

Upon hearing the latch of the door click, he spun around in the chair and screamed, "Who is in there?!" He looked frantic and afraid, as he got up from the chair, stomping to the bedroom door. He opened the door and pushed it all the way open, then stormed into the bedroom screaming, "WHO is in here!? Who are you?" He took a turn into the master bath where I heard him yell again, "Who are you!?"

I stood in the kitchen watching the entire scene. I couldn't believe it. He was out of his mind. He was paranoid, drunk, out of control and hallucinating. This was the worst binge he had ever been on that I had witnessed. I decided I would prop up my phone and record whatever would happen next. I figured it may be able to protect me if all this ended up in a messy divorce or worse yet, someone getting physically hurt.

After finally being satisfied that there wasn't anyone else in the house, he propped open the bedroom door and shuffled back out into the living room, taking his same seat near the wine bottle he had left on the floor. The expression on his face almost rendered him unrecognizable. It was like he had a look of both fear and anger combined. His wide eyes were darting everywhere, looking around in a state of paranoia.

As he sat there, looking around, he reached into the pocket of his shorts, pulled out his wallet, and awkwardly threw it across the room, somewhat looking like a monkey throwing the left-over peel of a banana. He didn't say a word, just threw it. I quietly picked it up and put it in a safe place.

He continued to sit and stare, and then started to cry. He cried, "I need help."

"Do you want me to call 911?" I asked.

"No, but I am sick," he started wailing. The crying was getting worse. I picked up his phone and dialed 911 for an ambulance. By the time the 911 operator picked up, he was wailing even more loudly. I explained to her that he had been on a four-day binge, had a history of alcoholism, abuses prescription medication, and had threatened to kill himself. After answering more of her questions such as if there were any weapons in the house, or did I feel my life was in danger, she dispatched the paramedic, police and ambulance!

While I was on the phone with her, he started to calm down, but also began fixating his stare on the ceiling fan in the living room. He looked like he was going to get up and give it a whack off the ceiling. As he jumped from the chair toward the middle of the room, I said, "Hey, it is just the ceiling fan. It isn't hurting anyone. Do you want me to shut it off?"

"Yes, please," he replied, "It is pissing me off!"

He then heard me say something to the operator about the location of the ambulance, and he looked at me and screamed, "What are you doing? Who are you calling? You're going to send me away?" He got up and stomped into the bedroom, looking frantically for his socks and shoes. He found them and struggled to put on a sock, all the time mumbling, "I'm not sick."

I was starting to go into panic mode, feeling like he would bolt out the front door at any minute. I was still on the phone with the 911 operator, who was keeping me calm and was giving me the status of where the help was. Dave started knocking things off the nightstand, then picked up an empty bottle and hurled it into the bathroom. He came out into the living room and started toward the kitchen, where I had strategically placed myself behind the counter for my safety. He reached for a bowl I had on the counter, ready to throw it, but I grabbed it from him. He reached for another object on the counter, which I grabbed out from under him, then yet another bowl that I managed to snatch from him before he threw it.

He finally stopped looking for things to throw and went back to the chair in the living room, sat down, and said repeatedly, "I'm not fucking sick."

I heard the faint sound of a siren, which grew more loudly as a small fire truck pulled in front of the house. Protocol, I was told, despite the fact I had just asked for an ambulance. I guess the fact he was drunk and had threatened himself warranted the police as well. The men in the fire truck stood outside the house and wouldn't enter until the police arrived, which was about five minutes later. This scene I was sure made for an interesting Sunday afternoon of "porch talk" in the neighborhood!

Two officers entered the house and walked toward Dave, who was still sitting in the chair, but had finally given up the bottle of wine (with about ¼ left). "Hey Buddy," said Officer 1, "How we doing today?"

"Fine," slurred Dave.

"Are you not feeling very good? Your wife here says you need some help today," stated Officer 2. By then Officer 1 had motioned for the rest of the gang to enter the house, which included two paramedics from the ambulance and two paramedics from the Fire Department. Needless to say, there were a lot of people standing in our small living room. Every time Officer 1 tried to pull me to the back of the kitchen to get the full story, Dave started having a fit, so Officer 2 kept coming around the corner to motion for us to come back to within view of Dave.

After what seemed like an eternity of them getting vital signs and taking my full report of what had transpired, they slowly walked him out the front door and to the ambulance. Off he went to the Emergency Room for further detoxification and hopefully some much needed treatment.

The relief I felt as I watched the ambulance pull away was enormous. I was completely exhausted, both physically and mentally, and had been on a frantic emotional ride for nearly four straight days.

Chapter 71

You're What?

With Dave on his way to the hospital, it was time to clean up the house. I entered the master bedroom, looking under the bed, in drawers and finally behind a chair to find all the empty vodka and soda bottles from the four-day nightmare.

The bedroom smelled. It was time to de-Dave the bedroom and bathroom. Wash everything, wipe it down, scrub it up and spray it off. I had to do whatever it took to reclaim that part of the house. Reclaim it I would! He was not coming back into this house with me sleeping in some other room. The dogs were also exhausted, but relieved. The poor animals had been through about as much stress as I had been!

I warmed up some left-over food, but hardly had any appetite. I was too tired to eat, which was a rarity for me. I had been through this too many times; the sense of relief, the "reclaiming" of the house, the reclaiming of my life!

No sooner had I finally sat back to relax, then my phone rang, displaying the number from the hospital. I figured someone from the ER was calling me to ask me some questions about medication or to hear what happened.

It was Dave! "Hey, they are releasing me to come home," he slurred.

"What? Are you kidding me?" I screamed. "Give the phone to someone else there. I need to talk to a doctor or someone else there!"

Some tech from the ER took the phone, "Yes" he said.

"My husband just told me he is being released from the hospital! He just got there two hours ago! I had the police, fire and ambulance here at the house plus he threatened to kill himself, and now someone is saying he can be released from the hospital!?" I exclaimed.

"The doctor said that he was cleared to go, but I'll talk to someone else and have them call you," said the tech.

I panicked. He absolutely could not get out nor could he come back to the house. When I called the hospital a few minutes later for an update I was told, "There had been a mistake and the doctor has written Dave in for an involuntary committal for detox." Thank God! The system had failed me in the past, but thank goodness it hadn't failed me for that one day!

Chapter 72

On the Road Again!

I did not go to visit him for his less-than- 24-hour stay at the local hospital. I did, however, pack a bag and drop it off right before they loaded him up to transport him back to South Carolina. He was heading back to the same facility he had just been released from two weeks prior.

He looked like Hell standing with a hospital gown and socks on, paramedics and a cop standing by. He was very grateful that I made it there in time with his bag of clothes. At that point I still couldn't stand the sight of him nor did I want to be around him. I just wanted him taken away. I wanted him away from me. I wanted normal.

Chapter 73

Who Really IS the Victim Here?

The first call he made to me the following day after his arrival back in South Carolina, was peppered with, "You should see this place," and "I'm going to see if they can transfer me back to Wilmington to the treatment center." He talked slow and sounded like he was highly medicated.

Day two's call brought a different Dave to the phone. "Hello Sunshine!" was his phone greeting. I remained distant. He needed to know that this was serious and he couldn't just expect me to chat with him like nothing had happened. We didn't talk about much of anything.

By day three, he was getting a bit paranoid, asking me if I was "doing something bad." What he really wanted to know was if I was looking for a place to move to. Little did he know at that time that it wouldn't have been me to move out. He would be the one to find a place and move. I assured him I was not and basically left it where we would just take this one day at a time.

Upon my visit to the facility, I presented my patient's security code before they would even acknowledge that Dave was there. In situations like this, protecting privacy was very important. I couldn't take my purse or my phone back to the unit with me to visit him. I had to transfer all the items I brought for Dave to a larger clear blue plastic bag so they could put his name on it as well as see the items inside. They had to be sure I hadn't brought into the facility with me anything that could be used as a weapon or toiletries with alcohol in them.

A counselor took me to the visiting area. As we walked through the rather sterile appearing hallways of twists and turns through a maze of units, I took quick note of the people inside. We passed by the adolescent unit, which I later found out was comprised of teens that mostly had issues with heroine and prescription drug addiction. We made our winding path through and past the adult Psych unit, where most of the issues there were related to schizophrenia, bio-polar, and other mental disorders. There was also the detoxification unit where the addicts went first, then on to the substance abuse (SA) unit.

The counselor indicated that the daily activities within the SA unit were very structured and didn't leave much free time on their own. The intent was to ensure that patients didn't try to isolate themselves. There were three beds to a room and only one centralized and rather small area within each unit to watch TV. Meals were held in one large cafeteria for all the units combined at the same time.

A typical day started off with waking up by 7:00 a.m. for medication, then dozing back to sleep until 8:00 a.m. Breakfast started at 9:00 a.m., with group meetings starting at 10:00 a.m. for two hours. Lunch was served at high noon, followed by more group meetings and group activities all afternoon. Supper was at 6:00 p.m. then AA meetings started at 7:30 p.m. for an hour. Phone time was allowed from 9:00 p.m. – 11:00 p.m. with lights out in rooms at 11:00 p.m. They did have TV time each evening from 8:30 – 11:00 p.m., which oftentimes included a movie with a theme. This theme usually centered on alcohol or drug abuse.

It was awkward seeing Dave after the horrible weekend prior. He gave me a hug and cheek kiss.

I stayed for about an hour and a half, of which the first few minutes were spent with Dave pulling out the victim card. He said he had been treated like a second-class citizen at the hospital. They treat alcoholics like dirt and he remembered the face of that ass of an ER doctor that treated him that way. Once he got out he was going to find out who he was and send the hospital a letter. He complained about the facility moving him out of detox a day early. He didn't want to leave there. He was having a blast and had made friends. All they did there was take medication and watch TV. It was great. He complained about the nerve of that nurse that was working on moving him. He heard her say to someone on the phone "This ain't his first rodeo." How unprofessional was that! He said that he certainly wouldn't be expected to go through that whole AA drill again with a sponsor. After all, Dave was special, right?

All that complaining and commentary gave me a headache and made me wonder what good any of this treatment really was. I figured some of it was due to the fact he hadn't really had any true therapy yet, and that after a few more days the whining and victim talk would subside.

He seemed overly hyper and very intense. He was clearly worried that I was plotting some move from the house, or was going to have separation papers delivered to the facility. That issue had obviously been stressing him out. He was on anti-anxiety meds, but I could hardly tell.

He seemed to calm down after convincing him that papers weren't going to be delivered to him nor was I moving out. I didn't have the heart to tell him that if anyone was going anywhere it would be him moving out. I told him that I was not going to ever be in that house with him in the state he was in the prior weekend. I was not going to be around him as a drunk any longer. He told me that he understood perfectly and wanted to know what I needed to help me feel more comfortable with him coming back home. He indicated that if it was truly over, there was no need for him to stay in treatment, and that coming home to his family was the only thing that was keeping him going.

That was when I dropped the "interlock" bomb. I had done my research and they could also be installed on a voluntary basis. For the low cost of $75 a month, I could feel confident that this man would not be able to drink and drive. Tight budget or not, it would be worth every penny.

He looked surprised, but then responded, "Ok, I will do that. If that is what you need me to do to make you understand I am serious, then I will do it." With that agreement, came further comments of him needing to have a meeting with his attorney to get the whole DUI thing expunged from his record as it was a job hindrance.

He told me there were many people in and out of that facility from Wilmington, as Wilmington no longer has a dedicated detoxification facility. People were coming and going out of detox, many not able to stay past four or five days due to not having insurance. More people were there due to heroin addiction than alcohol. He had a 27-year old roommate that was there due to heroin addiction that stroked out in his room. It was a mild stroke and after going to the hospital returned the next day for the remainder of his detox.

Chapter 74

A Well Deserved Break!

I had almost three straight weeks of a break from Dave. I was full of energy and motivation. I had time to do a lot of thinking. I hadn't thought Dave would be in rehab again, which threw a kink in my plans for separation. How could I separate now if he came out a sober and changed man?

My thinking was centered on giving him one very last chance. He needed to know that this was it and that if he were to drink again, our relationship would be over. The few friends I had shared any of this information with were telling me to be strong and not to fall back into his spell and believe what he said. I understood their point. However, they didn't know that I had been married to two men, one of which was a very kind and considerate man, whom I would consider my best friend. It was holding out for the appearance of this best friend one more time for me to make my final decision.

My three-week break consisted of no stress, knowing exactly what I was coming home to every night after work, and being active. It was great! It was normal. It was different. I had a mind-shift that when he did come home, I would no longer put my life on hold trying to prevent him from drinking. I would prevent the drinking and driving, and that was enough.

Chapter 75

Home Once Again

When he called to tell me that insurance was no longer going to pay for his stay in treatment, I was very nervous. I was scared to have him come home, not knowing what to expect. I didn't want to hover over him. I didn't want to nag him. He should have his plan from treatment and should act on it. I couldn't make him go to meetings or do what he was supposed to do. If he was serious, he would follow his plan.

The drive home that Friday afternoon was quiet. He shared some information with me about what he had learned. He was very surprised that I had the interlock appointment set up for him so quickly. We just had to make it through the weekend and that interlock would be installed by the following Monday afternoon.

I had many questions, but didn't want to pry. The weekend was better than expected and he frequently acknowledged that he understood when I mentioned not wanting to go through more roller coaster rides with his alcoholism and that this was it.

Time would tell as to whether this would work and if this in fact was the bottom he needed to hit before the light bulb came on. It was now on him as to whether he wanted to change or whether he would continue down the same path of destruction, which would eventually lead to his death.

He knew where I stood on the situation. He had more than enough warnings of what was to come if he drank again. I was utilizing the tools I had to ensure he didn't drink and drive. I was at ease with my decision on staying with him for that moment in time. At ease in giving him the one of many "last chances" he has had over the years.

I had changed my attitude and my mindset. I would no longer let his life take priority over my own well-being. I would stop preaching to him about what he should and shouldn't do. I would stop obsessing about him going to AA meetings. I would stop the constant worry about what he was doing, whether he was lying, or if he was drinking. The rest of these years would be more about me, regardless of if we remained together. I had finally learned how it needed to be. I had the experience, knowledge and tools needed to break away and take care of myself if he didn't stay sober.

Chapter 76

Fire Alarms

The confidence I felt didn't last all that long, which was no surprise. The inter-lock device was installed, which gave me a huge sense of relief. He could no longer drink and drive. However, it didn't take long to find an excuse to drink.

Within a week to the day after I picked him up from treatment, he drank. This was the Friday prior to the arrival of his family. I had surgery scheduled for the following week, and they were coming out to have the talk with him and see if they could convince him to go back to the Midwest with them, or perhaps go back into treatment. They would be there while I was in the hospital overnight. Quite frankly, I had zero trust in his ability to be responsible and I was worried about the pets in my absence and during my recovery.

I came home to the Jeep in the garage, his bike gone, and the smoke detector chirping. Shortly thereafter I received a text from him, asking me to come pick him up at a bar and grille about two miles from our home. He was drunk and couldn't ride his bike back home.

When I arrived, he was sitting at the bar with a glass of hard liquor, which he guzzled as he saw me come through the door. The looks of pity from the patrons at the bar didn't even bother me. It was just another day in the life of being married to a drunk.

When he sobered up enough to have a conversation with me later that evening, his excuse for drinking was that the smoke alarm started to chirp and he couldn't make it stop. He tried changing the battery and hitting the re-set button, but it just kept chirping. The most logical way to handle such a situation was to get on one's bike, ride to the nearest bar, and get plastered a week after spending three weeks in treatment.

Timing was everything, and with my surgery less than a week away, and relatives on the way, I just washed my hands of his situation mentally and focused on the fear of going under the knife. His family could deal with him and would hopefully convince him to leave with them.

Chapter 77

On the Mend

My surgery went well, but surprisingly I was written out of work for a month! Maybe it was meant to be, as Dave clearly was not going back with his family and he was not going to seek treatment. He had remained sober since the smoke alarm incident and pledged that he was a changed man, despite the fact he didn't do anything he was told by professionals to do, such as go back into AA, get a sponsor, etc.

The month went well. We were joined at the hip most of the time. I couldn't move around very fast or drive for 10 days, so he was at my beck and call. He was very helpful and supportive and aside from me not feeling that great, it was a good month.

The nerves set in when it was approaching the day for me to return to work. He assured me he would be fine and would again start to look for a job. He threw himself into projects around the house, hiring painters, pulling up carpet, getting hardwood floors installed, and running errands for me.

His court date came as did his sentence. He received a restricted license, where he could drive from 6:00 a.m. to 8:00 p.m. Monday – Friday for interviewing, a job, doctor appointments and household necessities. No driving on weekends at all unless it was for a job interview or medical emergency. He paid a fine and got one-year probation along with having to pay $600 for classes. It could have been worse.

In typical Dave fashion, he felt the rules didn't apply to him and continued to take the dogs for a ride, and drive for no legitimate reason.

With no job on the horizon, Dave had cashed in his 401k. He took some of this money and paid off my car, which was not something I had wanted him to do. However, he wanted to "do that for me." He used the remainder of his money to offset some of the expenses, but primarily used it for his spending money.

By early October, he was talking about taking a trip to Florida to see his long time friend, Hamid. I put in for the time off as well and we were going to make a long weekend of it. I even had dog sitter arrangements made. However, as time progressed, he changed the plan, stating that he was going to meet another friend there. This was a manipulation to get away from me and have an excuse to be out on the road with the ability to drink.

Rule breaker that he was, he would drive to Florida despite the fact he had limited driving privileges. If pulled over, the reason for driving down there would be to look for work. He had it all set up where if the cops called Hamid, he would say he was coming for an interview. I was very uneasy about the trip. The week prior to his departure his demeanor changed. He became very defensive, and would lash out at me for no apparent reason. He shifted focus and blame and told me that I needed to see a counselor and work on myself if he had to work on himself. By the time he left, I was glad to see him go.

Chapter 78

Missing in Action

He left a day early, telling me he was going to spend time with Hamid before his other friend arrived. He left later in the morning than he should have to make it to his destination prior to his driving curfew. His stories and texts to me weren't adding up.

He took two days to get to Florida, stopping and staying at hotels and checking out luxurious golf courses and posting on Facebook pictures of his travels. He told me that he didn't tell me what he was doing as he thought I would be worried and upset. I was thankful when I received confirmation that he had finally arrived at his destination in Florida.

We stayed in touch via text and phone calls. I was enjoying my little break on my own and he appeared to be enjoying his time with his friends, golfing, eating out, and lounging by the pool.

However, by the following Sunday something didn't feel right. He took longer than usual to reply to texts and he didn't call. He would only text. By Tuesday, he was supposed to take his friend to the airport in Orlando then head for home early in the morning. I texted him that morning, and he indicated that he had just dropped him off at the airport and was hitting the road to home.

The lies had begun. I found out later that he had left early Monday morning after going to the airport. He had texted Hamid on Tuesday indicating that he had made it home safely, when he was staying in a hotel somewhere in Florida.

To top it off, when I attempted to find Hamid's contact information in my phone to call and see if he had heard from Dave, the information was gone! Prior to his leaving for Florida he had taken my phone and deleted all contact information regarding Hamid from my phone! He had neglected to check my deleted voice mails, where luckily, I still had an old voice mail from Hamid from months ago. That showed the prior planning and manipulation that went into the preparation for that trip.

He was giving those of us in contact with him different answers, if he answered at all, as to where he was. First, he stated he was in Savannah, Georgia. Then to someone else within the same hour, said he was in Jacksonville, Florida, then added a story about being in Hilton Head, South Carolina, when he was actually stuck in a hotel in Daytona Beach, drinking and gambling, unable to start the Jeep due to the interlock device.

Hamid offered to pick him up in Daytona Beach and bring him back to his house where he could sober up for a few days. Dave refused and insisted on taking a cab from Daytona Beach to Hamid's house. When Hamid told me that my radar went up and I wondered if he could be trusted to even have the cab driver take him to Hamid's. Hamid seemed very confident, as he had the cab number, driver name, etc. and would be monitoring the trip.

Dave never showed up at Hamid's and after a call to the cab company, it was determined that he had stopped somewhere prior to Orlando and checked into yet another hotel. Through multiple calls, Hamid found the hotel where Dave was supposed to be. He drove there to pick him up only to find an empty room with all his belongings and no sign of him anywhere. He was not responding to texts or phone calls. The hotel staff hadn't seen him since he checked in. Hamid had the staff search the entire hotel, including stairwells for him only to find nothing. Hamid drove up and down the main roads near the hotel, hoping to find him, even going in the nearest bars.

At this point, Hamid was rather frantic and called Dave's family, and they decided to call the police and list him as missing. Meanwhile I was having so much anxiety to where bedtime one evening brought me the feeling of my insides vibrating. It literally felt like I had a vibrating phone inside my torso. There wasn't any pain and I could breathe fine, but while lying in bed at 11:30 at night with vibrating innards, I debated on whether I should call 911. I had no idea what was going on inside me and hoped it wasn't something serious.

I broke down and pulled out a little devotional called Jesus Today that a friend had given me after my surgery. I had prayed before, but I needed more. I needed to read something that would give me hope. I sobbed as I read the first three days-worth of reading in that little book. Since that night, I have made that little book a part of every morning. I needed to turn to God. I needed to just let go and turn it all over to him.

No word from Dave for two days. He was missing. He had fallen off the grid. Numerous thoughts went through my mind. He was dead in a ditch. He had gotten involved with bad people at a casino. He had pissed somebody off while being drunk. His body finally gave out and he died alone somewhere.

The following Saturday morning at 2:00 a.m. I was awoken by the doorbell ringing and the dogs freaking out. My mind was foggy and I was trying to wake up. Once I saw the police officer at the front door my heart went up into my throat. He saw the panic in my face as I opened the front door and told me right away after he confirmed who I was, that my husband was ok.

The Wilmington Police Department had received a call from the Osceola County Sherriff's Department in Florida that they had found Dave and had taken him to a hospital. He gave me the phone number of that Sherriff's office for me to call and receive more details. The sad thing was that when I saw the cop at the door, the thought flashed through my mind, that he was dead. He had finally killed himself off and this nightmare of a roller coaster ride was now permanently over. Those were thoughts from a very sick person as well. I was that desperate for it to be over for good.

When I spoke with the Osceola Sherriff's Department I was told they found him at yet another resort in Florida. He had taken another cab and left all his belongings at the other hotel off the interstate. They Baker Acted him and had taken him to a local hospital where he was transferred to a detox hospital. The maximum amount of time they would keep him there would be 72 hours.

The Florida Mental Health Act is commonly known as the Baker Act. It allows for involuntary examination, which can be initiated by judges, law enforcement officials, physicians, or mental health professionals. There must be evidence that the person may have a mental illness or is in danger of becoming a harm to self, harm to others, or is self-neglectful. The minimum period of time someone can be held under the Baker Act is 72 hours.

Chapter 79

The Beginning of the End

Needless to say, I finalized the separation papers and had them ready for his return to Wilmington, once he made it back. The treatment center released him after two nights. Hamid picked him up and let him stay at his house for a few days. The hope was he would stay a couple weeks and sober up. That was not the case. He left after two days, then took almost another week to make it from Florida to North Carolina, due to the interlock on the Jeep and the fact he couldn't stay sober long enough to start it and drive.

Not knowing his mental state, since he did know via phone that this was it and it was over between the two of us, I had the locks on the house changed. When he finally made it back to Wilmington, despite the separation agreement, he seemed to think he would be able to stay at the house and just live in the bedroom above the garage "while he works through this." That was not the case and he checked into a hotel room.

The separation agreement was signed shortly before Thanksgiving. A few days later, he said he wanted to talk and would meet me at the house after work. When I got home, I noticed all his laundry in the laundry room, the washer running, and him sitting in the living room watching TV. He had checked out of the hotel! This wasn't a case where he was coming by to talk. He was taking advantage of my kindness and the fact I left the door unlocked for him in case he got to the house before I did, and basically moved back in upstairs! A few days later, he finally left once again to go back to the hotel.

This entire time he continued to drink, didn't look for a job, and refused to look for an apartment. He couldn't make a decision. He would just spin and spin, clinging to the notion that we still had a connection. He tried to make deals on going to treatment if I promised he could move back into the house when he got out. There was no more 'we' and he just didn't understand. Even after leaving a very large suitcase on the back porch for him to pick up, he still didn't get it.

I wanted an opportunity to talk about the separation. I was met with "Talk about what? The fact I am kicked out of my fucking house? Not fair. Can't get a job in Wilmington. Neighbors know people. There is no reason I can't live in this house until I get better. Can't get a job here other than flipping pancakes and will live on the street before I do that!"

I wanted to hear that he would flip pancakes for me. That he would do what it took to show me that things will be different and that he would be a changed man.

He took Hamid up on his offer to come back to Florida. He could stay there until he found a job and Hamid would help him stay sober. While down there he asked me what I was doing for Christmas. Hamid's family was coming to stay and he didn't want to be there with all the family coming in. Again, he got to my heart and I told him he could come back to the house and stay through Christmas.

He arrived the Friday before Christmas, smelling of alcohol. The next week through Christmas he spent all of about two hours total downstairs, which was just long enough to eat. He would drink and take pills. He disrespected me and the agreement and had the nerve to drink in the house. There was no hiding it. A couple times he asked me to take him to the liquor store as he had the shakes. Right or wrong, knowing he would be gone after Christmas, I took him. I just didn't want the fight. I didn't have it in me.

Chapter 80

All About Me Now!

While he was full of indecision, continuing to manipulate and drinking himself to death in a hotel room, I started working on me for once. I attended the Al-Anon meetings that I had once despised. I had support of friends as well as the support of his family.

I decorated for Christmas for the first time in two years, took the dogs for rides to look at lights, went to a neighbor's house for Christmas Eve, and had two holiday gatherings at the house. I was living. I actually had a life. The dogs were more content. My attitude had changed. I was no longer willing to get caught up in his drama.

I had grown. I was a slow learner, but I had finally learned to set boundaries on what I would and would not accept. I was getting better each day. I could look back on the good times and not burst into tears. I had acceptance that I couldn't make a difference in what he did. I couldn't control it and it wasn't my problem any longer.

I had hope for a wonderful new year. Once I finally let go and let God, positive things started happening. I still had my moments as the healing process takes time. I was as sick as the alcoholic, allowing the alcohol and addiction to control me, yet in a different way.

I looked forward to each day, even the work day, as I knew what I would come home to. I controlled my day as the addict no longer had that control over me. I was at peace.

Chapter 81

Cold Turkey and AA

January 7, 2014 was the day Dave decided, in a time of despair while alone in a hotel room, to stop drinking. He called me the next day and asked if we could meet. I agreed to meet him a couple days later to simply go for a drive. During that drive he indicated that he had stopped drinking and that he would prove to me that he could stay sober, turn his life around, go to AA meetings and get better. That revelation was followed with a plea to allow him to come back home. He was the master liar and manipulator and time and time again I fell for it. He started begging me to give him a chance. I would say that after a couple days of not drinking, his eyes were the clearest I had seen them in four months. I told him I would need time to think about it and would get back to him.

The following day he called me again, wanting to meet and know what my decision was. I was torn. My heart wanted to open back up to him. However, I had been hurt so very badly and mentally was in a good place. I didn't want to go back to the darkness I had experienced over the years of being married to an addict.

Against everyone's advice, I told him I would allow him to come back for two weeks. Actions speak louder than words and if during those two weeks I saw a change for the better, a sincere and honest change minus the manipulation, he could stay two more weeks. We would take it a few weeks at a time to see how it went.

He proved to me over the next couple months that he was walking the walk and talking the talk. He attended AA meetings. At times, after those meetings he would open up to me about them, how he was feeling and how drinking had impacted his life. He helped around the house. He became more of a considerate and appreciative husband. He became what a husband should be. I hadn't seen it for a very long time, and I was surprised at how different things seemed at home. Life was getting better.

He ran errands, looked for a job, and started doing some home improvement projects. He even started researching recipes and took up cooking. I was glad I took that one last chance on him.

Chapter 82

Boca Bound – A New Start!

The year 2014 was a whirlwind of excitement. Not only was Dave maintaining his sobriety, but my life was also beginning to take on a whole new life of its own.

We had been invited to Hamid and his wife, Kathy's house in Florida for three weeks to dog sit while they went out of the country. Those three weeks in Florida sparked even more interest in making the attempt to find a job in Florida and make a move.

I was sending out resumes right and left. At some point not even bothering to do a cover letter. I figured if it was meant to be it was meant to be. It was on the way to Florida for the three-week trip that I submitted a resume that would change everything. After being in Florida for one week, I received a call from a company located in Boca Raton, wanting to set up a phone interview. A few days later, I had my first phone interview with the recruiter, who then called back a day later to set up another phone interview with the person that the position reported to. The day after we returned to North Carolina from our trip, I had an hour-long phone interview with who would eventually be my new boss. Three weeks later, they flew me down to Boca Raton, and the rest was history. Within a week I was offered a great job with a relocation package.

I was on cloud nine. It appeared that my luck was finally changing. I had lost 45 pounds, my confidence was brimming to the top, and good things were coming my way. A sober husband. A new job. A fabulous adventure. A new start!

Less than six weeks later we wrapped up our house hunting trip, found a place to rent with a pool, had loaded up a moving truck, three dogs and a caravan of vehicles and headed south, never to look back. I was more than ready to say good bye to the place that had been my home for over 17 years. There were some good times, but there were more bad memories there than any other place I had ever lived.

The excitement I felt on the way to Boca and that turn into the driveway of what would be our new home was indescribable. After all the unpacking and organizing was over, I was literally pinching myself and staring in wonder at the palm trees above my head as I floated in our pool. Could it be real? Did I really deserve all this goodness and happiness?

Dave helped get the house set up and took care of the dogs as I set off for my first few weeks at my new job. He started looking for a job as well and had many interviews and a couple offers. After trying out a couple different places, and much discussion, it was decided that the employment market in Florida was very different from that in North Carolina. The pay, the environment, and the people. Unless one were to obtain a management level position, the pay was pitiful and most didn't even offer benefits.

However, we were not to be discouraged. Life was good. We had rented out the house in North Carolina and everything was falling into place.

Chapter 83

Two Great Years in a Row?

In the Spring of 2015 Dave was approached by a former competitor of his past employer, offering him an opportunity to manage a renovation project in the Orlando area. The money was great as was the opportunity. However, it meant that Dave would be staying in Orlando for four months during the week and would come home only on weekends. After much discussion and soul searching, Dave felt that he was strong enough to take on the challenge, despite the fact it meant he would be staying at the resort during the week. All I could do was pray that everything would be fine and put the rest in God's hands.

We were paying way too much rent for the house near downtown Boca, which led me to get the urge to look for a house to buy. Dave was in Orlando and I went to look at a house that had only been on the market for two days. I was the last of three showings for that second day on the market. It was perfect. Good price, had a pool, low maintenance and just a few cosmetic things to change when we were ready. I made a full-price offer that night and beat out three other offers that had already come in. Blessed again! The house was mine!

You see that fact that I said the house was mine was really a big deal for me. I had done all the legwork on getting approved for a loan and it was only based on my salary and the house would only be in my name. The feeling of pride and accomplishment that I felt the day of closing as I drove to the house with my new set of keys was beyond words. I became very emotional and cried. I felt that I had come so far and to think that two years prior I was at my wits end, without hope. It was truly one of the best days of my life.

The blessings kept coming. An opportunity presented itself at work where which led to a promotion. Bought a great little house. Dave sober. Dave working. A promotion. Life was awesome!

However, just when I thought the tidal wave had hit, the aftermath was over, and there was nothing but calm and serene seas ahead, I got smacked in the face with the hard and cold reality of addiction. Again.

Chapter 84

Addiction Treatment Capital of the World

Unbeknownst to me, the move to Palm Beach County, Florida put us smack dab in the middle of what was considered the addiction treatment capital of the world. Who knew? Was it one of those "things happen for a reason" items I often mentioned? Fate? Karma? I had heard from various sources that God has a sense of humor. Was it God playing a trick on me? In any case, I found myself spinning out of control in situations and scenarios that I had hoped were over and long gone.

I started getting suspicious in January 2016, when Dave's behavior started to change. He was such a routine oriented person, so when he changed the routine I instantly became suspicious. However, I truly thought that he would never go back to drinking again as he knew he had so much to lose. I was once again in denial.

He had received a couple offers of employment for some good jobs. One started in January and was a referral from someone I knew. It lasted a week. They decided he wasn't a good fit. He then interviewed and received another job offer from another company. He resigned after two weeks. The last job offer was for a construction company as a purchasing manager. They let him go after less than two weeks, stating he wasn't a good fit.

All this time through these on again off again jobs, he was telling me his side of the story and I was believing it. Hindsight is 20/20. He had been drinking more frequently and the mix of the booze with the pills was impacting his behavior and ability to function properly in the workplace.

I was once again coming home from work to him sitting on the couch, blindly staring at the TV. He became puffy eyed and lethargic. I blamed it on depression due to job loss. It got to where I dreaded coming home like I had when we lived in North Carolina. I wasn't sure what I would come home to. He also started texting me about the time I was on my way home, telling me he was going to an AA meeting. Was he?

In April we got hit with a pretty substantial tax bill for 2015, which he found out about on his 50th birthday. He freaked out. All the work I put into trying to make his landmark birthday special was ruined. He was obsessed about the taxes and became extremely agitated. I had left work early to help him celebrate and came home to a fight. He took off and said he was going to a meeting. When he got back a couple hours later, my feelings were hurt and I was confused. All this about taxes? Something wasn't right. We ended up ordering Chinese food and having it delivered. Happy 50th Birthday and way to start a new chapter of his life.

I was finding myself getting pulled back into his insanity. His behavior was having a direct impact on me, despite my efforts. I ate. I ate a lot. I didn't care. I stashed food and ate it.

By early May he started to go to bed around 7:00 p.m. each night. He wouldn't eat much. I searched the house for any signs of alcohol and found nothing. However, he admitted that he had filled another prescription of Seroquel without me knowing it and had been taking extra pills during the day to help him with his depression. I started monitoring his pill consumption once again.

I asked him if he had been drinking and he would always tell me no, that he would never resort to such a thing ever again. That was until one night he replied with the word, "yes." I knew it. I knew it all along but didn't want to admit it. The pattern had started once again and it took off with full force. The trust that had started to build back was gone. My cloud nine feelings that life was so good and I was so blessed changed to feelings of despair, grief and depression that I was back on the roller coaster of addiction without any way out.

Chapter 85

Back on the Crazy Train

Quite frankly, it was almost a relief to hear him admit it. It validated the fact that I wasn't jumping to conclusions. It was all on the table and I knew what was coming. The weeks leading up to Memorial Day were a roller coaster of emotions and chaos. He spent a lot of time in the back bedroom, in bed, out if it and oblivious to anything going on around him. The holiday weekend was a disaster, which started Friday night and finally ended with me leaving him in the emergency room at the local hospital at 1:00 a.m. on Sunday.

He had indicated he was going to quit cold turkey and was lying to me all along. He said he was detoxing, so I put all my efforts into trying to make him comfortable and offering to help him get help.

My first experience in Florida with trying to get him help was not an easy process. First, I called an urgent care center to see if they would be able to see him and prescribe any medication to assist with withdrawal. I was told he needed to go to the ER.

I called a number that I thought was for a local treatment center, as he had finally agreed to maybe go to one, and ended up at a national call center where they were literally trying to sell me costly treatment. They required a deposit to even be put on a waiting list! They were clearly taking advantage of people calling them when in an extremely desperate and vulnerable state of mind.

I frantically began searching online for any place locally that would have a bed. I found one that had a "chat" option on their website and reached out regarding space. Total relief filled my entire being when they told me they had space and could coordinate detox and treatment for him as soon as possible. They would call me back after they ran our health insurance information.

While waiting, Dave started going into a panic mode, pacing, crying and sitting down and frantically rubbing his hands up and down on his legs. He began looking for his keys, threatening to leave. I grabbed the keys, ran in the bedroom, shut the door and hid the keys. When Dale from the treatment center called me back I explained to him what was going on. He told me that to calm him down I should just get him some alcohol.

While waiting again for another call back regarding the plan for detox, I loaded my drunk and manic husband into the Jeep and proceeded, while crying, to the closest convenience store to buy beer. Dave directed me to where he wanted to go, which was a little dive of a joint with bars on the windows. Dave told me that this was the closest place for him to hit in the mornings first thing when he got the shakes. I listened in disbelief, gave him some cash, and watched him walk in then out with a six-pack.

Off we went to the first of what would be three detox adventures in the following four weeks. As I pulled into the parking lot of the facility, Dave immediately started rambling about how there weren't any cars there and what kind of place was this. Dale from the center came outside to greet us and led us inside to the quiet lobby. Dale told Dave, "I'm one of you bud, and I know this is a scary thing." The entire time that Dale was speaking, Dave was wide-eyed, looking around in a state of paranoia, interrupting Dale with questions like, "How old were you when you took your first drink, where are the people, who is watching us, where is everybody, what kind of place is this?" Dale had the patience of a saint, and I once again felt blessed to be surrounded by people who got it. They had lived it and been a part of it, which meant I could drop my mask of deception that life was good, and truly expose my feelings. Anyone looking at me could tell that my life wasn't good.

A nice young man, Alan appeared, who would be the one driving Dave to the Detox center, a few miles away. Alan would be sure he got checked in.

Dave in his full state of paranoia started giving Alan the grand inquisition, to which point Dale told him that Alan was also "one of them" and could be trusted. That didn't stop Dave from demanding that I take a picture of the license plate of the car before he climbed inside.

I chatted a bit longer with Dale after they left, who assured me that Dave was in good hands and they would get him the care he needed. As I drove home I realized how physically and mentally exhausted I was. Upon arrival at home, all I wanted to do was to change my clothes, curl up on the couch and fade into a state of calm.

That wasn't to be the case. Within 30 minutes of my arrival at home I received a call from the detox center. The nurse asked me if he had mental problems. I asked her why. She told me that he thought the nurse's pen was a scalpel and that the belt a worker was wearing was a snake. I told her that he did hallucinate some when he was overly intoxicated and she seemed to be fine with that.

I sat down, ready to relax in jammies when I received yet another call, this time from Dale, who indicated he received a call from Detox who said they were transferring him to the hospital because "they couldn't handle him." I was supposed to meet them at the hospital. Then Alan called and wanted to know if anyone called me. Then Dale called me back and told me to just meet him back at the facility where we had met previously, as Alan would bring Dave back there and we could figure out where to go from there. I burst into tears as I changed back into street clothes and made my way back out to hit the road again. By now it was after 8:30 p.m. and I was completely wiped, still hadn't eaten anything and felt there was no hope.

I arrived back at the facility, parking lot empty and all lights off. As I sat on the step of the entryway, I wondered what the heck had happened where I had allowed myself to be put back into a situation such as this. It was like I was trapped in a bad Lifetime mini-series that would never end.

Dale arrived and shortly after that Alan pulled up with the drunk. It took everything both Dale and I had to convince Dave to get back in the Jeep with me to follow Dale to the county mental hospital, where Dale indicated they couldn't turn him away. He would help me get him in there and we would be good to go. They would evaluate him, then transfer to detox or hospital if needed later. There was still drama though, as Dave grabbed his bag and took off on a quick walk through the parking lot to get away. We corralled him back and got him loaded into the Jeep.

As I was following Dale to our next stop, closer to home, Dave kept grabbing the door as if he would open it and flop out into the street at any given time. It seemed like the 15-minute drive took hours, but we finally arrived.

This was not a place that I would have picked to take him to judging by the exterior of the building, but desperate times called for desperate measures. We got out and approached the non-descript government looking building. There was a buzzer near the door that Dale pushed for a staffer to come.

A worker came and barely opened the door wide enough for Dale to explain to her why we were there and the help we needed. She went on to explain, despite all his attempts to convince her otherwise, that they couldn't take him and he needed to go across the street to the emergency room at the hospital. Dale requested to speak to a manager, who happened to be standing behind the other worker, who simply responded "what she said" while laughing. I had no words. While all this was going on, I was trying to get Dave to stay close and stop rambling. He kept trying to take off walking with his bag.

We loaded him back up in the Jeep and drove over to the ER at the hospital. After what was a speedy check-in they got him in a gown and on a bed. The problem was the ER was full and there weren't any rooms. We were herded into the hallway, with beds lined up in the hallway, to wait. And wait. And wait. While we waited, my drunk husband kept getting up to try and wander around, despite being told by several nurses and two security guards to go sit back down.

As we sat waiting, three Sherriff's deputies (two women and one man), along with a police officer and three paramedics wheel in a guy on a stretcher, half clothed, in restraints, and passed out. He had been Baker Acted. It was amazing to see all the government resources it took just to bring one big drunk that had been Baker Acted into the ER. Here I sat with my drunk, threatening him every few minutes that if he didn't sit down and stop telling me he was going to leave, that I was going to Baker Act him. I certainly had all the people there I needed to do it.

The clock kept ticking. We had been there for an hour, without any nurse or help. I was exhausted, and at that point didn't care who saw me, heard me or what they thought of the drunk I was with or me. The two women deputies kept looking at me like they felt sorry for me. One very nice security guard came to stand closer to me to help me keep Dave settled down. I finally got up and demanded that the nurses station send someone over to at least take a urine sample or something to get him settled in. She had the nerve to tell me "We can't help him unless he is overly intoxicated." I said, "Look, he has been getting up and wandering around here, threatening to walk out, we have been turned away from two other places because of his levels, one of which he indicated the nurse's pen was a scalpel and her belt was a snake, and he needs help now!" I think she was a bit surprised, but it at least started the process.

After multiple attempts to keep him seated, a guard stepped in and helped me. After two hours dealing with him in ER I found myself starting to have what I assumed was a panic attack. I couldn't breathe very well. I was exhausted and crying. At the point when the deputies were ready to leave, one smiled at me sympathetically and said, "Good luck."

After they got his urine results back, along with me voicing my concerns once again that he was going to walk out, they got him into an ER room. This happened 2 ½ hours AFTER we joined the herd. After double checking with a different nurse that he would be watched and would not be allowed to leave, I left. It was 1:00 a.m. and I was exhausted.

No rest for the weary as by 5:30 a.m. he called me, threatening to leave. The doctor was stupid. Nobody cared. He didn't need this. He was going to walk out with his backpack and walk home. I managed to convince him to stay and move over to the detox unit once a bed became available.

He was released the following Wednesday. I went through all that hell, only to have peace and quiet for less than five days. He had insisted on being released so he could come home and help me get ready for my friend that would be arriving for a long weekend visit. I was exhausted.

He was drunk the entire time she was visiting. He basically stayed in the master bedroom, except for going to get her coffee in the morning. It was odd. Anyone on the outside would think it was strange. I was covering for him once again.

Chapter 86

Call of the Wild

Less than a month after emergency room and crazy ward detox, we were back in business with yet another trip to another detox center. It always seemed to happen over a weekend. After calling multiple places, many of which wouldn't call me back, I was referred to one of the facilities they use for detox. Thankfully, they had room.

On this event-packed trip, Dave continued to talk about wanting to end his life. This was occurring while he guzzled beer and continually hooked and un-hooked his seatbelt. This was a very long and anxiety ridden 40-minute drive.

Upon arrival, an extremely thin and tattoo covered guy met us in the very small lobby. I looked around, wondering what in the world had I gotten him into. However, looks could be very deceiving, and despite the skin and bones, large number of tattoos and a few missing teeth, this guy was extremely welcoming and kind to Dave. He started off by explaining that "he was one of him" and understood how scared he must be. One thing I had learned through the years of detox, treatment centers and the psych facilities was that you can't judge a book by its cover, nor should you.

Dave was extremely anxious and paranoid, with his wide eyes darting back and forth, even up in the corners to see if there were cameras. Similar to his last bout with detox, he began interrogating the intake guy, who was very patient with him. Dave kept asking me if the place was safe, and "what are they going to do to me here?" He was threatening to leave on multiple occasions.   The tech left us in the lobby while he went to find the administrator to sign Dave in.

Dave was threatening to leave when suddenly, looking out the front glass door, there was a small raccoon. There he was, just wandering by and pausing to look through the glass just long enough for me to direct Dave's attention to our furry friend. This pulled him back from his state of paranoia and anxiety and calmed him down. He stopped threatening to leave and sat there and watched as the racoon stared back for a time, then opted to continue his journey. This little wild ball of fur was sent from above, as he came just at the right time.

Back to reality when the technician reappeared in the lobby to take Dave beyond the steel, locked metal doors, hopefully on yet another road to recovery.

Less than seven days later, he was back home, after refusing to be transferred to long term treatment.

Chapter 87

Happy Independence Day?

There was no "Happy" in this year's Fourth of July. My holiday was spent with a drunk that opted to start drinking mouthwash to get his fix. Shortly thereafter, I was making more calls to facilities to see if there were any beds available. Luckily, there was.

Another crazy ride north on I-95, not to mention the constant consumption of booze on the way. The stench in my car was enough to make me vomit. As we pulled up to the gate to announce our arrival, I took some time to examine the area. It appeared to have once been a large hotel, which had been converted into a treatment center. The entire property was fenced in with 8-foot black fencing, complete with security gate and speaker.

Upon entry into the lobby I received a much better vibe than the other places we had been over the past few weeks. This was more elegant. Elegant was a strange word to use to describe a treatment center, but that was the first word that came to mind. It had a spiral staircase, a very large tropical fish tank, professional looking people sitting at the check-in desk, ready for intake, and non-sterile looking lobby furniture. Granted, the bar had been set pretty low given where we had been before, but this just had a different feel to it.

Quick and efficient. We had him out of my hair in less than five minutes and I was off to enjoy what I would hope to be 30 days of calm. Again, rules didn't apply and despite being told there would be no contact for seven days, as he called after two days with his counselor because he needed to hear my voice and needed "cheering up."

He called a few days later after his seven-day block was up, indicating it was a good place. He was going to be in treatment this time for him, not just for me. He went on to say that many professional athletes have also come through there. I guess that made it more of an acceptable place for him.

A few evenings later when he called he told me he had been having nightmares and they needed to increase his anxiety medication. They thought they found something that would work for him, and he was starting to feel better. He had a lot of group sessions, where they talked about feelings and childhood. The counselor told him this was a good break and was needed.

He earned a two-hour in-person visit after 21 days. This meant that he had a pass to be able to leave with me for two hours. He would have to submit to a drug screen and urine test as soon as I brought him back. When I saw him come out of the building he looked like a completely different person. The red, puffy-faced and fat guy that I had dropped off 21 days prior was replaced with a leaner looking, healthier and clear-eyed guy. Amazing what 21 days without alcohol can do for an addict.

During our visit, I told him I would do what I could to support him, but could not go through this again. He said he understood, and knew that even with me no longer believing in promises, promised it wouldn't happen again.

Chapter 88

Home Sweet Home ... Again

Dave was probably as nervous as I was when the black Lincoln pulled in our driveway to drop him off. The first couple days were awkward, almost like we didn't know each other. I tried to let him do his own thing and not "mother" him or quiz him. This was a new day. One day at a time.

The next couple months was a flurry of activity. He was scheduling doctor appointments, dentist appointments, doing yard work, house work, and errands. You name it, he did it. He had a new morning routine and managed to fit AA meetings into his new schedule.

My 50th birthday came and went, but not without some very thoughtful surprises from Dave. The week before my birthday, he surprised me with new tint on my car windows. The day prior to my birthday he surprised me with satellite radio hooked up in my car, Thai food, the house decorated with banners and balloons, a full bouquet of flowers, a card and gift from him and the dogs, and a movie. My birthday was spent with a trip to Miami and a boat tour. It was a great time. Dave said he had a lot of fun working on the surprises for me. That was the Dave I knew and loved. The thoughtful and motivated Dave.

His knee pain was becoming unbearable though, and it was time to get the long awaited full knee replacement surgery scheduled. I was very anxious about this as I knew he was very routine oriented. Having this surgery just a couple months out of rehab would completely throw off his routine, plus what about the pain medication?

Since we had already reached our out of pocket maximum for the year for health insurance, this meant that as long as he had the surgery this year it would be 100% covered. Dave scheduled it for October 11, 2016.

Chapter 89

Worst Fear Realized

The surgery was successful and he was released from the hospital three days later with a prescription of a low dose narco. This was a combination of Tylenol and Percocet, which he was supposed to take every four to six hours for pain. One pill. In typical Dave fashion, one pill wasn't enough, so he called the doctor's office for a consult. They indicated that if he needed to take two at a time, that was fine. If someone was in pain they couldn't do their physical therapy and that therapy was extremely important to achieve full recovery.

There was a roller coaster of new prescriptions, hiding pills, taking more pills than he should, and starting to drink again less than three weeks after surgery. The spiral into drunken chaos had begun.

I found the first evidence under the bathroom sink, where he had evidently poured Vodka into a water bottle. This led to ongoing suspicion. The trust had been broken again. The words "why me" circled chaotically through my head. His personality was off, he was short-tempered, dis-engaged and had extreme mood swings.

I found myself looking for booze, catching a whiff, watching him as he fell asleep on the couch in an upright position four nights in a row, going to bed right after eating supper, and sometimes in bed when I returned home from work.

We were approaching our 30th wedding anniversary and I didn't even care. I had zero desire to do anything special. Did

I celebrate 30 years of marriage or mourn it? I was so tired of life with an addict. I wanted normal.

There seemed to be consistent tension, like a smoldering campfire just waiting to burst into raging flames, engulfing a forest. It wasn't easy to live this way. I wanted more. I needed more of me and less drama.

My little patch of paradise in Florida, my dream of a new and fresh start had been crushed. This was changing me for the worst.

One evening, Dave made the comment, "I can't believe we aren't going anywhere, geez it's 30 years!"

Three treatment centers over the summer, multiple binges and fights, stress, lies, more trust shattered and he thought I would want to go somewhere to celebrate 30 years of marriage? I looked at my wedding picture and thought about the 20-year old girl in the picture, how happy and excited she looked. Zoom ahead 30 years later, not so much. That girl was long gone. The innocence and trust gone. Lost.

As I sat three days before the anniversary, I started to attend yet another pity party. I was numb. I had become indifferent and disengaged. Was that how I was supposed to be nearing what should have been a time of celebration? Or was I celebrating that I was a survivor after 30 years, 20 of which had been riding through the roller coaster of life with an addict.

I was tired of not trusting. I was tired of being indifferent. I was tired of feeling trapped. I wanted to live again.

Chapter 90

Tacos Anyone?

I had planned many months prior to take the day off to celebrate 30 years of marriage. I had gone shopping for the perfect anniversary card. The problem with that was all I could find were cards with mushy, lovey and romantic words of togetherness and eternity. I was having a really hard time finding the right card. Maybe I needed to start a line of greeting cards for families of addicts!

When the bar set is low, it's hard to be disappointed. That morning started out with me trying to find the right thing to post on Facebook. I had to keep up the masquerade of this fabulous high school sweetheart couple thing. I found one of our wedding pictures and posted that.

Dave's morning started out with taking Seroquel, then going to a morning appointment with his counselor. He came home after his session as we had planned to go out for a nice waterfront lunch. Unfortunately, he returned from therapy smelling like a brewery and thought he was covering it up. He denied it completely. My morning was going downhill quickly. This anniversary was tanking faster than the Titanic.

I offered to drive for obvious reasons. He wouldn't commit to anyplace to eat, seemed like he didn't care, and we started to argue. Despite my attempts to control myself, the tears started coming and we ended up eating at a small taco joint. We ate in silence. The drive home was in silence. He took another pill and went to bed early afternoon on our 30th wedding anniversary. He texted me from bed an hour later telling me to wake him up at 6:00 p.m. so he could shower before going to another AA meeting. That was code for "I took a pill to knock myself out, probably a shot of vodka as well, and will need more later so will use an AA meeting as an excuse to leave the house and get booze."

A friend ended up coming to the house to take a smelling and puffy looking Dave to his home group AA meeting.

This anniversary was as unspectacular as the 20th one was (drunk in Mexico). Number 26 we spent at an attorney's office to figure out ramifications of his 3rd DUI. It just kept getting better. He promised me on this day that the next 30 years would be better. After hearing that, more of me died inside.

Chapter 91

More Lies and Prying Eyes

December brought more of the same. I found tiny vodka bottles hidden in drawers. His pores were once again reeking of sweat and alcohol. He was falling a lot. Not sure if that was from the booze, the meds, the knee or all the above. He made constant excuses as to why he couldn't do anything with me on the weekends.

I came home one Sunday after lunch to an out of it, blurry eyed, Seroquel induced Dave, which was most likely included a few shots of Vodka. He admitted to me that he had been taking a couple shots before his physical therapy visits.

I thought I was out of tears, but I wasn't. I wanted a vacation from my life. I hated my life. It wasn't supposed to be like this in Florida. I made a promise to myself that I would no longer live like this.

Christmas was coming and it appeared I would have another holiday of misery and despair. He wouldn't leave. He wouldn't stop. I hated coming home. I wanted to be by myself. I was finding it more difficult each day to keep faking happy.

One day mid-December he had an appointment with his primary care physician, who prescribed him Librium. He had lied to the doctor and told him that he had a job coming up and needed to be sure he could stay off the alcohol. Time to dry out at home again.

However, he was a no-show for that next physical therapy visit. He had been double dosing on Librium and Seroquel. He quit taking his anxiety meds. This man couldn't be trusted to take his medication as prescribed. He was a zombie. He was drooling when he ate. He couldn't walk in a straight line.

I took the pills away. I started handing them out to him as prescribed. We were back to him stalking me, temper tantrums, lies and driving off to meetings to get booze. He even tried to mow the lawn while dosed up on something. I dared him and he did it. It took him twice as long and he was exhausted when he was finished. A part of me thoroughly enjoyed watching!

The following week I took him to the primary care physician for a follow up visit. The truth also came out at that visit that he has been drinking while taking Librium, which is a drug used to curb cravings and withdrawal!

The following day after snooping around in my bedroom, he found and read my journal. Many of my most deep and personal notes and thoughts. He read them and used it as an excuse to fall further into a state of addiction.

The feeling that I promised myself I would never be in a position to feel again came back. The feeling of hopelessness and gloom, the feeling of being cornered and trapped without any reasonable way out. I knew I was changing into a different person. A person that I didn't want to be. I would catch my reflection in the kitchen window and didn't recognize who was looking back at me. Who was that sad and joyless person?

I had resigned myself to being stuck in this rut, with the only option being how I handled it day by day. I would no longer try to control his drinking. If he wanted to drink, go for it. I would no longer obsess with whether he was drinking, or fire a line of questioning at him that would only result in him lying to me, again. That would be insane, right?

I would simply live my life and he could continue to rot his away. I would basically be biding my time until he drank so much one day that he just wouldn't wake up. With the amount of alcohol and the constant abuse of prescription drugs with it, the pre-mature death was bound to happen sooner or later. Dark thoughts. This was what I was left with. My new attitude for a fresh start for 2017. Very sad.

Chapter 92

Pillow Time

After yet another week of coming home to a drunk passed out in the back bedroom, only coming out to eat supper, it all came to a head.

Saturday started out with the same routine of him waking up clear eyed, going to a meeting and coming home over an hour later with an excuse as to why he wouldn't participate in life. You know, the basics, like running errands, mowing, going out to lunch. These were the things that normal human beings did each weekend unless you lived in the "normal" of addiction.

He spent the majority of the day in bed. At 4:15 he decided to get up and come out into the living room, dressed like he was going somewhere. Another "meeting" which was the code for needing alcohol. He came home a few minutes later and stayed in the driveway. I wasn't sure how long he had been there but I figured he was talking on the phone. Forty-five minutes later he was still out there. I peeked out the window and couldn't see him. All I saw was something white.

I went outside to check it out. He had the driver's side seat pushed all the way back, and the back of the seat on the furthest decline possible, basically laying down. He was clutching the pillow (the something white I had noticed) that was left in the Jeep from when he was recovering from knee surgery. Stone cold passed out. It took me three bangs with my fist on the window before he came to. When he opened the door, he almost fell out of the Jeep, swaying back and forth and attempted to make his way to the front door.

He staggered around the couch and fell back onto it, sitting in his usual position. I went back outside to get the Jeep keys and anything else he had left and took a drink out of the large class he had full of liquid in the console. For the most part, it was straight vodka.

Had he drove that impaired back to the house after picking up booze or did he wait until he got back to the house before he started drinking it? How could he have passed out so quickly and have the mindset to lean the seat back and pass out? He had once again put other people's lives in danger.

I came storming back into the house and shoved the glass of 90% vodka and 10% soda up to his mouth, pushing it against his lower lip, screaming "Drink it... finish it why don't you... just drink it!" He was moving his head back and forth trying to avoid the glass, all while looking at me through half open eyes. I kept on, relentless in my effort to force him to finish the glass off. I pulled my right arm back and slapped him across the right side of his face, then proceeded to verbally shame him.

He rose from the couch, staggered over to the kitchen counter and kicked the bar stools across living room. He moved on to the other side of the counter, doing a couple quick fist pounds on the counter and slurred, "Give it to me, give it to me!" I put the glass on the counter and he grabbed it, tipping it back to guzzle the booze inside, some of which poured out the sides of his mouth down the front of his clothes. He staggered to the back bedroom and passed out for the rest of the night.

I was left shaking. What just happened? Did I try to force him to finish a glass of liquor only to top it off by slapping him? My previous rage turned into shame that I had snapped. That was horrible and I shouldn't have done it. He was sick. He didn't mean to do the things he did, right? This was a disease. Would I force a cancer patient to do something? Would I slap someone with diabetes simply because I didn't like what they were saying to me? This had to end. I was also sick. No matter how hurtful short term to him or me, it had to come to an end.

Chapter 93

It Stops Now!

I was awakened at 4:00 a.m. on Sunday morning after hearing water running. Dave was taking yet another bath due to insomnia. Around 4:30 he knocked on the locked bedroom door. "Hey... you up? I want to talk to you about something." I ignored him. A few minutes later there was another soft knock on the door, "Hey, did you dump out everything that was in the Jeep? I'm shaking really bad and need to drink. Can you unlock the Jeep?" I got up and unlocked it through the window and went back to bed. I could hear him in the kitchen, getting ice, pouring a drink.

At 8:30 a.m. he said, "In about an hour and a half I'm going to start having withdrawal. I'm in trouble. My body needs it. Can I have my keys?"

"No, keys," I replied. "You have been drinking and you are not about to drive."

Ten minutes later I found myself buying an 18-pack of Coors Light. A few short hours later, after him telling me that he was in trouble, understood that the marriage was over, and to let him go to a hotel and drink himself to death, I managed to convince him to go back to treatment. I made the call and was hopeful that they would accept him back and that insurance would approve. It would be an hour or two before they could confirm.

I decided I would take the dogs for a walk while I waited for the call back. While walking a few houses down from our house, I found a penny on the side walk, picked it up and said over and over as I proceeded down the sidewalk, "Find a penny, pick it up, it forever means good luck. Today could be the first day of the rest of your life. Find a penny, pick it up, it forever means good luck. Today could be the first day of the rest of your life. Dear God, please let this be the first day of the rest of my life. Please let them take him. Please let this be over."

Imagine driving on I-95 with an in-coherent drunk of a husband only to see an extremely large billboard flash by stating "Imagine Being Sober" with a super-font 800 number listed. As we hit the exit ramp off the interstate and waited at the stoplight, there was an older, homeless man, perhaps in his sixties or seventies. He was holding a cardboard sign with words that were too faded out to read. His face leathered by the sun and too much of something other than the sun spoke volumes to the path he had to have been on. He was begging for money. The timing of seeing this homeless man in tattered and dirty clothes, begging for money made me wonder if Dave would ever end up this way. Was this going to be his path? My thoughts were interrupted with Dave saying "Who is this guy? What is he doing?" I replied, "He is homeless and is begging for money," to which Dave responded, "We should give him some."

He was fading in and out of a normal state of mind, one time turning around quickly and looking in the back seat asking me if Ripley was there. There were various hand motions and mumbling on our journey to detox, along with six different times when he unbuckled the seat belt like he was going to open the door and jump out. He kept asking where we were going, so finally I lied and replied, "Sonny's BBQ." "Sonny's?" he asked. "I love Sonny's. I'm hungry." As of that moment he hadn't eaten anything in two days.

At one point he started staring at my hand on the stick shift. As I watched him out of the corner of my eye, he reached for my fingers with one of his fingers. I asked him what he was doing. He took my hand and placed it up to his mouth and kissed the back of it. He began to cry. He said he was sorry and that he was sick and that he would go away for a long time to get better, and hoped to someday be the husband I deserved.

Tears were pouring out of my eyes, which was making it most difficult to drive. I was also trying not to look at him or let him see me cry. It would make things worse. All I kept thinking was this was going to be the end. This would be the last time I would be driving him in a drunken state to detox. The last time I had to buy him booze to ease his shakes. The last time I would come home after work to misery.

As we drew closer to the facility, he once again asked where we were going. I told him we were going back to rehab, where he could get better.

Once we arrived in the lobby, I found it hard to hold my emotions together. Here we were again. Everybody was so nice and a guy walked up to Dave and welcomed him back. He assured me that Dave would be fine and they would once again take good care of him.

As I left the facility, waiting for the security gate to open, I had a feeling of nervous relief. However, I knew this wasn't really the end. There would only be a few hours respite in the ongoing saga of Dave and addiction. It wasn't matter of if my peace and calm would be shattered, but rather when.

Chapter 94

No Rest for the Weary

I hadn't even arrived home when I received a call from the facility stating that due to his blood alcohol level and history, he was on his way to the emergency room of the nearest hospital to be cleared. They wanted to be sure to let me know in case "I wanted to be there for him." He was on his own. Two hours later, I received a call from Dave in ER.

"I'm in the emergency room," he stated. "They won't give me any medication. I'm starting to shake."

"Well, you are definitely in the right place if you start to have a seizure," I replied in monotone.

Two more hours pass and I received yet another phone call. "Hi, it's me again," he stated. "I'm waiting for someone to come pick me up and take me back to the facility. I have been cleared to go. Can't believe I have to lay here and wait. They won't give me anything to help me. This is ridiculous."

I had very few comments. An hour or so later I received a call from the facility stating he was back and going through the formal check-in. Thank goodness. I should receive a break for at least seven days as there was a seven-day block on outgoing phone calls.

It was less than 24 hours later that I received a call from him in facility. "Hi, it's me," he said. I couldn't believe he was calling. After asking why he was able to call, he indicated that his counselor, Kory was there and it was an introduction call. He said he would be finished with detox in about seven days and then would be coming home to hit meetings again. I responded with a resounding "No, that isn't happening. There is no way that you are coming home after only seven days. You need to stay the full 30 days and get the help you need."

After going around and round while on speaker phone with his counselor, it was quite apparent that he was trying to manipulate me once again. Not even 24-hours sober and he was back to his old tricks. Laying the guilt on me "If I don't have you I have nothing" garbage that was spewed numerous times from his lying lips.

Even Kory told him he was missing the point. When she asked him why he stopped going to meetings last time and what would make this time better, he didn't really have an answer. I was proud of myself, sticking up for myself and leaving Kory with the obvious impression that he wasn't welcome. He agreed that we would talk further on Friday when she made another call with him.

While home after work making supper, I received yet another call. This time it was from the Administrator, indicating that Dave was in the office with him saying he was going to leave against medical advice. The Administrator wanted to know if I would please talk to him and try and convince him to stay.

Round two began with me trying to talk him off the ledge and convince him to stay. Same old crap again and again. Twenty minutes later he finally agreed to stay through detox and we would talk on Friday. He was trying to suck me in again. I needed to stay strong this time. Not just for me, but for him. Maybe if I considered this as saving his life it would make it easier, despite the fact it was the most difficult thing I could ever do.

Dave's family called me with an offer that was sent from heaven. Dave was welcome to come to their house in the

Midwest and stay after he was released from treatment. They had a friend that was willing to give him a job on a construction site, would have free room and board, and would have various after-care recovery programs available to him there as well, such as AA meetings and Celebrate Recovery. The question remained whether he would accept the gift.

The following Thursday evening after his admission I received a phone call from his counselor. She told me that she felt he still hadn't taken accountability for his actions. She had been there a few years and had worked in the industry for quite some time and didn't feel that he had another relapse left in him. She wanted to give me a heads up and would be calling me back a few minutes later with him on the phone. I was preparing for yet another battle to convince him to stay.

I was shaking like a leaf with the anticipation of the phone ringing. This next call was much of the same, with him making every excuse in the book and trying to manipulate me into giving in. I figured now was the time to bring up the move to the Midwest. Before I could even finish explaining, he cut me off.

"Crawl back to family, tail between my legs, a 50-year old with no money and nothing, picture that," he snarled.

My reply was quite simple, "Picture this, divorce papers and total and complete shut out from this marriage. It will be over. Now you decide which picture you prefer. You stay in treatment for 30 days you would at least have hope. Don't you at least want that? I have given you 30 years; can't you give me 30 days?"

The counselor stepped in and started doing what good counselors do best. I told Dave that what I wanted was very simple. I just wanted to be a normal couple. I wanted to hang out, go out to lunch, go bike riding, watch movies and take the dogs for walks. That was all.

After hearing those words, he agreed to stay the full 30 days. So much for the seven-day block of peace and quiet.

Chapter 95

Brave?

After 21 days in rehab, the kind and trusting Dave was starting to return. The twice-weekly phone calls were a time of healing, for both him and me. He had hope, which oftentimes gave me hope. I didn't know where this would go. I only hoped that with my faith, everything would work out for the best.

Day 30 brought another black Lincoln to our driveway, dropping off a rejuvenated and hopeful Dave. One day at a time with prayer was needed moving forward.

It was easy in a time of crisis to say that this was it. No more chances. There was so much hurt and emotion. Raw emotion that ran deep. People on the outside that were aware of our situation must have thought I was either stupid, insane or in denial. Some called me a saint, others said I was brave.

They didn't know. Nobody knew how one should react to living with an addict. You can't know unless you have walked in my shoes. Alcoholics are people that don't do the things they do on purpose. They really can't help it. It's so very hard to understand and I'll never be able to know what Dave went through with his struggles each day or why the good Lord made this part of His plan for Dave or His plan for me.

He is still a human being. Human beings deserve love and compassion. Dave was a kind man, with a big heart. I couldn't bring myself, despite everything that had happened, to shut that door on him just yet. He had said all the right things and had done what I asked him to do, which was stay another 30 days. I have given him 30 years. He gave me 30 more days. I had 30 days to start my healing, for now.

I later had found a letter that he wrote to me on January 31, 2017:

My beautiful little Tulip,

Ever since I laid my eyes on you I have been madly and deeply in love with you. Something happened to me when we first met, I knew right then that we would be together in love for the rest of our lives. I don't know what it was, I just knew you were something very special. Knowing now of course it was fate and God brought us together. You are as beautiful today as the day we met. What I've never told you is that deep down inside of me I felt I did not deserve you, and somehow, I twisted it in my mind and thought I had to hold on tight to keep you, which is why I treated you so shitty sometimes in high school not "letting" you go out and so jealous every time I saw you talking to other guys. In short, I was fearful of losing you. The happiest day of my life was when I found out you actually wanted to and would marry me, even then I still didn't think I deserved you. I want you to know, you are as beautiful today as the day I laid my eyes on you.

If my disease only affected me, I could easily forgive myself, but knowing what my disease has done to you is so unbearable to me, I just try to push it to the back of my brain. It has been just crippling to me and my recovery and I've never "felt" those feelings emotionally until now. I have never cried so much in my entire lifetime as much as these past three weeks. I've got a lot of work to do to be able to let go of the self-hatred and turn it over to God, but I feel I'm on my way. I do not want to die a drunk and have that be my last chapter. I intend to take all the steps in my recovery that will ensure I will never relapse again. I want to live long enough to give us more years and memories of good times, than all the shitty years we've had due to my alcoholism. I have failed miserably as a husband, friend, lover, and provider for you, and I refuse to fail at this any longer. I can't express to you enough just how so so sorry I am for all the shitty things I've said to you, how I've treated you at times, and all the emotional pain I have caused you. I want to spend the rest of my life making my amends to you by living sober and healthy one day at a time, and by loving myself which will allow me to love you properly as your husband, friend and lover. I long for the day we can regain our closeness like we had when we first met. My disease has cost me and us an unbelievable wreckage, but no more.

In closing I know you're scared about me coming home. I'm terrified in a good way. I want to assure you I will not put you through anymore turmoil. I honestly think I will never relapse again, but you've heard that before. You have my word on our wedding rings that if I relapse, I will leave peacefully with no animals. Again, I will never put you through another relapse or put you in a position to act as my mother. Pray for me every day, as I pray for you every day, night and morning.

Kiss the pups for me and tell them daddy loves. Miss you all, Lifetime Love, Dave.

I never thought I would be quoting a song from Lady Ga Ga, but the first time I heard it brought me to tears, and pretty much summed up my feelings at that moment.

Million Reasons –

You're giving me a million reasons to let you go

You're giving me a million reasons to quit the show

You're giving me a million reasons

Give me a million reasons,

Given' me a million reasons

About a million reasons

If I had a highway, I would run for the hills

If you could find a dry way, I'd forever be still

But you're giving me a million reasons

Give me a million reasons

Given' me a million reasons

About a million reasons

I bow down to pray

I try to make the worst seem better

Lord, show me the way

To cut through all this worn out leather

I've got a hundred million reasons to walk away,

But baby, I just need one good one to stay

Thirty Days was that one good reason.

Chapter 96

Around and Round We Go

That would have been a good ending had he not started drinking again less than three months later. Upon arrival home from his 30-day treatment stay, he went to his orthopedic doctor regarding pain, redness and swelling in his replaced knee.

That visit led him to emergency surgery on February 14, 2017 to go back into the original incision area, clean it out, then pump him full of antibiotics via pic line. He had extreme infection. This meant he would have a catheter for three months and had to visit a medical office for IV drips of antibiotics every day.

This was yet another excuse to start drinking. The man was full of infection, on high doses of antibiotics, and started to self-medicate once again. I even took him for his treatment on weekends drunk. I couldn't imagine what the other patients or nurses thought.

This all led up to another over the top binge weekend, which left him babbling incoherently, gagging and coughing up blood at the kitchen sink while clinging to a bottle of wine, him saying he wanted to die, and me calling 911. Again. Baker Act to the rescue!

This time he was in the hospital for over a week detoxing. Given that he had a catheter and had a medical condition, they couldn't take him to a psych ward or treatment center. As usual, upon being discharged, he vowed that he would never drink again.

Chapter 97

The Great Last Summer

Dave kept his word for a few months following that last Baker Act episode. He finished up his treatments, got good news on prognosis, stayed busy with projects around the yard and house, and started looking for a job again.

He accepted an offer for an office job that started early July. He had hope, goals, income and felt that he was back to normal. Things were going so well, we planned a week vacation to go back to Wilmington to see our friends. We were excited to load up the dogs, take a long road trip and have the first vacation we had been able to have in years.

However, by mid-August Dave was having some issues with his job. He said he wasn't being valued for what he could do. He would come home from work and often complain. This was raising red flags for me again. Despite the fact he promised he would never quit a job without first having another job to go to, I had a feeling that it would happen again. His ego and unhappiness led him to apply for a different job closer to home in Boca.

The interview went great. The second interview also went great. So great, they made him a verbal offer of a salary, and said they would follow up in a week with specifics and an offer in writing. Dave felt this was a perfect fit. So much so, that he quit the job he had.

A few days later after Labor Day weekend, Hurricane Irma came. Her aftermath left more than rising waters, uprooted trees, and power outages. When she left, I was left with what would be the beginning of the end. For real this time.

Chapter 98

Insanity and Hysteria

The promised follow up with a formal job offer never came. The week after the hurricane, upon my return home after work I found him soaking in the tub with his arm in a brace. His explanation to my inquiry about what happened was that he sliced open a tendon near his thumb with a sharp piece of bamboo when he was cleaning up the yard. He gave me details, which sounded off.

Here we went again. I could tell something was wrong. He was trying to hide it but not being very successful. The real story was that he had drank a six-pack of bottled beer, then drove to the nearest gas station to get rid of the evidence. He was trying to force the six pack of empty bottles into the garbage container, like trying to force a square peg in a smaller round hole. He was annoyed that it wasn't going through the hole and raised up his arm, bringing it down to force it through, breaking a bottle, which sliced his tendon.

He had driven himself home first, to get towels due to the extreme bleeding, then took himself to the nearest urgent care center. They put a temporary fix on it and referred him to a specialist due to the nature of the cut.

Within two weeks at 6:00 a.m. I was driving a completely wasted Dave to the hospital for his scheduled hand surgery. He was so drunk that he tried to open the car door to get out at a stop light at a major intersection.

I didn't care. It didn't matter to me that he was drunk out of his mind and falling asleep on the 15-minute drive to the hospital. I would dump him at the entrance with his admission papers, driver's license and medical card. They could deal with him. I figured as soon as they saw how drunk he was they would get him some help.

I dropped him off. The valet looked at me like I was crazy as I pulled away, watching in my rear-view mirror a drunk attempting to have a conversation with a valet about his surgery.

Nobody called to tell me he was too drunk to operate on and a few hours later I received a call from a nurse indicating he was ready to be picked up. That's our healthcare system for you. I later found out he had drunk a pint of vodka in the middle of the night prior to his surgery. Dave also told me that the surgeon was joking around with him about it and that he probably didn't even need anesthesia.

Within a week, I was calling 911 to the house again to deal with an extremely intoxicated Dave that had driven himself home from a "meeting." I received a call on my cell, which I ignored. Then I received a text. I checked my phone and it was a friend of his. I called him back. "Quick" he said, "I have Dave on the other line and he told me the cops followed him to the house."

I put the phone down and ran out the front door to a crookedly parked Jeep, motor still running and a limp, incoherent Dave at the wheel. He didn't even know I was there or that the vehicle was still running. I reached across his lap and shut it off, as he slumped and basically fell out of the Jeep onto the ground. He barely made his way into the house.

There weren't any cops around and nobody had followed him. However, after two straight hours of him in the house, screaming profanities and demanding that I make arrangements to take him to North Carolina for treatment, I called the police.

In typical Dave fashion, he had completely coherent conversations with them and they left. He stayed. There wasn't any reason to take him or do anything.

After another month of insane drinking, I called the police again. He was out of his mind and was Baker Acted, and taken to the county mental facility. He was released within 72 hours and drank upon his return home.

He continued the constant pouring of poison and upon arriving home from work on November 7th, I found him gray in color and shaking through his entire body. I took him to the emergency room where he was admitted for intoxication and extremely low sodium levels. He was released three days later and returned home only to start drinking again.

I later found the following handwritten note dated November 11, 2017.

Sobriety Date: 11/8/17 (In hospital)

First full day out of hospital after hitting my bottom – brain swelling, body shutting down, sodium level low enough for permanent brain damage. Priscilla has papers for divorce, but for the grace of God she has given me one final chance to get my life together. I don't understand why I continue to turn to alcohol, when I get fearful or depressed. I have done so many horrible things that I think people are going to find out about. So much shame in my heart but I have to get passed it in order to live a life again. Today I feel hopeful only because Priscilla allowed me to stay at home and have one last chance at a normal life. I also feel scared people know I've been a total loser for so long. I have to let go of my pride and ego and accept the help that is out there. Today's going to be a great day!! Prayer: God I pray you will come into my heart today and change me for good. Take me away from fears and anger and replace them with faith, hope and love. Crush my pride and ego, walk with me today and please please keep me SOBER!!! Amen

Time flies while having fun and before I knew it our 31st wedding anniversary had arrived. Thirty-one years of marital bliss. Living the dream here. I was going to take the day off, but decided there really wasn't a point since he was drunk anyway. I picked up food on the way home for the two of us and he was too drunk to eat it. Happy Anniversary.

A few days later I forced him into the Jeep and physically dragged him from the Jeep into the ER. It took every ounce of strength and determination that I had. I didn't care that people were looking at us like we had lost our minds. I was crying and pulling on his sweatshirt and he was grabbing the concrete barrier pole and wouldn't let go. I managed to pull his fingers off it and he lost his balance, allowing me enough momentum to get him pushed through the doors into the ER lobby.

There was more public humiliation but I didn't care. The check-in desk took one look at us and let us go in front of others. However, Dave was not going to agree to even being checked out so they were telling me that there wasn't anything they could do. By this time, I was in tears which worked as one of the intake nurses started trying to convince Dave to allow them to just take his blood pressure and check his heart. After much convincing, Dave agreed and he was eventually officially checked into ER.

The next hour as we sat in the hallway of the ER, which had unfortunately become a very familiar place for me, was hell. He would not sit still, he would not listen, and he was manic as he paced the floor, threatened to walk out, and continually caused a scene. I was trying not to cry. I was once again in a public place where I tried to keep my wits about me, but eventually got to the point where I didn't care what anyone thought of me.

Dave made a comment that he wanted to kill himself. That was my opening to try and get the ER doctor to Baker Act him once again. Otherwise, they would be sending him back home with me and the cycle would continue to spin out of control. It worked! At that point, the security would play a larger role in keeping him in check, even if he was still sitting in the hallway. I headed home, completely exhausted with no hope.

While hospitalized under the Baker Act, he manipulated and conned everyone once again and managed to get released four days later on a Friday night. Just in time for me to have another great weekend. He started drinking within a couple days at the same insane pace as he had been previously.

Chapter 99

The Loneliest Christmas Ever

The couple days of sobriety that he had after being released prompted Dave to commit to our neighbor across the street that he would take care of their puppy while they went out of town. He said it would be good for him and give him something to focus on. He would be the one to go to their house multiple times a day to feed him, let him out, and take him for walks, and play with him.

Needless to say, he started drinking again and was three sheets to the wind by the time the neighbors left on their trip. I got stuck with not only watching over my drunk of a husband, caring for our three crazy dogs, and working full-time but also taking full responsibility for the neighbor's puppy.

Aside from that chaos, December of 2017 was a time where I hit one of my lowest points emotionally. The stress of everything was taking its toll on me daily. I was an emotional wreck. I had to put on the good face, my normal "happy" and dedicated to my job face, Monday through Friday, knowing that every drive home would lead me to a night of chaos, stress, and agony.

Just to get some time away and spend time with an out of control and bored puppy, I would load him up and take him for rides. It was a ride on Christmas Day night that I was in a particularly low point, and as Christmas carols were playing on the radio, while driving around the puppy to look at lights, I recorded a message to myself:

A year after recordings I made last year at this time, I'm making this recording to remind myself how horrible this weekend has been. This last four days leading into Christmas has been a total nightmare. Nonstop drinking, nonstop harassing me for pills, pacing around. He conned me. I got him put away and he conned me to get him out. Less than two days later, he started drinking again. And here we are again. I can honestly say this has been the worst Christmas of my entire life. I feel trapped, like there is nobody that can help me out of this. He won't go away. He won't leave. He tries to manipulate me and con me. Always conning. Always trying to suck me into ...making comments like "you're my wife, you're the only reason I'm alive." What kind of crap is that to say to somebody? Meanwhile he is sucking every bit of joy and life out of me. I think I have done my time. I have said it before but it's got to end. I just can't make myself do it. But I have got to do something I have to do something, it's got to save him and it's got to save me because it's turning me into this horrible ugly person with a foul mouth and a bad attitude. It is sucking the life out of me. I really can't handle this anymore. I want it to stop. It's like this nightmare that never ends. I don't want to wake up in the morning knowing that I have another day like this ahead of me. I'm so tired. I'm so tired. Meanwhile, I'm driving around the neighbor's puppy for another week. He's supposed to take care of the puppy. I'm not supposed to take care of the puppy. He's supposed to take care of the puppy. I feel hopeless right now. I'm desperate for some help.

Like the above wasn't enough, after driving more and composing myself, I recorded another voice memo to myself. I wanted to be sure I captured my emotions so if I started getting conned again, I had something to listen to.

Something to remind me of that really dark place from Christmas 2017.

I have never felt so alone as I feel right now. As I drive around and look inside of people's windows on Christmas Day night. There are cars. All these neighborhoods and lights. People walking around outside. It's a beautiful night. Went by a house that had a huge picture window in it and there is this guy in there wearing a Santa hat dancing around. People are having good times with family and friends. I feel so alone. It's horrible. I have never felt this bad. I don't think I ever have except maybe time just makes it go away. The move to Florida was supposed to be a fresh start. What a joke. Still I drive around with a puppy in the car. How is that for pathetic and lonely with a drunk husband at home? I keep hearing Christmas carols that remind me of home. Like when I was little. With my mom and dad. What would they think of me right now? What would they think? What would they think of me on Christmas Day?

My home life insanity continued through the holiday right into the new year.

Chapter 100

The Struggle

The new year of 2018 brought me to a point where I had to make a choice for myself. What to do? Do I finally make that final decision to cut the cord? I looked at the list of random thoughts I compiled at a time of despair locked in my bedroom. That master bedroom had become my sanctuary. The place I could go with the dogs and lock him out. My safe place. That list said a lot.

Paranoid

No AA meetings

Manipulates

Lies

Not dependable

I'm not happy

Ax under his bed

Drinking

Pilling

He is an adult

Should take care of himself

Can't trust with dogs

No conversation

Can't believe what he says

Lies about little things

Drinks and drives

Liability to me

I need to live

Need to be happy

Stop enabling

Stop enabling

Stop enabling

Stop

Stop

Stop

Question – Can this ever be fixed or has too much happened?

Police to house 5 times in FL

1 Court order

4 Baker Acts

3 DUIs

Over 10 treatment centers

Chapter 101

Blood, Poop and the Super Bowl

I came home from work on January 2ⁿᵈ to find the dining room table and chairs moved, blood all over the floor and rug and drops of blood leading into the guest bathroom. It was eerily quiet in the house, with the dogs being shut in the bedroom, but strangely enough not barking.

I cautiously approached the bathroom and peeked around the corner to see Dave sitting in the bathtub with his legs hanging over the side. His face and hands were completely covered in blood, as well as his clothes. He was conscious and just stared at me with this bloody "Walking Dead" type of look. I told him to stay where he was and not to move. I called 911.

He was loaded onto a stretcher and taken via ambulance to the hospital. I received a call approximately four hours from the time he was removed from the house, from the ER nurse asking me if I was ready to come and pick him up. When I asked how he could be released, and what about blood tests, like a blood panel to check on sodium levels, I was told "We have treated him for his injuries. We did not run a blood panel. CT scan came back fine. Nothing broken." I told them I was not going to pick him up, thinking that would force them into a different type of action. Nothing. I explained that a couple months earlier he had been hospitalized at a different hospital with extremely low sodium levels. I inquired about detox, stating he needed help. I pushed back, but received very matter of fact answers and was clearly not going to get anywhere in speaking with the nurse. If I didn't pick him up, they were going to release him into the street, fully loaded on Vodka, bloody and no shoes on a rainy night. The answer I got was "We don't treat for detox here." They obviously didn't care either. He was just another addict.

I picked him up from the main hospital lobby around 10:30 p.m. His face was barely cleaned up. No stitches, just some tape and his eye was almost swollen shut. He was out of it, but not out of it enough to refrain from demanding a drink. "I need it ... I need it Cilla... you have to stop and get me something to drink. I'm shaking. I'm going to go through DTs if you don't get me something." I told him to shut up and wait until we got home.

The minute he walked in the house, he went for the fridge and pulled out a diet soda and filled the remainder of the glass with Vodka. I should have thrown it out, but deep inside I knew that I would be harassed to death until he got some. So, my answer was to keep it but hide it until needed. I left him all bloody in the kitchen with his booze and locked myself and the dogs in the bedroom for the night.

I could hear him stumbling around in the kitchen, when around 2:00 a.m. I heard a loud noise. I opened the door to see nothing going on in the kitchen but noises coming from the guest bath. I walked toward the guest bathroom, where the sounds were coming from. He couldn't breathe well. His face was still bleeding from the previous injury, with the one eye swollen shut and the other one wide open, wild and crazy looking. He was trying to get to the toilet, and kept falling. He fell and landed sideways on the toilet pushing it off its base. He kept trying to get up and I kept telling him to stop and to be still and stop moving. He was completely out of his mind. I tried to lift him but he was dead weight so I managed to get him eased flat on the tile floor. His shorts were off as was his underwear. There was poop all over the toilet, the floor, and some on the walls. He was literally laying on the floor in his own feces, drunk out of his mind, and in a state of insanity. I called 911. Again.

Some of the same paramedics that had been to the house a few hours earlier arrived. They couldn't believe it. They had to take blankets off the stretcher into the bathroom to roll his feces and blood covered body onto it to get him out of the bathroom onto the stretcher. They Baker Acted him immediately and took him upon my orders to a different hospital. I had explained that the previous one had released him and shouldn't have. By the time they left it was 3:00 a.m. on January 3, 2018.

He ended up in ICU for four days due to critically and life threatening low sodium and potassium levels, then moved to the cardiac wing of hospital for another four days, and then moved to Fair Oaks due to the Baker Act on January 11th. He was transferred to treatment back up in Palm Beach on January 17th.

Dave was released from treatment the Saturday prior to the Super Bowl. Just in time to have our little party with the dogs and enjoy some wings. He was a changed man and would never drink again he said. This was the wakeup call he needed, he said. I caught him in a lie two days later, and left him a note when I left for work that he needed to move out. He was drinking less than a week after completing another stint in rehab.

In typical Dave fashion, despite promises to never put me through his hell again and that he would move out if he drank again, he didn't. He threw the note away like he never saw it and continued to drink non-stop.

How was he getting his supply of booze? I was getting it for him. It was hard to explain and one can't know what it is like until one has walked a mile in my shoes. What would people think of me? I was both ashamed and embarrassed. It was pathetic. I kept going to the same places at 7:00 a.m. every morning, hoping people didn't think I was the one with the problem. I felt like I had to explain myself to the cashiers. "This isn't for me," I would say. I was stuck. I felt like a robot, just going through the motions of what had become my insane daily routine.

Chapter 102

It's 2:00 a.m.

By the late afternoon of the 12th of February 911 was called yet again with both the ambulance and police arriving. He was taken to the hospital and released by 2:00 a.m. the following morning. I was awakened out of a dead sleep by banging on the front door. I peeked out the front window and there was a cab in the driveway. Dave was banging on the door demanding that I let him inside.

I had previously disengaged the garage door from the opener so I had thought I was protected from him coming in through the garage. However, I had failed to lock the side bolts, therefore allowing him to manually open the car garage door and start banging on the door between the garage and the house. He was screaming that he needed to come in and to please let him in and that he needed to pay the cab driver.

I grabbed his wallet off the counter and figured I could open the garage door really quick when it was quiet and he had moved back to the front door, and toss his wallet out there. He then had what he needed to pay the cab, but more importantly his money to be able to go to a hotel for the night.

He tricked me and despite it being quiet in the garage, he was there waiting. There was a fight to get in through the garage door. I was trying to pull it shut and he was pulling it open. We struggled for what seemed like eternity and he reached in, grabbed my arms and pulled me out of the house and into the garage, pushing me back so he could get around me to get into the house shutting the door behind me. My arm hurt and I was devastated. He got back into the house once again and would never leave unless it was via ambulance or police.

I walked out in the driveway in my nightshirt to pay the cab driver, came back in and locked myself and the dogs in the bedroom until 5:30 a.m.

Chapter 103

Let's Make a Deal

I watched the security cameras on my phone while in the bedroom and he was pacing most of the night. He knocked on door at 5:00 a.m. wanting to know if there was anything at all in the house he could drink. I told him I would take him to get booze if he would please just sign the divorce papers. He agreed. I felt horrible, like I was being manipulative in trading a trip for booze for his signature on a legal document. He was "sober" enough to know what he was doing and it wasn't like he didn't know it needed to be signed. I justified it all in my head. He had manipulated me so many times, now it was my turn. I was holding the cards.

An hour later, I took him to a convenience store a couple miles from the house. This was one that I typically did not go to. He went inside, then came out, got in the Jeep and told me to pull around to the side of the store near the back alley. Since it was too early, they couldn't legally sell him alcohol. A minute later some guy came out the side door by the trash dumpster with four tall boys in a brown sack. Dave slipped him $5 and off we went. I felt like I was part of a covert operation, plus I felt dirty.

By 8:00 a.m. I was searching desperately for a place to go as soon as possible to get the papers signed and notarized. He was desperate for booze. He held it together long enough to get papers signed and notarized by 9:00 a.m. The relief for me was indescribable. This was the start of a new life for me. I stopped at another convenience store on the way home so he could go in and purchase another 12-pack after signing the marriage away.

We got home and I left for work, leaving him at the house with his 12-pack. By noon he was calling me to tell me that he called Rehab. By the time I got home for lunch he was even more drunk. I took over making the arrangements on the phone, as he was incoherent and the intake counselor couldn't make sense of what he was saying. They said they could come get him within the next three hours. I told them there was no way we could wait that long, so I loaded him in the Jeep and sped up I-95 to get him there before he changed his mind. He tried to get out twice while on the interstate.

He was welcomed with open arms at rehab. They all knew him. On my way back to work I wondered if this vicious cycle would ever end.

I had my answer five days later when he checked himself out of rehab, against medical advisement. He drank the next day.

Chapter 104

Around and Around We Go

The remainder of February into middle March was hell at home. Multiple calls to 911 for ambulance and police. They take him in an ambulance only to be released a few hours later to come back home. His behavior at home was deteriorating more each day. He couldn't stop and I couldn't stop him.

I was locking myself in the bedroom almost every night. His constant stumbling, mumbling, drooling and drinking around the house was out of control. I couldn't stand the sight of him. He wouldn't eat much and when he did, he would have a hard time getting the food to his mouth, drooling onto the counter, food falling on the floor, the fridge door left open, and dogs being completely freaked out.

He had this zombie way of walking when he drank the hard stuff. He would zombie walk out of the bedroom and then just stop in the middle of the house, standing there, drooling and staring, both arms dangling on each side. Then he would "wake up" and just start zombie walking to the bathroom or the kitchen. He would hit the wall, fall, and slide out of bed. It was like this every day and every night, after I got home from work and on weekends. It was a nightmare that I couldn't seem to escape.

My daily routine had become getting up for work in the morning and making a WalMart run for beer to bring it home before I went to work. That was followed by purchasing more beer over lunch on my way home to check on the dogs.

And finally, on my way home after work I would stop at the ABC store to get Vodka as needed. Lots of it. It was insanity.

It's like I knew it was wrong and it was going to kill him, yet him drinking non-stop and passing out or going to the hospital was better than when he was coming down off his high and harassing me for it. It was a hopeless situation and he refused to leave, despite my tearful pleas.

I tried to change my tactics and take the advice of a female police officer that had ticked me off after arriving at the house one night. She asked me how he got his booze, and I told her I bought it. She told me to stop buying it, take his keys (which I always did) and his money and don't let him buy it either. I mentioned to her she didn't understand and that I was afraid that he would get violent with me. Her answer to me, "Then you call us."

Fine. Let's try that. I let him go without and hadn't brought any home after work, ate my supper and locked myself in the bedroom waiting to see what would happen. He started knocking at the bedroom door with little light tap tap tap tap. Then he stopped and started again, tap tap tap tap. "Cilla, can you go get me a 12 pack? I'm out. I need some." My reply was no.

Tap tap tap tap. "Please, you need to get me some."

I replied, "No, I'm not getting you any."

The tapping on the door continued, becoming louder and more frequent. As he continued to knock and bang on the door, verbally harassing me and demanding his money and keys, I pulled out my daily devotional and started reading one page after another out loud through tears. The louder he knocked and screamed, the louder I read my devotional.

The knocking eventually stopped. As I watched the security camera, I saw him pacing back and forth. He started to swear and drop F bombs about how could I do this to him. He just needed some. Then I saw him collapse and fall on the floor, laying on his side for a moment. I continued to watch the camera, uncertain as to whether I should call 911 or what I should do. A few seconds later he stood up like nothing happened and continued his verbal tirade. He told me later that he did a "fake fall" thinking it would get me to open the door.

This went on and on for about 30 minutes, then the doorknob to the bedroom started to jiggle, then jiggle more and more. Then it sounded like he was trying to pick the lock to the bedroom to get to me, his keys and/or his money. This was a bedroom doorknob that only had that little hole that you could poke with something to unlock it.

I waited until it was quiet, then opened the door and told him to stop it. I slammed and locked the door again. He continued swearing and trying to pick the lock. This continued for another 10 minutes or so until I braced myself, opened the door, and told him I was going to call the police if he didn't stop it. He was standing at the bedroom door with a paring knife! Not sure if that was what he was trying to use to pick the lock, or what, but I called the police.

While waiting for the police, I moved my tall dresser in front of the bedroom door in the hopes that if he did get it open somehow that I would have more leverage and protection. The police arrived about 15 minutes later and pounded on the door, demanding that he open it, which he did. When they arrived, I had moved the dresser and was ready to open the bedroom door. After realizing he was away from the door and I should be safe, I opened it.

There were two police officers, both with guns drawn at him. One was at the door, the other one a few feet back. They told him to come out of the house then grabbed him. They proceeded to have a lengthy conversation with him, then one officer came in the house to talk to me.

I explained everything to the officer who had, unfortunately, been at the house before. He kept asking me if he had touched me in any way. I could have lied, but didn't. If he had physically touched me to "harm" me, they could arrest him for assault and take him away right then and there. But he didn't, so they didn't. Instead, they offered to drive him to a hotel for the night to cool off and of course, he refused.

About an hour had passed and they allowed him back in the house. An officer asked him if his bedroom was in the back of the house, to which Dave replied that it was. The officer got in his face and said, "You go back to that bedroom and shut the door and stay in there all night. Do you hear me? You stay in there. If you come out of there and if she has to call us again tonight, I will come back here and arrest you so fast you won't know what happened! Do you understand me?" Dave's answer was that he did and he shuffled off to the back room and shut the door.

Chapter 105

Angels on the Way!

Dave's family was fully aware of what was going on. One evening I received a call from them, stating that they had talked as a family and they would be coming down to Florida to pick Dave up and take him to the Midwest. I cried. The relief I had was indescribable. There was hope. He had to get out of the house. I didn't know how much longer I could go on as I had been.

The date of March 21st was the big day. Family would fly down, stay overnight on the 21st, then head out with the Jeep loaded with everything Dave needed. Dave agreed to it, but he wasn't sober long enough to really understand it all. I really don't think he was. The next three weeks continued as the past few had.

He needed to stop drinking and be sober for the trip back, but he didn't. He continued to drink beer continually. I was counting down the days in my head over and over. One more week and they would be here. I can do this. Four more days and they would be here. I can do this. Twenty-four hours and they would be here.

It was a battle to the very last minute until they pulled out. He was guzzling cans of beer as he was finishing his packing. He wasn't even really packing. I was packing. He was just drinking.

We hugged goodbye and he was crying. I wasn't crying. I was saving my tears for when they were gone. My tears were going to be tears of relief. Tears of joy.

Chapter 106

Missing in the Midwest

Dave drank the entire trip back to the Midwest. Upon arrival, he refused to stay at the house, so they took him to a hotel nearby for a few days. While there, he kept drinking until they went to pick him up a few days later.

I felt bad for them. I had warned them, but they had no idea what they were getting into. I knew what to expect. They didn't know just how powerful the desire to drink was for Dave and that he would put that desire above everything else.

I later found out just how much Dave had put them through. He went into their garage into the garbage can to find the empties of beer and drink the stale, warm droppings that were left in the cans. He drank their mouthwash. He clutched beer cans to his chest like a baby when they tried to take it away.

It was a horrible time for them and it only lasted a few weeks. He basically hadn't been sober more than a day or two off and on the entire time he was there.

Our divorce was final on April 24th. As I sat in the Courthouse with my attorney, waiting for the doors of the courtroom to open, Dave started texting me non-stop. He asked me if I was ok. He said he loved me and hoped I loved him. Like this time in my life wasn't hard enough, but he had to continue to intervene and try to manipulate me.

About 30 minutes later, it was over. Divorce final. I did it. It wasn't easy. As the judge was asking me to repeat my name and answer a couple basic questions, I broke into tears after I answered the question about how long we had been married and if I felt the marriage was irreparable. He smiled at me and said "Hey, this is supposed to be a happy time." He stamped and signed the paperwork and just like that, I was a divorcee.

On April 27th Dave loaded the Jeep once again and hit the road, telling everyone he was going back to Boca.

I sent him a text "Heard you left. Not sure where you are heading but if you come back to the state of FL you will be Marchman Acted. I could tell you had been drinking based on our phone call last night. You have lied to me since you left here. I told you I would continue to have a dialogue with you, talk and text, and stay in touch as long as you were sober, honest and on the right path. That clearly isn't the case. I will no longer communicate with you and you should refrain from trying to contact me."

The Marchman Act would be a last ditch effort for us in forcing Dave to get treatment. It is a Florida law that provides a means of involuntary and voluntary assessment and stabilization and treatment of a person allegedly abusing alcohol or drugs. The court gets involved and a judge can order mandatory longer-term treatment, which could lead to jail if treatment is refused.

Nobody knew where Dave was. He was telling multiple people different things. He was in Nashville. He was in Louisville. He would see me "tomorrow."

For the next few days, I received multiple ranting texts to call him, stating he had a right to his dog, he would get lawyers and would sue me, threatening to show up and take Ripley, cursing, and on and on. He called a couple times and left voice mails, threatening to come and get Ripley. I refused to respond.

A week later, on Friday, May 4th I received an email with subject line "Please.... Hey, I'm in trouble, and about to be homeless. Credit cards are not working. Please just be my friend and help me. I am sober, struggling but sober. Please call me." As hard as it was, I didn't respond.

The following day, I logged into my cell phone account, which also had all his phone and text activity, to see if he had made any calls from his phone to cab companies or convenience stores. That would give us an idea of where he was physically located.

Sure enough, I saw multiple phone calls made to phone numbers indicating he was still in the general vicinity of his family's home. I started copying and pasting the phone numbers into Google.

My heart both sank and began racing at the same time. Most of the phone calls were made to three different escort services. How does one process knowing that as you worried about his health and where he may be, was he driving drunk, or was he dead somewhere, the addict had not only continued to lie and drink, but also called an escort service? How exactly was one to process that?

My physical being felt like throwing up. The images I conjured up in my mind refused to leave, no matter how hard I tried to push them out. He was hurting, I got it. We weren't married any longer, that was a fact. But the hurt was still there and it was deep.

I cried. I felt nauseous much of the day. Finally, toward the end of the day, I decided to pull up my big girl pants, get dressed up so I felt good about myself and go out for a drink. As I sat enjoying the one and only drink I ever order, a strawberry daiquiri, I thought I would call one of those numbers. Would someone answer? Was it a computer-generated phone sex thing or was it an actual escort service? I had no idea what to expect.

I called it from my cell phone and received a very professional phone message of a female voice that indicated nobody was available to take the call at that time and to please leave a message. I hung up. Within 10 minutes, I received a text from that number stating "Hi! Sorry I missed your call!" I was disgusted and blocked the number. I didn't have the guts to click on the web link to see what the website(s) looked like. I had enough image burned into my brain cavity. I certainly didn't need to see more.

The next month or so was a nightmare of trying to figure out where he was, if he was alive, as well as dodging random phone calls and texts from him. He eventually reached a point where he felt he needed to go to treatment so he enlisted the help of his family, who came to his rescue at the hotel to pick him up and take him to the hospital. Once they reached the hospital, he refused to get out. He ended up going home with them again, still refusing to stop drinking.

A couple weeks later he hit the road again, stating he was sober, and was going to drive to Boca. However, this time they had put a tracker on his phone so we all could keep track of his progress and where he was.

Once he made it to the Atlanta area, it was a cycle of hitting three different hotels within the next couple weeks. One of those hotel stays resulted in him calling 911 and going to the local ER. They released him within hours and he was taken back to the Super 8. His family was aware and at that time had started the conversation of coming to pick him and drive him to Florida. Yes, back down here a couple months after I had been so relieved that he had left.

The plan had initially been to drive him to the Orlando area and leave him there, closer to Hamid, hoping he would hit a treatment center in Florida. After they picked him up in Atlanta and started the drive to Florida, Dave agreed to go to treatment in Palm Beach again.

The drive from Atlanta to Florida was a nightmare, with Dave drinking non-stop. They stayed in a hotel one night, then made the drive to Palm Beach the following day. Dave was making a point to spend every last waking moment he could drinking on the way to treatment. Finally, they made it to their destination.

Full circle back to southern Florida. What I had thought would be the beginning of healing and a new life for me in March 2018, clearly ended up with me still being consumed with Dave drama.

Chapter 107

The Final Blow

After having lived with someone for over 30 years, and with them since High School, it wasn't a surprise that even after all the emotional pain and roller coaster, wasted money, time and energy, that I still felt a sense of loss.

I was excited about the new chapter in my life, yet sad that so much time had gone by. There was also the grieving of the loss of the person as I knew him at one point in our lives. When he wasn't drinking, life was good. We never really argued about anything other than his drinking. We spent so much time together. We were two peas in a pod.

The thought of him being out there struggling to stay sober, not having a job, and at this point only a few thousand dollars to his name made me continually think about him. How could he manage to recover from all of this? Would he ever recover? Did he WANT to recover?

I found myself feeling the need to be kind, compassionate and to feel empathy for him. I wanted to be helpful and understanding, once or IF he made that turn to recovery.

That was the case until a Saturday in early June 2018. Hamid's wife Kathy came over for our first ever "girls weekend." As we sat for lunch, I received a call from rehab. I picked it up, thinking it may be them calling me to get more information on what had been happening with Dave over the past few months. However, it was him.

The conversation started out with him telling me he was thinking "clear as a bell" and was just waiting for them to medically release him at some point the following week, most likely on Tuesday.

He then indicated that when he got out he was going to come and see the dogs, and that we needed to sit down and "talk about some things." I asked what and he indicated "things." I pressed further and he said, "We need to talk about me staying there a couple days when I get out until I get situated."

This blew me away. He went for weeks doing nothing but spending what little money he had left on booze, hotels and God knows what else, and he had the nerve to think he could stay at the house a couple days. No! No! No!

After telling him no, he pulled the manipulative spin on me with "Wow, after 35 years together this is what happens. This hurts my heart." I replied with "You hurt? Seriously? Try finding out that you used the phone and service I pay for to call an escort service." His response was "Can't you just forget about that?"

The call ended abruptly after a few more jabs at me for how horribly I had been treating him, with him saying "I'll be there on Tuesday when you got off work to see the dogs."

Kathy was listening to the entire conversation, and when the call ended she started to look very anxious and began to cry. She clearly had to tell me something.

The episode with calls to escorts a few weeks prior wasn't the first time. He had been calling for and receiving service from escorts before. Hamid had confided in her and told her. It happened back in North Carolina when he would go "missing" for weekends, oftentimes driving to Pinehurst. This evidently happened on multiple occasions. It happened when he was "lost" in Florida back in 2013, where Dave told Hamid about it.

I felt sick to my stomach, and went on to repeat some of what she told me back to her, thinking that I may not have heard her correctly. She was crying. I was in a daze. My insides were shaking. More images, worse than the ones I had conjured up previously were racing through my mind.

We were married. How could he? How could he when he always told me that he would never be one of those horrible men that would cheat on their wives? He said we were soul mates. He said we were meant to be together forever. I had always thought that the one sacred thing that we had, was the fact that we had always been faithful to each other. It was that one thing that had been making it hard for me to leave, as I felt that the disease was something he couldn't help and that he was sick. I could forgive.

This may have been God's way on this Saturday to get me information that would make me even stronger, with more will than ever to say no to him and to not allow him to suck me back in as I had been so many times before.

Even so, the feelings of despair and regret, along with disgust kept hanging on. Those images. I just couldn't get them out of my mind. All the efforts made to conceal it, then come home to me. Me. The one that was always there to pick up the pieces, the one to get him to rehab, the one that drove him to and from work for multiple years due to losing his license, the one that spent so much time alone, self-medicating with food.

I wanted to burn every picture that was ever taken of the two of us. They were lies. I wanted to burn my wedding dress. I wanted to rid the house of anything and everything that had a direct link to him. I wanted him to hurt. I wanted him to ache like I did. I wanted him to know that I knew. I wanted that smug "I'm here and I'm going to win you back" look on his face replaced with a look of despair and a type of regret that he could never overcome. I wanted revenge. This wasn't something I could forgive and would certainly never forget.

Just the thought of seeing his face again made me want to vomit. I wanted to hurt him. As I watched TV, any scenes of infidelity or sex started me on a mini meltdown. Strange as it sounds, I wasn't upset or sad for what could be in the future, because I never had any intent whatsoever to get back with him once he had proven he was a "changed man." There was too much at risk there for me. Rather, it was the memories and the flashbacks to what I thought was going on versus what was happening.

What a sham. The notes indicating he was sorry now meant something completely different. The trips where he would disappear for weekends and not come home until late Sunday, now had a completely different meaning. The ring he gave me with the engraving on it; was that a guilt gift? Everything meant something different, and that was what made me sad.

Staying busy had been a way to attempt to push thoughts out of my mind. However, staying that busy was exhausting. I was finding the only way to get past those thoughts of sadness were to look at the multiple pictures and videos I took of him when he was drunk. Now there was a catch. A grown man in his early fifties, stumbling around in a drunken stupor, falling, pooping himself and babbling like an idiot. Karma's a bitch, and maybe the unfaithfulness was why he was landing where he was now.

My previous feelings of compassion for him were gone. They were replaced with feelings of resentment, contempt, and anger. All this made me feel that the 15-20 years of my life had been wasted. Those years of my life were prime years.

However, God's timing on revelation of facts is often much later than we would like to see. Financially and professionally I was in a much better place in my life and could more than care for myself, the dogs, and my home. Ten to fifteen years prior, that wouldn't have been the case. This all goes back to things happen for a reason, and I do think that all this mess of my life had been for a reason. I was a strong, independent and successful woman. I felt that I could basically conquer anything.

Chapter 108

A Hurting Heart

The following Monday, June 4th, after the big revelation from Kathy, I received a voice mail from rehab at 3:30 a.m. to call them back regarding Dave. Upon calling I was told that Dave was taken via ambulance to a local hospital due to claims of chest pains and shortness of breath.

The nurse went on to tell me that he had been restless that evening and had requested more medication to sleep, which they could not give him. He was doing a lot of pacing, so the usual technician checks that occurred every hour, were moved to every half hour, along with further monitoring of him on the camera.

More pacing and very large quantities of water prompted them to check on him every 15 minutes. In watching him on the camera, they noticed that he would pace, then stop and hold his chest, break for a moment, then start pacing again. After multiple occurrences of this nature, the nurse went to ask him if he was ok. It was at that point he complained of chest pains, which warranted the call to 911.

Dave had started refusing all his detox medications that prior Friday, stating that he had to get back to work on Tuesday and pay his bills. I told the nurse that he didn't have a job, had been on a two-month binge and road trip, and that we were divorced and he had no home. Dave had told them that he still lived locally. It was no surprise that Dave had not told anyone at rehab the truth. The nurse indicated he would send an email to the clinical people, letting them know this information and wanted to know if I would be willing to talk to them. I agreed and of course, nobody ever called me.

That was, except for Dave. He always called. By Monday noon, he had been released from the hospital and was back at rehab. He had called to tell me he was back, and that he was going to stay there longer and they were putting him on a different detox protocol.

He wouldn't be showing up at the house as he had planned after all.

Chapter 109

To Tell or Not to Tell

After all of this I could always count on calls from Dave while in rehab. June 6th was another one of those days. However, this time seemed to be the right time for me to let him know that I knew about the escorts.

I needed to do this so he would get out of his head once and for all the thought that he would be welcome to come "home" and stay with me. He needed to get rid of the hope that we would ever get back together. So, after the usual "how are you" and chit chat, I said, "I know things. I know things, Dave. I know things that you don't think I know. Let's just leave it at that."

He kept pushing and pushing, trying to find out what I was talking about. He said "You said on the phone the other night that there was hurt in the house. Are the dogs ok? Are you ok? Are you still mad about the escort numbers? That wasn't me. You know I'm insane when I drink that much. It isn't what you think."

"Which do you like better, girls from the Midwest, girls from North Carolina or girls from Florida?"

"What do you mean?" he replied.

"I know, Dave. I know about Pinehurst." There was silence on the other end of the line.

"What are you talking about?" Followed by more silence, then "That wasn't me, I was insane. I'm not that kind of person."

He didn't deny it. It really happened. After over 30 years together, it was confirmed.

Chapter 110

A Razor and a Pen

I had learned over time that if I wanted to get any sleep at all, to put my phone on Do Not Disturb when I go to bed. It was the morning of June 7, 2018 that I was greeted with a voice mail from the treatment center from a nurse telling me to call back as soon as possible. That voice mail was left at 1:30 a.m. that morning.

Dave had attempted suicide early that morning while in treatment. They had checked on him at midnight and he was fine. When they went by a few minutes later they saw a light on under the door. When they opened the door, he came running out of the room. He was hearing voices and "agents" were after him. He was extremely paranoid.

The room was bloody. He had cut himself on his wrist and neck. He had taken the little round razors out of his electric shaver and had continually run them across the veins on his left wrist until they started to spurt blood. He had also taken a pen and repeatedly stabbed himself in the neck, with one successful full puncture.

He was taken via ambulance to a local hospital then shortly thereafter transferred to a different hospital with a trauma unit due to the puncture in the neck.

I was shaking all over as I was taking notes. Was this my fault? Did he do this because I told him the night prior that I knew he had been unfaithful? I felt like I was going to throw up. When was this going to end? A small part of me had hoped it had really ended. Ended like he was gone forever. Gone to a better place. What was going on with him wasn't living. It wasn't even existing.

He called me the next night from the hospital, asking if I could bring him some clothes as they were going to be moving him within a couple days back over to Fair Oaks. He had been Baker Acted again. He started the conversation by telling me that he tried to kill himself, then shortly thereafter asked me if I would bring him some Diet Pepsi.

When I saw him in the hospital his color looked bad. His left wrist was bandaged and there was a bandage on his neck. He was weak and frail looking. He had been moved to trauma due to the possible permanent injury he had to his neck. Luckily, after multiple tests the doctors felt that there wasn't any permanent damage, and that over time the internal bruising would heal itself. Had my conversation with him the night prior drove him to do what he did?

I left the room hoping that this was finally the bottom that we had all been praying for. Maybe this would be the beginning of the change.

Chapter 111

Hotel Tour of Boca

As they say, "things happen for a reason" or in Dave's case, things don't happen for a reason. He had numbers to call and an appointment to meet with a guy regarding a sober living home. However, that wasn't meant to be. Within two hours of me picking him up from Fair Oaks and coming back to the house to get his Jeep, he had left to hit the local liquor store.

After leaving the house to pick up prescriptions thirty minutes later he pulled back in the driveway, drunk. Drunk as a skunk and looking me in the eye to lie about it. I told him he wasn't welcome at the house and since he was so drunk, offered to take him to a hotel.

He ended up at the Holiday Inn Express four miles from the house. One night he had left me over 30 incoherent voicemails. Within four days, he had called 911 on himself and ended up at a hospital. He was Baker Acted yet again and while at the hospital we were told he tried to eat soap.

Five days later he was transferred to detox in Boca. Four days later he had given them a very hard time, refused to stay on for longer treatment, and left. Within two hours we knew he had hit a liquor store, thanks to the tracker on his phone. He ended up at the Hilton Garden Inn, which was about four miles from my house.

Three days later, he managed somehow to get himself picked up and admitted to another treatment center in Palm Beach. However, three days after that he checked himself out and ended up at the Hampton Inn, which was directly across the street from where I worked.

Five days later, 911 was called again and he ended up back at the hospital. However, this time they released him a few short hours later. He didn't go back to the Hampton Inn. My guess was he didn't remember where he was staying, so upon release from the hospital that time, we didn't know where he was. However, I received a call from the Hilton Garden Inn that night, which I didn't answer and nobody left a message. I received a call from a local Fairfield Inn the following morning which I also let go to voice mail. No voice mail left. That Sunday he ended up at a hospital a couple cities away. I had learned later that he had been at the Fairfield Inn (no bags, clothes, or anything) and there been an "incident" with him and the police were called. They decided he needed medical help and called the ambulance and he ended up in Boynton Beach. They released him later that day (on a Sunday) and he ended up back in Boca at a disgusting hotel.

The following morning, 911 was called by the hotel management and he was taken to South County Mental and was once again Baker Acted.

During this tour of hotels in Palm Beach County, I had been going back and forth to hotel rooms to pick up his stuff, locate the Jeep, apologize to hotel staff, and on and on. The condition of the hotel rooms was disgusting. There were empty beer cans and bottles everywhere, broken bottles in the bath tub, and empty vodka bottles. It had been eight weeks of chaos.

Chapter 112

Treatment by the Sea

After spending a few days in the county mental facility, Dave was transferred to another inpatient treatment center. He showed up in donated clothes from the psych ward due to not having any of his bags, or even knowing where his belongings were.

Now he had an opportunity to get better ocean front! Seriously? I was working my ass off every day of my life and he got treatment at the beach?

He was assigned a counselor by the name of Matt. Matt had called me to get the real back story, which I was more than happy to share. He also asked me if I would write an impact letter that he could share with Dave when the time was right. After being there a couple weeks, I met with Matt who told me that Dave would be awarded the "stubbornness award." He had never seen anything like it. Matt felt Dave was damaged. As an example, he would be doing fine and thinking straight in the morning, then by 1:30 that day was completely defiant. Matt went on to state the obvious to me, which was it was a chronic condition for Dave, and that Matt felt that he was on his last gasp. Matt had been doing this for 35 years and had never seen anything like it. Dave thought things were there or things happened and they weren't or didn't. He would "get" recovery, but if he was in it long enough, recovery would get him. That in itself, confirmed the point that limits on treatment for addiction by the insurance industry was hurting those with a desperate need for long term treatment.

Dave had said while in treatment about half of the day he wanted to get on track and recover and the other half he just wanted to drink himself into oblivion. Matt indicated that Dave still didn't really have a plan. His hope was that he could be with me.

My impact letter dated July 20, 2018

Impact – A strong word that can have a negative meaning or a positive meaning. This is the case with me. I have also included a letter I wrote to you in 2002.

Your drinking and all the behavior that goes with it has had an enormous impact on my life over the last 20+ years.

It has lead me to guarantee myself that I will never allow myself to be hurt like this ever again by anyone.

I am in it for me now. It is now my time to live for me. I have covered for you, lied for you, sacrificed for you, and for years put you, your addiction and needs above my own. That is to be no more. You are a master manipulator that has had an ability to continually suck me back into believing what you say.

That has left me with no choice but to limit my conversation with you. The less we talk, the less opportunity there is for you to weave your manipulation back into my thoughts. I need space and time for healing.

I put my phone on "do not disturb" every night before bed so I'm not awakened by the constant drunk calls, sometimes over 20 times in one night, or the calls from wherever you may be to tell me you are in the hospital again or have left.

My normal had become driving home from work with a pit in my stomach to an unemployed, drunk husband. My normal had become me having the expectation of not if but when I would be calling 911 for either the police or an ambulance. My normal was me logging into ADT multiple times a day while at work so I could see if you were coming, going, letting the dogs out, stumbling around the house, or had fallen. My normal was not wanting to go anywhere for long because I couldn't trust you with the dogs when you were drunk. My normal was obsessively looking for empty bottles, cans, or glasses with evidence to prove that you were drinking and lying to me. That makes me a very sick individual.

My life had come an obsession with your addiction.

However, through all this chaos of my so-called life, I have become very strong. I'm mentally strong and my faith is strong. That may not have happened if my life hadn't taken the turn that it did for me. That is the positive aspect of the impact of you and your addiction on my life.

It took me too many years to come to the realization that I can't stop you. That no matter what I do or say, or don't do or say, it won't make a difference. I'm finally there.

You said you want me in "your corner." I am. More importantly than being in your corner, I forgive you.

I hope that you will make the right choices for the right reasons to get your life back on a path of sobriety and happiness. - Priscilla

I had accepted an invitation to "family day" to visit Dave and be part of a 30- minute group session. I was nervous as I pulled up. When I saw him walking toward me I could tell he was extremely nervous. He looked surprisingly good. He was tan and healthy looking and his eyes were clear. We had an hour of awkward conversation, with him stating that this was it for him. He would never drink again and wouldn't hurt me.

Letter written late July/early August 2018 from Dave to "his addiction" which I found:

To my addiction.

You have taken everything in my life from me, and you make me fearful and paranoid every day of my life. I hate you so deeply that you have chosen me as one of your victims. The scary thing is that after all you have taken, I still want to drink so I don't have to feel these feelings of loss. I say goodbye to you today, crazy enough not knowing yet if I can keep you out of my life, or if I truly want you dead and gone and out of my life. I am no longer the person my wife and family knew before you entered my life, and that makes me feel really depressed and sad, and angry you chose me. You stole the most valuable thing in my life, an incredible best friend and wife, and I fucking hate you for that. But now you have me in a spot that makes me not want to live without her. You have done what you sat out to do and you make me sick, yet I know I may need you in the future. Please DIE before I have to find out.- Dave

Chapter 113

A Park Bench

He was to be officially released a few days later after completing the program. He had taken some tours of sober living homes and was set up to transition directly to one upon release.

I was on my way home from work to check on the dogs over lunch, when ahead of me a few vehicles I saw his Jeep. I had blocked his number so I had not received the calls from him a few minutes prior telling me he was released. He wanted to meet me at the house to see the dogs.

When we met at the house he looked nervous. I asked him why he was out early and that I thought he wasn't supposed to be released until 2:00 p.m., then go directly to the sober living home. He said they let him out early and they didn't want him sitting around the property until then. Something didn't sound right about that.

He seemed jittery and antsy. He saw the dogs, then left to go drive around until his appointment with the people at sober living. Something was off. I could tell he was lying. On my way back to work I had a sinking feeling in the pit of my stomach. The type of feeling where I wanted to throw up. I called his family, letting them know he was out. They said they would check the tracker on his phone later to see if he showed up at sober living.

A few hours later I received a text of a google map screenshot area where he was, which was the vicinity of the Boca Raton Inn and Suites. I drove by there on my way home from work, and sure enough, his Jeep was parked in the back of the parking lot. He never made it to his appointment at the sober living home. The same day he was released from 30 days of inpatient treatment, he drank. He spoke with family on the phone for 45 minutes where Dave said he just wanted to drink himself to death and wake up in heaven. He didn't want to go on any longer.

Four days later, on a Saturday afternoon I received a call from a Boca Raton police officer indicating they had been called twice about him that day with reports of a suspicious male wandering near businesses. He was in the back of their car and had told them to bring him to my house. The officer noticed in the records that there had been a domestic call earlier in the year and wanted to check with me to be sure it was ok that he was brought to the house. I told him no. The officer indicated he would then take him to a park where he could be near a restroom and bench and hopefully sleep it off. He told me if he showed up at the house, to call the police.

Sure enough, a few hours later at 2:30 a.m. he showed up at the house, banging on the door wanting to come in. The dogs went crazy as I peeked through the front window. He was stumbling around and had one little orange bag with him. Where he had been or how he got to the house was beyond me. He was drunk. He was pacing non-stop. I told him through the door that he needed to leave or I was going to call the police. He begged and pleaded for me to let him in. He said he didn't know where the Jeep was or where his clothes were. He said he couldn't go to a hotel and didn't have any money. For 20 minutes he paced, begged, banged, rang the doorbell, walked in the landscaping to knock on the front window, then over to the master bedroom window, back and forth. He was begging for water, so while he paced over to the bedroom window I opened the front window and threw out a bottle of water for him. He grabbed it and guzzled it within a couple minutes. His coloring looked bad. He was completely out of it.

I couldn't take it any longer and he clearly wasn't going to leave, so I once again called 911. The police wanted me to make a formal statement to him in front of them that he was not to be on the property. They told him that if he came back to the house, he would be arrested for trespassing. They loaded him up in the car and took him to another hotel.

The roller coaster of emotions that I had from the time the police officer called me in the afternoon until he showed up at the house in the middle of night completely drained me. All I could think of was him in his drunken, zombie like state, wandering around a park, the roads, and completely out of his mind. I had to make myself stay home and not go drive around to check on him or look for him. It took all that I had to even function. I cried, then I would be fine for a bit, then I would cry some more.

I had thought that once he had left Florida back in March and once the divorce was final, that I would have some sort of peace and could try and move on. That was not the case.

Chapter 114

Unresponsive

The following afternoon I received a call from Hamid. He had received a call from Dave's phone which was made by a Boca Raton paramedic. They had been called to the Quality Inn by the manager due to Dave not being responsive. Hamid gave the paramedic some history and Dave was taken to the hospital and was admitted to ICU, and eventually Baker Acted. He didn't know who he was and for a couple days didn't speak.

I stopped by the Quality Inn on my way to work to inquire about his belongings and to find out what happened. I was able to speak to the Manager that had called 911 the day prior. Dave had been in the hotel room past checkout time and despite multiple attempts to get him to come to the door over a several-hour period of time, he didn't. Finally, around 2:00 p.m. that afternoon, he did. The Manager said his behavior was off. He couldn't speak properly, which left him wondering if he even spoke English. His clothes were soaking wet and there was water all over the floor. He said that Dave sat down and then couldn't get back up or communicate. It was at that time the manager decided to call 911.

Five days later he was transferred from the hospital to a mental health facility in Fort Lauderdale. Six days later and a few phone calls to me resulted in me driving to Fort Lauderdale to pick him up upon his discharge. He supposedly had set up an appointment with the same sober living home that he was supposed to have gone to earlier. He assured me it was set up and he had a place to go.

He lied. He had called them but he had not been officially accepted. Upon his release, he looked weak and shaky. He most definitely did not look stable. There we sat in the admissions office, trying to convince them that he was sober and able to function there. They denied his request due to the fact he did not have paperwork from a medical facility that "cleared" him.

As we walked out to the Jeep, I broke into tears. I was a nervous wreck. Here we were again, in a position where he had no place to go and he would most certainly try to stay at the house. They had given him some other numbers to call, but none of them could meet him until the next day.

I was torn. Did I dare let him come back into the house for even one night? Just one night to be sure he was safe and could move to a sober home the next day? Would doing so start another battle for him to leave? He promised me it would be for just one night, but then again, he had broken hundreds of promises before. I was nervous and scared, but I did let him stay. I prayed that night that I had done the right thing.

Chapter 115

Back Home

Dave was subdued and grateful as we pulled in the driveway to the house. He stated that he understood how hesitant I was about letting him stay in the house for one night, and assured me that he would leave in the morning when I left for work.

It was a very uncomfortable time, as we had both been through so much. I ordered some take out and we ate at the counter, barely speaking other than to murmur the usual comments about the food. We watched TV, but neither of us were actually "watching" it. It was brutal. He remained very quiet and thanked me again for letting him stay for the night.

As promised, the next morning as I was ready to head out the door, he followed behind me. He asked if I minded that he stayed parked in the driveway while he made the calls to set appointments for the other sober living homes.

A couple hours later he called me at work and said that none of the places would take him without him first officially going through detox again and going through a medical release and direct transfer. I got another pit in my stomach. I was certain that this was leading once again to a very bad place.

An hour later he called to tell me that he had made a phone call to detox to see if they would take him back as a self-referral. They would and were working on verifying insurance coverage before he could check in. I was so relieved that he had for once in a very long time, made the right decision. The relief I felt when the intake person from detox called me to tell me he had arrived safely and was admitted sent a surge of hope back through me again. Maybe this time it would work.

Chapter 116

A Battle, but Still......

In typical Dave fashion nothing was ever easy. He started giving them a hard time at detox when it came time to transfer directly to a treatment center. They were going to try a different one this time, and unfortunately it was out of network. However, they thankfully granted him a scholarship and would simply take whatever insurance would pay, leaving Dave without anything extra to pay for the first 30 days in treatment.

After a couple weeks there, I went for the weekly Sunday visit that was allowed. I could tell he still wasn't clear in his head and he was worrying about his bills, his Jeep, what would happen to us, etc.

After his 30 days in treatment were completed, he was to transition to their sober living home. This was set up as a type of apartment complex where everyone had a small one-bedroom apartment to share with someone they paired them with.

Initially, all he could do was complain about his roommate, but after a week he settled in and seemed content. By then the Jeep had been re-possessed due to lack of payment and Dave had no transportation.

His family and I had a conversation about splitting the cost of a vehicle for him that would be in his name. He had been doing so well and would be very limited on getting a job, or moving forward without transportation. This resulted in the purchase of a 10-year old Honda.

Chapter 117

Getting Back on Track

The next three months went very well for Dave. He made friends at his complex, attended meetings, "gave back" by giving guys that didn't have transportation rides to meetings or to work. He formed an especially close relationship with a guy named Brett. They were inseparable to the point where his counselor mentioned to me that it was a bit of a concern. Real life wasn't hanging with a buddy, playing basketball and eating out. What would happen when it was time for Brett to move on and go back to his home? We were both concerned.

He came to the house regularly, especially on weekends to see and walk the dogs, take them for rides, along with helping around the house by trimming trees and mowing. I never asked, but he always offered.

He was being exposed to new music and technology, which he excitedly shared with me. He was fun to be around. We went out to eat some, caught a couple movies and life seemed good. He was working out regularly as well as attending church on a weekly basis. We had good conversation about what had transpired over the past few months, and what he needed to do to stay on track for the future. He said all the right things. He started interviewing for jobs and after a few weeks landed a job that included a company truck, credit card for gas, and full benefits after 90 days.

He was coming over so much though, that I was starting to feel like I did when we were a couple. It was too much time. On weekends, sometimes he would come and go three times in a day. I wasn't getting my "me" time or the time I needed to process. He wasn't moving on and taking care of what he needed to take care of to function on his own. He was slowly sucking me back in, and unbeknownst to me at the time, was getting the wrong idea about our relationship.

He was really excited about the holidays and said that everyone at the complex could get overnight passes for Thanksgiving and Christmas. He wanted to stay at the house over Thanksgiving and Christmas, to which I agreed to. He kept saying this was going to be the best holiday ever.

Thanksgiving and Christmas were great. However, little did I know at the time what the new year would bring.

Chapter 118

Not Exactly
a Happy New Year

Homeless, broke, no car, and possible charges pending was how 2019 started and where the finality of my relationship in any form ended with the man that I had been with since the age of 16.

After over four months of sobriety, making good decisions, landing a great job, and earning some trust back with me, Dave blew it.

Looking back, I started to see a slight change in behavior after his roommate moved out, which was a couple weeks after Dave started working. Within a couple weeks after that, he started making comments about work that made me feel he was slowly sinking back into a place where he was getting back inside his own head. In other words, he was once again about to be his own worst enemy. He stopped working out, stopped going to church regularly and seemed obsessed with moving out of Sober Living. He refused to wait any longer and maintain the structure and accountability that he desperately needed.

I had found a small efficiency place on the backside of someone's home. We went to see it on New Year's Eve. He seemed very preoccupied and nervous while we were meeting the people and discussing background check, deposit, and the fact they would let him move in the very next day. I was going to loan him the deposit he needed to get started.

One would think that knowing that the next chapter of one's life was going to take another positive spin would have him excited. That wasn't the case. He was off and I started becoming concerned. Especially when after we got back to my house, he left to go start packing, indicating he would be back in a couple hours.

When he came to back to the house after packing, he was acting distant. He came in the door and went directly to the bathroom, avoiding eye contact. He was also chewing gum. My radar was up, but I thought there was no way after the past four months and what he had talked about that he would drink anywhere close to me.

We ate then sat down to watch a movie. More distance. He wasn't "present" and for the next few hours was dozing off and on. I poked him at one point and said jokingly "Hey, I don't need to get a breathalyzer, do I?" His response was an eye roll and "Don't be ridiculous."

He didn't want to stay up until midnight, didn't even say goodnight. I ended New Year's Eve with a very unwelcomed yet familiar pit in my stomach.

New Year's Day 2019 did not begin with a Happy New Year greeting and a state of being positive, but rather with him getting up and out of the house by 5:45 a.m. to take a drive.

An hour later I received a text that he was at his apartment packing up the rest of his things and cleaning. A couple hours later, another text that he had loaded up (complete with sending me pictures of his vehicle completely stuffed with all his belongings), and that he was saying goodbye to everyone.

Around 9:30 a.m. I received a call stating he needed to talk. The pit in my stomach, which had continued from the day prior was churning and I started to feel sick.

He told me that he had been talking to his sponsor and that his sponsor told him that he needed to ask me if there was "a chance ever, ever, ever, ever for us to get back together." I was stunned. I knew he was lying as no sponsor would tell him to call me and put me on the spot and ask such a ridiculous question. He said, "I need to know this. I need to know what path I need to take, because if there isn't any chance ever, there is no reason for me to be in Florida. I'll just quit my job and move."

I replied, with tears flowing and voice volume rising that I couldn't believe he was calling me to ask a question like that, nor could I believe that he felt he was owed an answer at that time. I was not ready to answer that question.

He showed up at the house around 1:30 that afternoon. I took one look out the window and instantly knew he was drunk. He had "the look" and as he walked toward the front door his head was down and his gate was off. He was carrying the usual large plastic Big Gulp glass.

He walked in the front door, put the glass on the counter and immediately went to the bathroom, avoiding eye contact with me. I went to the glass and took a sip, tasting the bitterness of Vodka. I took the glass to the bathroom and confronted him, stating that I knew he was drinking and he needed to leave the house at that moment and he was not welcome back here ever again.

He stood there with that stupid "drunk, small eye" look and denied it as he shuffled out of the bathroom. I dumped out his drink and escorted him out the front door. At first, I was going to take his keys, then I thought back to the insanity of the past years and just let him go. Whatever happened would happen. I could not control the situation. As he backed out of the driveway, he rolled down his window and yelled "Have a nice fucking life."

That was how my 2019 started, but there was much more chaos to come.

Chapter 119

Was It Worth a Cold Taco?

The next few days were filled with drunk texts and voice mails. I was not responding to him. He was staying in a nasty hotel as he didn't have much money left. He had recently cashed his paycheck which left him with $700 to spend.

It was during my lunch break on Friday, January 4th when he called me once again for money. I asked him where he was and he said he was at work. I didn't believe him so I told him to send me a selfie of him at work. He was extremely agitated and said "Really? Just a minute, I need to pull over. Good grief Cilla." A minute or two later, he texted me a picture. The problem with the picture was that it was a picture he had taken a few weeks prior that he had already shown me.

He called me again. While on the phone with him I decided that I would drive up to where I had last seen his car at the nasty hotel, which was only a couple miles away. If it was there, he was lying. We were on the phone as I was speeding up the highway toward the sleazy hotel. His car was parked where it had been for days. I snapped a picture, then said "You are lying to me. You aren't at work."

He screamed back at me, "Yes I am at work. I told you I'm not drinking." My insanity continues as I drove toward the halfway house where I assumed his company truck was still parked from the last time he worked. Sure enough it was there. I took a picture and screamed back at him "You are lying, your truck is parked at the halfway house. I'm done," hung up, and texted him the pictures.

It had happened again. I had allowed myself to get sucked back into his insane and toxic life. I actually left my lunch to speed to a gross hotel just to prove that he was lying to me. What did that get me? Nothing really other than a cold taco. Satisfaction that I was right? Proof that the manipulator that was known to lie all the time once again lied to me? Big deal.

Chapter 120

It Finally Happened

The barrage of crazy texts continued, over the next few days with him pleading for help or money or to pick up food for him. I received a text from him on January 8th:

Please think about it. I'm so desperate right now. Need to keep my job. I promise no bs.

Also I need to eat, got no money. Not trying to guilt you. I'm just so desperate.

So much for 36 yrs together. What heartless money doesn't come from your heart.

Not even a fucking shower.

Can I at least sleep in the driveway?

My engine light came on and I don't want to get stranded.

Please. I won't try to come in promise. Maybe Rip could sleep with? Please give me something.

I'm really afraid its gonna break down.

Just give me a yes or no

So that's a no?

Getting late. Would you please change your mind? Just want some time with my boy.

Do u realize it is illegal to park overnight anywhere around here?

Need an answer

I'm parking in the street. Gonna arrest for that.

Hello yes or no!

Technically if I'm not on the property I can park in the street but I can't take the chance and fuck up my job how do you not understand that.

I'm here please tell me yes or no.

Wow.

The constant texts and requests for help and to stay at the house were making me a nervous wreck. I pulled blinds, checked the locks, and every time I would come and go from the house, I would drive by slow and look around the house before getting out of my car, key in hand, as I walked quickly to the front door.

After putting my phone on do not disturb and going to bed for the night I woke up the next morning to another barrage of texts from him in the middle of the night. Reading them made me very emotional, as he was once again being the master of his craft of manipulation. However, I couldn't help but feel bad and pictured him out there somewhere in his car, with no place to go, parked in some random place and sleeping… homeless.

12:10 am – January 9, 2019

Do you remember when we used to enjoy the stars together sitting out in your back yard

And you jogged and I road ur bike? I remember your famous cut off shirts

OR sit out on the porch with your parents when we both had perms. And I wore his pajamas

The glass switch? Pizza Pit, the theatre where you lost $8 bucks? The time you puked in the ditch?

Or the time I surprised you with the 3000 GT?

Then made you drive the civic? All that stuff was before I transformed into the alcoholic. Oh and that great apartment where the Camaro got egged?

I could have been happy there for the rest of our lives.

Oh and Dunkin Donuts every Saturday.

Like clockwork

Oh and beautiful you were singing Desparado

I could go on and on. But I'm taking my Seroquel now.

Your obsession with taters.

Your failed first attempt to cook when I had my appendix out. You buying the house all by yourself when I was working in Orlando.

Venice, London, Aviano AFB, Grand Bahamas, Cozumel with the blue water, Coronado on our 10th. There were great times too I could go on and on but I'm tired.

A few hours later, by 9:00 am, the texts started again:

Are you gonna let me clean up for work tomorrow I'm filthy need to soak for a long time.

Or shave and dip in the pool. Have no money to buy razors.

And I need a little bit of make up for a bad fresh scratch on my forehead.

Just tell me if you're not gonna help so I can try something else.

And I need money for gas.

If you're not gonna help just freaking tell me and I'll except it and move on

All morning while at work I'm getting bombarded with these texts from him. This man that thought the world still owed him despite his continual toxic decisions. I caved and replied:

"I was in a meeting. You can meet me at the gas station by the WalMart by the house and I will fill up your tank. Meet me there at 12:30. I'll have razors and makeup for you as well."

After stopping at a drug store to get razors, I stopped at a Panera Bread for a $30 gift card. I figured he could have a nice warm place to get some hot food. The stress I was feeling knowing that he was out there with all his belongings in his car, no money, probably lost his job by now, lying and drinking was taking its toll on me. Unfortunately, I just couldn't get it out of my mind.

I met him at the gas station. He looked grey in color and had a large gash on his forehead, most likely from falling and hitting his head while drunk. I hadn't seen him since New Year's Day. His facial hair was very grey, eyes bloodshot, and he avoided eye contact with me. When I gave him the Panera Bread card, he stated "I have food stamps." I then told him that I thought it would be nice for him to have a warm meal sometime. To that end, we departed in our cars.

Approximately three hours later I received a call from the Police Department that Dave had been in an accident. He had hit someone on a bike, who had a "bunch of broken bones" and was taken via ambulance to the hospital. Dave was ok, but was also taken via ambulance to the hospital. I was supposed to call the officer.

I was shaking from head to toe. He finally did it. He was driving drunk and he hit someone, as well as a parked car. He had admitted to the officer that he had been drinking earlier in the day, but that the reason he swerved off the road was because he "choked on a Wendy's burger and blacked out."

He was taken to a local hospital due to chest pains and to check out his claims for blacking out. While there, the barrage of texts continued, some of which included threats of killing himself. This landed him the opportunity for another Baker Act stay. Once he was medically released, he was to be moved back to Fair Oaks.

January 12, 2019 - Texts to me and his family

So you all fucking screwed me again so much for fucking family. Family like this who needs enemies.

Does anyone of you actually give a shit about me? Sure doesn't appear that way.

Gag order hurts the worst. They are indefinitely incarcerating me.

How is that treatment?

January 13th text to me

Can you please talk to me? I need some moral support. Pls.

For the love of God dear, please communicate with me.

Who knows where they're taking me and if I'll survive. Please just tell me you love me and will pray for me.

You really helped me this time I'll be escaping first chance I get. You all think u get it but you just damn don't. Thx again for nothing.

Thanks for the help when I needed it most.

He was released from Fair Oaks on Friday, January 18th. They gave him a bus ticket that he could use to go anywhere and of course, he ended up in a hotel. Later that evening I received a yet another text from him.

Dave: Can u bring my charger to the whole meeting in room 109? My battery is dying and I am I got like 7% left.

Me: No, I can't today. I have plans.

Dave: I need help. Please. Just drop it off at the door. I also need cash for a bus fare

Please. Maybe please pick up toys

Me: I told you I have plans. I am not dropping it off.

Dave: Wow. When did you fucking turn evil?

Dave: Thanks for nothing

Dave: So you're not going to drop me off the power cord or any cash for a bus?

At that point, I blocked him. That was enough verbal abuse via text from this drunk. However, unbeknownst to me, voicemails from blocked callers can still be left. On the next day, Saturday the 19th of January I received a voicemail from an extremely intoxicated Dave at 6:24 p.m.: "Please call me.

Can you please call me hon. Please. I don't have a place to go to. I'm sleeping on the street. Can you please call me. Please."

And another at 6:39 p.m. where he was completely intoxicated and slurring his words: "I wish you would come and get me. I'm gonna...I wish you would come to get me. Help me. I'm gonna jump in front of a fucking train. Ok? I'm gonna jump in front of a fucking train. Yeah. So. See how ya like that."

I hadn't realized he had left that voice mail until a couple of days later. However, on train night, his family called me to tell me he had been picked up by the police, taken to a hospital and Baker Acted. Someone had called 911 when they saw him by the train tracks. However, the hospital only kept him a couple of days and he was released on January 21st.

January 21st – group text to me and his family

Family: Yes evidently addiction isn't enough. Not saying it's not but when someone reaches out and makes arrangements for u to get help and u rebel against it what in the hell are we supposed to do. Dave, you have a place to go. Arrangements have been made for u. All u have to do is make that call.

Dave: Sorry. I'm going out in a blaze of fire. Hoping I die.

Family: What?

Dave: I want to fucking die.

Family: You're talking stupid. You could be going to a treatment center. Call the number Joe gave u.

Dave: Nope fuck him. He's just going through the motions I don't trust him.

Family: No he's not. He's trying to help u. Dave for God's sake take some help.

Dave: I'd rather die. Sorry.

Family: That's ridiculous. Call the stupid center Dave.

Dave: Fuck that I rather die and I'm gonna.

Family: You know you're really killing me. Where are u at?

Dave: That's fine at least the last time I kill you.

Family: That's not even funny. Just straighten up and get help.

Dave: Sorry I'm going out I will have. I don't want to live.

Family: Well too bad I want u to live!!! Evidently, you don't care what you're doing to me.

Dave: Goodbye heaven us for me. Fucci Ella there breaking down the food. I'm gonna run out and get shot in Plano and me I don't think you both are happy I love you both I think as hell I'm going I'm not going down easy I'm gonna do is hurt myself I don't wanna hurt anybody else. I'm going for it I'm gonna drive out and I have a shoot me, sorry this is the way I feel.

Me to Family: He could be serious or paranoid or hallucinating. I don't even know what to do or say.

Family: Not really anything we can do.

There was something I could do. I turned on the local news and was glued to the TV to see if there was any breaking news about a standoff with police at a local WalMart. Nothing. I called the WalMart that I assumed he would be at and after being transferred to customer service, inquired whether there was a middle-aged man ranting and raving, police standoff, etc. The answer was no.

So, all this was just an act in a state of delirium. Was he hallucinating and out of it to that extreme that he really thought he was at a WalMart in the middle of a police standoff? The nightmare would never end.

Chapter 121

More Insanity and an Arrest

The next couple weeks brought more of the same, with him almost being hit by a bus due to wandering in traffic, Baker Acted, released a few days later than hitting a treatment center for less than a week. He received his final paycheck and opted to blow it on hotel rooms and alcohol.

On Sunday, February 3rd I came home from lunch to find him standing in the middle of my driveway. He was just standing there, obviously drunk. He had brought three small bags of his things and had put them on the side of the garage. I told him to leave and he refused. He said he had no place to go. I told him again to leave, or I was going to call the police, and he refused to leave.

I managed to get by him and enter the house, quickly locking the door behind me. He proceeded for 20 minutes to go from the front door to the side garage door and back and forth, knocking and jiggling the door knobs. I told him through the garage window he better leave or I was going to call the police. His response was that he didn't care. I called the police.

While waiting for them to arrive, he continued to knock and act in a manic way, then somehow climbed over the 6-foot privacy fence into the backyard to try and open the back sliding door, as well as the kitchen window, looking in at me and begging me to let him in as he had no place to go.

The police arrived and arrested him for trespassing. While in the back of their car he started to rock back and forth, then let out a gut-wrenching scream while he shook his head. Who knows, maybe all the rocking and screaming was an act.

He was booked in jail, then Baker Acted and transported to a different psych ward. Five days later the angels from the Midwest came to my rescue again. They were coming to take him away one last time.

Chapter 122

Back to North Carolina

The stay in the Midwest didn't last long, as on March 13th Dave was heading to North Carolina. The days leading to his flight were met with more drinking. The little bit of freedom that had been given him had once again been abused.

He had taken his food stamps card from Florida, purchased food then returned it for cash and bought alcohol. He even drove his family's car while drunk and got lost. That was the final straw.

He was supposed to stay with a friend in North Carolina but ended up going on a multiple day binge at a hotel in Cary, North Carolina then calling 911 on himself. He was released less than 24 hours later, with his friend picking him up. He had blown his $700 tax refund on hotels and booze in less than a week.

He had received a small settlement from the insurance company for his car being totaled, so his family sent the money to his friend, then washed their hands of him. They were going to cut off contact. I had cut off contact with him again on the day of the accident.

Chapter 123

Moving On

I don't know how Dave's story will end. After everything thus far, he still hasn't hit his bottom. He has lost almost everything, his family connection, and support, marriage, home, credit, car, savings, and hopes for employment. He has done so much damage to his body and brain. He isn't the person he used to be.

Does he want to live another day to face the uphill battle that he has ahead of him or will he continue to zone out, spending the little money he has left on hotels and alcohol only to die alone as an addict?

I am angry at the system and how broken it is. The mental health system and the insurance guidelines on how to treat and how long to treat addicts are a joke. It's a vicious cycle of the same people in and out of treatment repeatedly.

On the news, all we hear about is the opioid crisis and the meth problems. Where is the attention on the legal drug that destroys the lives of so many people each and every day? Why isn't there a "crisis" for alcoholics? Why aren't there better methods for treatment? Why do insurance companies get to dictate when someone no longer needs detox or treatment? Like a 30-day treatment program is going to be the cure-all?

Dave had been in detox and treatment 16 different times, not to mention the 15 times he had been to an emergency room. The police had been called on him 23 times, of which 13 of those times resulted in him being Baker Acted. He tried to commit suicide. He has had three DUIs, was missing once in Florida, and finally hit someone. What was it going to take!?

I have been forced to learn a lot more than I ever dreamed I would about addiction, mental health and the ins and outs of treatment. I hope to be an advocate for family members that are experiencing the pain that I did. How I can pull that off is yet to be known.

My journey has been a wild ride of ups and downs. The past year since he moved out of the house had left me with a different kind of trauma. If I heard a noise from the back of the house I jumped, thinking it was him falling or pacing the floor. When I drove by one of the many hotels he had stayed at, I had flashbacks to how the rooms looked when I came to get his things. If his family called me, I thought it was to tell me that Dave was dead. Every time I would hear a train or cross railroad tracks near my home, I would think of him. When he was out on the road or wandering the streets and we didn't know where he was, I would anticipate coming home to a police officer waiting to tell me he had been found dead. Every time I would hear the police or ambulance siren, I wondered if it was related to him.

It took some time for me to be able to make it through a weekend without having a sight of something or a song or thought trigger me into a weepy mess. I would be driving along then suddenly get an image of him in my head, which triggered tears. I had painful headaches and couldn't sleep more than four to five hours a night. I was falling into a state of non-stop stress and hopelessness.

It's incredibly hard to let go of someone that you had been with for over 30 years. There were good times, despite the fact I had learned so much of his past that tainted it. I didn't want to be a single person in my fifties. I didn't sign up for this, yet it was where I landed.

Time heals and over time I will think of him less. The triggers will be fewer and farther in between. The restful sleep will return. The focus will no longer be on him and his addiction, but rather on me. It is MY turn to live a full life.

I feel liberated and free. My faith has carried me through these most difficult times and I pray for him daily. I can do anything. I am strong. I am brave. I'm a different kind of brave. My story really begins here. Where it will end, only God knows.

Made in the USA
San Bernardino, CA
27 November 2019